A Paddler's Guide to Everglades National Park

Other books by Johnny Molloy
Trail By Trail: Backpacking in the Smoky Mountains
Day and Overnight Hikes in the Great Smoky Mountains National Park
Best in Tent Camping: Southern Appalachians and Smoky Mountains
Best in Tent Camping: Florida
Day and Overnight Hikes in Shenandoah National Park
Beach and Coastal Camping in Florida
Best in Tent Camping: Colorado
Day and Overnight Hikes in the Monongahela National Forest
Best in Tent Camping: West Virginia

Visit the author's web site:
www.johnnymolloy.com

A Paddler's Guide to Everglades National Park

Johnny Molloy

University Press of Florida

Gainesville / Tallahassee / Tampa / Boca Raton

Pensacola / Orlando / Miami / Jacksonville

05 04 03 02 01 00   6 5 4 3 2 1

LIBRARY OF CONGRESS CATALOGING-IN-PUBLICATION DATA
Molloy, Johnny, 1961-
A paddler's guide to Everglades National Park / Johnny Molloy.
p. cm.
Includes bibliographical references (p.).
ISBN 0-8130-1787-4 (paper: alk. paper)
1. Canoes and canoeing—Florida—Everglades National Park—
Guidebooks. 2. Everglades National Park (Fla.)—Guidebooks.
I. Title.
GV776.F62 E937   2000
917.59'390464—dc21   00-025638

The University Press of Florida is the scholarly publishing agency for
the State University System of Florida, comprising Florida A & M
University, Florida Atlantic University, Florida International
University, Florida State University, University of Central Florida,
University of Florida, University of North Florida, University of
South Florida, and University of West Florida.

University Press of Florida
15 Northwest 15th Street
Gainesville, FL 32611
http://www.upf.com

This book is for my three brothers—Steele, Pat, and Mike.

This book is a guide to the paddling region of Everglades National Park. Every effort has been made to make this book as accurate as possible. Neither the descriptions nor the maps in the book can be assumed to be exact or to guarantee your arrival at any given point. Use your good judgment in this and any wilderness endeavor.

Contents

Preface

To paddle the Everglades was a dream of mine for nearly a decade before my first trip in the early nineties. Everybody has heard of the Everglades, but I had heard of paddling the Everglades while canoeing the Boundary Waters Canoe Area Wilderness of Minnesota. About that time, an old college buddy from the University of Tennessee, Tom Lauria, had taken a new job and moved to Miami. It seemed only natural that we would combine a reunion with a trip to the Everglades, as by this time I had become completely immersed in the outdoor life.

We drove to Flamingo, rented a canoe, then struck out for the Glades, completely ignorant as to what to expect. I still remember the first night at South Joe chickee—watching the sky turn red, not believing we were camping in the Everglades! The fishing was good, but the water was far more open than we had expected. The following year, we took off from Everglades City and hit the Gulf. The scenery was incredible and so were the waves, nearly swamping us after a cold front blew through. Every year thereafter I went on some new Everglades adventure. The first trip around Cape Sable just blew my mind. It made me realize how precious this natural preserved coastline is in our era.

The trips became longer and longer, culminating in a 15-night experience that is still as clear as if it had happened yesterday. By this time I had started writing outdoor guidebooks. I could see a comprehensive guidebook covering all the commonly paddled waterways of the Everglades was needed. Also needed was more information on the campsites, gear, and just what it is like out in the Everglades. I ran into so many paddlers who were surprised, as I was on my first adventure, about the Everglades back-country, from the vastness of the water to the mazelike mangrove. I decided on that long trip to write a guidebook about the paddling area of the Everglades.

After hooking up with the University Press of Florida, I set off for the Glades, meeting with park personnel, getting their helpful input, then striking out on trip after trip one winter, paddling more than 500 miles while researching the book. I would rise from my tent in the morning, load my craft (I used both a canoe and a sea kayak), then set out on a new route. While paddling, I would record information on a microcassette recorder and make notes on maps, eventually landing at a backcountry campsite. After unloading at a campsite, I would have a bite, set up camp, then hook up my laptop computer to a power inverter, which hooked up to a portable power pack. I would then type up literal on-site reports while the information was fresh in my mind.

While paddling, I stored the computer inside a dry bag inside another dry bag, then crossed my fingers. The miracles of modern technology made writing the book easier, but they never stopped a headwind, or made the tides turn in my favor, or made the mosquitoes go away. But overall, writing this book was a wonderful experience and a dream come true. I hope you enjoy the Everglades as much as I did and as I will far into the future.

I would like to thank the following folks for their invaluable help in writing this book. From the Flamingo campground kiosk, the very friendly Chris Cagle, Chris Ryan, Jase Harris, Holly Bartlett, and Tim Downey. Especially helpful were my Volunteer friends from Minnesota, John and Barb Haapala, and the Michiganers John and Donna Buckley. From the Flamingo Ranger Station: Kris Stoehr, Steve Robinson, William "Buzz" Botts, Sarah Beckwith, John Waters, Lori Rome, Nancy Holman, Roy Wood, and especially Allyson Polocz, who all answered my persistent questions. I wouldn't have blamed Allyson if she had hidden when I kept coming around. I also would like to thank the folks from the Park Head-quarters: Reed Detring, Deborah Nordeen, and Rick Cook, and Cal

Singletary of the Florida National Parks and Monuments Association for his guidance. From the Gulf Coast Ranger Station I thank Mike Mayer, Judy Hayes, Tom Iandimarino, Eugene Wesloh, Greg Podany, Kathy Clossin, Candace Tinkler, Carl Hilts, Noreen Brown, Dola Berg, Patrick Buerkle, John Russell, Sid Capo, and Gary and Gail Eaton.

Thanks to Steve and Sharon at Perception Kayaks, whose high-quality service and better boats made many a mile of paddling that much more pleasurable; Bud Heath at Jet's Florida Outdoors in Miami; Vivian Oliva for typing on Turkey Key; T. J. Keefe, Alex Peterson, Tom Rodgers, and the guy from Manhattan at Lopez River campsite who entertained me with his tales of life in the city; the folks at the Ivey House and North American Canoe Tours; Linda and her daughter Meredith from Rabbit Key. And a special thanks to Sharon Collier for being friendly and looking better.

Thanks to Caroline Fleischer at Freebairn & Co. And thanks to Eureka! for a quality bug-proof tent that kept me dry and the skeeters at bay, to Silva for a reliable compass, and to Slumberjack for the canoe chair, sleeping pad, and bag.

Thanks to Ken and Meredith at University Press of Florida for backing the book.

Thanks to Debbie Lauria, Tom Lauria, Anthony Lauria, and Kristina Lauria for boarding me in Coral Gables between paddling trips. Thanks to Ellie Connally for accompanying me on a trip. Thanks to Bill Armstrong for coming down to lend his photographic expertise and fish-cooking artistry, and to Danny Johnson for his help, too. Thanks to Bryan Delay for letting me store my boats at his house, and to my reliable friend Cisco Meyer for capably holding down the fort. Thanks to Keith Stinnett at Patrick Sullivan's Saloon in the Old City for feeding me and keeping me busy. Thanks to Dana Rizer for her good voice, great laughs, and better smile.

A final thanks to Will Fontanez, Tom Wallin, Hilary Burns, Will Albaugh V, Susan Carney, and all the other Volunteers at the University of Tennessee Cartographic Services Laboratory.

Leave No Trace Principles

Plan Ahead and Prepare
Travel and Camp on Durable Surfaces
Dispose of Waste Properly
Leave What You Find
Minimize Campfire Impacts
Respect Wildlife
Be Considerate of Other Visitors

Introduction to the Everglades

The national park system of our country is an American legacy. This system preserves and protects special and unique natural features scattered about the land. If these parks had not been established, many scenic and environmentally important treasures would have been lost. Everglades National Park is no exception. A century ago, South Florida was perceived as a swampy no-man's-land, where a few settlers and the last of the Seminoles survived in an inaccessible vastness. Then, Henry Flagler completed his railroad to Key West, and the appeal of this warm country became apparent. The rush for land and water to accommodate the homesteaders was on. The Everglades had both—if they could be drained and canalized. The realization that this ecosystem should be preserved competed with the realization that much money could be made by "taming" the Everglades. A struggle ensued, and by 1947 Everglades National Park was established. Even though the park is the most sizable east of the Mississippi and contains the largest roadless area in the lower forty-eight, the entire Everglades ecosystem has not been not preserved. Far from it. Vast tracts to the north have been drained, Lake Okeechobee has been diked, the natural flow patterns of the River of Grass have been changed for good.

But all is not doom and gloom—there is much to see in the Everglades and even more to realize and appreciate. Imagine South Florida today, with its population bursting at the seams and vying for all the resources available, without an Everglades National Park. Condos in the Pinelands, strip malls on the old Ingraham Highway, high-rises looking over Florida Bay from Cape Sable, bridges connecting the Ten Thousand Islands—it could very well look exactly like that.

The Everglades have been permanently altered, but they aren't dead. On the contrary, they retain many of their original characteristics. The Everglades are a vast spread of seemingly endless sawgrass, mangrove, sea, and sky. You can see birds, fish, gloomy tidal creeks, dolphins rising for air on wide rivers, and the world's best sunsets from Cape Sable and un-spoiled islands in the Gulf of Mexico, where deserted beaches are yours to walk. All you have to do is get in your craft and paddle.

That is the purpose of this guidebook—to help you most effectively paddle the Everglades. With this book, you will have a realistic idea of what paddling the Everglades is like, how to get on the water, what to take with you, and where to go and stay in the Everglades backcountry. There are more than 50 routes described in this guidebook, covering not only the Wilderness Waterway and the Gulf of Mexico, but all the commonly and many not so commonly paddled routes in the entire park.

Each route description has an easy-to-read information box that gives you a brief overview of that route. The beginning, end, distance in statute miles, and estimated paddle time get you oriented. Potential tidal influence, potential wind influence, navigational challenge, highlights, and hazards help you size up the route. Campsites on the way and connections with other routes help you plan your overall route while in the back-country. A verbal overview and running commentary of the route follow, giving general directions and alerting you to any significant natural or historical sites and other route connections along the way.

There is a special section in the book about campsites. Here you'll find details about each individual campsite in the paddling backcountry: where it is, what it is like, and how much use it receives. Everglades backcountry paddlers can then cross-reference this information with the route information to develop a comprehensive, realistic itinerary for a watery adventure lasting from one night to two weeks.

For reference once you're out there on the water, backcountry pastimes such as fishing and birding are also detailed. Using all the data in this book can add up to a successful trip. So reserve some of your precious time, study this guidebook, plan a trip, and then go do it!

What It's Like—Paddling the Everglades

It's seeing an osprey carrying a grunting Jack Crevalle in its talons.

It's paddling 9 miles into a head wind until your arms ache.

It's seeing porpoises jump out of the water in unison as the sun sets on the Gulf of Mexico.

It's looking out and seeing nothing but no-see-ums on your tent window.

It's sitting by a driftwood fire beneath palm trees on Northwest Cape.

It's being pulled into Lake Ingraham by a strong tide rushing through the Mid Cape Canal.

It's recognizing the constellations reflecting off a glassy bay as fish splash in the distance.

It's huddling behind your tent on Mormon Key, trying to make coffee with fumbling fingers as a north wind pierces you to the bone.

It's hooking a tarpon on a light rod with 4-pound test line.

It's spending the night lost somewhere near the Roberts River.

It's lying in the shallow waters, soaking up sun on Carl Ross Key.

It's watching motorboats parade by from Darwin's Place.

It's a picnic lunch and a laugh at Lopez River campsite.

It's a never-ending paddle on a hot still day in Florida Bay, where the mirages in the distance cause paddlers to believe their strokes toward an invisible goal are futile.

It's being cooked a fresh fish dinner by some fellow campers at Camp Lonesome.

It's frantically loading your canoe as the mosquitoes drive you to finish your morning coffee from the boat in Broad River.

It's walking deserted Highland Beach.

It's hearing gentle night breezes tap your canoe against the chickee as you drift off to sleep.

It's being stuck on New Turkey Key for two days by gale force winds.

It's paddling your sea kayak over topaz waters to North Nest Key.

It's drying out your gear on the dock at Plate Creek chickee.

It's seeing an alligator sunning himself at your campsite on Alligator Creek.

It's inhaling the pungent waters of The Nightmare as the winds howl through the canopy of branches overhead.

It's watching minnows dart about the crystal-clear water of Rocky Creek.

It's leaning against a cooler as an all-day rain falls at the Rodgers River chickee.

It's wondering in the middle of the night if the spirits of Mr. Watson's long-ago-murdered laborers really do haunt the Watson Place campsite.

It's looking out on whitecapping waves from behind a sheltered island on Whitewater Bay with miles ahead of you.

It's reeling in a red from the Lane Bay chickee.

It's seeing a manatee in the warm waters of Dusenberry Creek.

It's running aground onto a mud bar while shortcutting across Broad River Bay.

It's walking the sandy flats of Rabbit Key at low tide on a moonlit night and wondering if you can walk all the way to Fort Myers.

It's trying to guide your canoe to the safety of the Chatham River as stained four-foot waves batter your canoe into Gun Rock Point.

It's watching the red fireball of the sun drop into the Gulf of Mexico from Cape Sable.

It's the sense of fear that sets in when you realize that your navigational skills have led you astray, while the sky darkens into night.

It's mentally calculating how many strokes of the paddle it will take to cover the remaining miles of your day's journey.

It's realizing the ground on which you are camping was built up hundreds of years ago by the daily piling of discarded shells by Calusa Indians.

It's noticing sharks in the waters of Whitewater Bay while you fish, and realizing that your canoe lies awfully close to the water's surface.

It's battling through language barriers while exchanging tales of the day's experiences with your fellow campers at South Joe chickee.

It's paddling toward the rainbow's end after weathering an afternoon thunderstorm.

It's being awakened by a bull gator's bellow near your chickee and wondering whether he is looking for a mate or something to eat.

It's playfully surfing the waves in your sea kayak while being blown by a friendly wind to Pavilion Key.

It's being pestered by raccoons at Pavilion Key who leave their sandy footprints all over your boat.

It's exploring the interior of Mormon Key, looking for signs of previous inhabitants.

It's lying in a wet sleeping bag at the Oyster Key chickee after a midnight storm catches you with your tent fly down.

It's seeing a deer in the mangrove on Lostmans River.

It's seeing Chokoloskee Island after paddling in a storm through Rabbit Key Pass.

It's watching the sky darken at Canepatch, while you ram down dinner after paddling for 10 hours, then racing to the tent as swamp angels buzz all around you.

Natural History

The Everglades. Just about everyone has heard of them. But what are the Everglades? Ask twenty people and you get twenty different answers. Yet most conceptions of the Everglades center around two mental pictures. First picture: Everglades as jungle. This image has tall trees towering over gloomy swamps with snakes hanging from tangled vines. Alligators lurk beneath coffee-colored waters, while strange birds deliver stranger calls that echo across the ooze. Second picture: A limitless plain of verdant grass growing out of water. The sun beats over the harsh bleakness, punctuated only by violent thunderstorms. An occasional bird flaps its wings across an endless horizon.

Neither image is entirely incorrect. The jungle scenario comes closer to describing the nearby Big Cypress Swamp, while the river-of-grass scenario somewhat describes only one ecosystem of the Everglades. The vastness of the 1,500,000-acre Everglades National Park, the largest roadless area in the lower forty-eight, encompasses several environments that together form a fragile, complex ecosystem like no other on the face of the planet.

To describe the Everglades, we must first go back in time. Over the past 2 million years, the peninsula of Florida was alternately exposed and inundated as cycles of glaciation came and went. Sediments deposited from the Appalachian Mountains to the north formed the surface of the Everglades. After the final glaciation some 6,000 years ago, the sea rose to its present levels and the shoreline of the state took its present shape. A warmer, wetter, more tropical climate ensued. Some temperate vegetation stayed in South Florida, while other, more tropical, vegetation migrated north from the Caribbean. Then the Everglades, a mere infant as far as ecological systems go, began to evolve and dominate the South Florida landscape. To conceive just how dominant the Everglades were, consider that the Everglades National Park represents only one-fifth of the historic Everglades.

Water has always been a defining element of the Everglades. Its flow has been drastically changed by man over the last century. Before canals, agriculture, and Miami, this aquatic maze originated in lakes just south of present-day Orlando. Creeks flowed south from these lakes, merging to form the Kissimmee River and other creeks, which in turn flowed southward into massive Lake Okeechobee, more than 700 square miles in size. Water spilled over the south shore of this inland sea into a 50-mile-wide river only inches deep. The river was hidden by an expanse of sawgrass extending southward as far as the eye could see. Beneath the sawgrass, the water flowed, glimmering in the sun, heading southwesterly in a shallow trough with a slope averaging less than 2 inches per mile. This "sheet flow" was punctuated with dense islands of trees and other vegetation. The islands, called hammocks, stood slightly higher and drier than the sawgrass. Eerie-looking dwarf cypress trees formed other tree islands.

The water of the Everglades has always come and gone with the seasons. And down here there are two seasons, wet and dry. The wet season starts around the end of April, when warm moist air flows north from the Gulf of Mexico and the Caribbean, then dumps water in sporadic yet certain storms all over the Florida peninsula.

Plant life on Everglades key. Photo by W. W. Armstrong

This wet season climaxes as the days slowly get shorter and disturbances head west from Africa, building over the warm Atlantic waters, sometimes forming hurricanes, sometimes not, but dumping water all the same, often several inches in just a few hours. In times past, the waters of the northern lakes, along with local rains, filled the Glades. And then, sometime in November, the first cold fronts pushed all the way down from the north, leaving brilliant blue skies broken by very occasional storms. The flow of the Everglades slowly diminished until the wet season returned again.

Depending upon the season, fire has played an important role in shaping the Everglades. When thunderstorms reign over the region, bolts of lightning strike, starting fires that spread through the sawgrass. In spring, while the soil is still dry, fires can burn down to the layer of peat, slowing development of marsh and swamp habitat and allowing water to flow through the sawgrass. In the wet summer, when water levels are high, usually only dead growth burns, creating a fantastic sight as flames stretch across the landscape.

Today, as historically, the water flows ever south and west, merging into wide tidal rivers bordered by mangrove, inevitably mixing with the salty water from the Gulf of Mexico and Florida Bay. It is here that the world's greatest mangrove forest thrives. But as robust as these trees grow, they are flattened with frightening regularity by hurricanes, which shape the Glades as surely as does the flow of water from Lake Okeechobee. Surrounded by the mangrove forest and nearly inaccessible to humans are the coastal marshes, where sawgrass forms a plain. More accessible are the coastal prairies of Cape Sable. Salt-tolerant ground cover such as sea purslane grows atop limestone marl. Abutting the ocean on the continent's edge is pristine beach, rare in Florida today.

Beyond the sawgrass and mangrove of the mainland, in the shallow waters of the Gulf of Mexico are outlying islands, known as "keys." These mangrove islands, with occasional beach fronts, extend northward from Key West into Florida Bay and reach their greatest numbers near Everglades City in the storied Ten Thousand Islands. Rich tropical marine

Flock at Sandy Key. Photo by author

vegetation grows in Florida Bay, creating an important link in the web of life for the aquatic and avian animals of this salty side of the Everglades.

And there are other environments in the Everglades. The Pinelands thrive on a limestone extension of the Atlantic Coastal Ridge. This land is dry by Everglades standards, but it is often inundated for 2 or 3 months per year. Slash pine, cabbage palm, and palmetto dominate this fire-dependent community. Saline flats, brackish bays, and cypress heads, other elements of this complex natural world, subtly blend and merge and mesh to form a fascinating landscape worthy of a lifetime's study.

The historic Everglades are no longer; the flow of water has been permanently disrupted; the Kissimmee River has been straightened; the south shore of Lake Okeechobee has been dammed; the Caloosahatchee River has been channelized; sawgrass has been drained and planted over with sugarcane; canals have been dug all over the eastern Glades; Main Park Road acts as a dam; Florida Bay suffers aquatic blooms from exotic fertilizers; almost all wildlife has been reduced in numbers. The Everglades will never be what they once were, but with care and management as a national park their recovery can continue.

The Impact of Modern Civilization on the Everglades

The historic flow of water from central Florida has been the key component in shaping the Everglades. But since the mid-1800s, plans have been in the works to drain, channelize, and otherwise "improve" the Everglades. Between 1882 and 1916, several canals were constructed that diverted the historic flow through the sawgrass to the east and west coasts of the state. Then Lake Okeechobee was diked. More canals were added; others were enlarged to tame the Everglades. Yet problems like flooding, fires, and residents' disrupted water supplies led to more extensive water control, managed by the Central and Southern Florida Project for Flood Control and Other Purposes. This CS and F Project, authorized by Congress in 1948, was mostly in place by the mid-1960s.

The project eased flooding, created a more reliable water supply, and opened up a huge expanse of land south of Lake Okeechobee, formerly sawgrass, for agriculture. In the end, only 25 percent of the freshwater Everglades was left intact. Project engineers have attempted to mimic freshwater flows of the past with little success. Freshwater concentrations have become compartmentalized between levees and canals, instead of flowing naturally through the ecosystem. Phosphorous from agricultural lands to the north have overly enriched some areas, while the decrease in freshwater has led to higher salinity and attendant changes in Whitewater Bay and Florida Bay.

Wildlife, especially the area's once vast rookeries, has suffered accordingly, save for alligators, which thrive in manufactured canals. But their habitation strategies in the historic Everglades created trails and aquatic alligator "holes" that were havens for fish and birds during the dry season. In the changed Everglades, there are far fewer alligator holes and so less of the wildlife that is dependent on those holes. This is just one example of the alteration of the complex Everglades that park officials, agricultural interests, environmentalists, and the Army Corps of Engineers are playing tug-of-war over. This interaction of people, land, and water goes on to this moment.

Human History of the Everglades

The Everglades as we know them first took shape around 5,000 years ago. Human habitation shortly followed. The Indians who occupied South Florida quickly came to use what the region gave them. They often lived in open raised platforms with palmetto thatched roofs, called "chickees," on beaches, along rivers, or over sheltered waters. The chickees and a healthy dose of fish oil smeared on their skin helped cut down on mosquitoes. Smudge pots—smoldering fires of black mangrove—further kept the "swamp angels" at bay.

In other places, the Glades Indians lived on shell mounds that expanded from one generation to the next, accumulations of the discarded remains of oysters, turtles, conchs, clams, and other creatures that were the mainstay of their diet. From the land, they harvested white-tailed deer, turkey, marsh rabbit, hearts of palm, coco plums, and sea grapes, as well as birds such as ibis. More important still were the fresh- and saltwater fish abundant all around them. The waters from Lake Okeechobee, to the mangrove-lined rivers, to the Keys were their waterways, which they traversed in canoes made from hollowed-out cypress logs.

Conch shells broken open by Calusa Indians at Mormon Key. Photo by W. W. Armstrong

Several groups of Indians enjoyed the good life in the Everglades. The Calusa roamed the northwestern Glades, from the Caloosahatchee River down to the Ten Thousand Islands. The Miamis centered their lives around Lake Okeechobee. The Tekesta ranged along the Atlantic Coastal Ridge down to the Keys. The populations of all groups eventually declined and were assimilated after the Spaniards made the opening gambit in their attempt to conquer the people of the Glades.

The Calusa of the Everglades proved to be a fierce lot in the post-Columbian era, as Spaniards combed South Florida in search of gold and slaves to work the cane fields in Cuba and Hispaniola. The Indians and the Spanish were quite wary of one another. An early colonization attempt in 1521 by Ponce De Leon, who named Florida, ended violently with spears and arrows and Ponce De Leon's death. Slavers went after more docile Indians for plantation labor. Many Glades Indians stayed free, lurking to retrieve booty from galleons sunk by hurricanes, as the Spaniards rode the Gulf Stream back to Europe.

Florida passed into the possession of the newly formed United States by purchase in 1818. In the typical pattern, a signed treaty and further white settlement were followed by another treaty and more settlement. The Seminoles, as Florida's remaining Indians were known, were forced farther into swampy South Florida. Federal troops were deployed to get rid of them; white settlers were attacked guerrilla style. Back and forth went the slaughter during the Seminole Wars. Some Indians were sent to Arkansas, but a few remained unconquered in the Everglades to form the nucleus of the only current residents of the River of Grass, the Miccosukee and the Seminoles, on sites stretched out along the Tamiami Trail and a few other scraps of South Florida.

Then came the grand plan to drain the Everglades, proposed in the state legislature for the first time the very year Florida became a state, 1845. Reports were hurriedly written, and the Swamp Lands Act was passed by the U.S. Congress in 1850. The Civil War delayed further action until the great freezes of the orange groves in 1894 and 1895 drove more settlers south to get below the "frost line." Miami grew overnight. The Everglades were ripe for the taking. Plumes and alligator skins were, too.

By 1905, the dredges were at work in earnest. "Land" in the Everglades was selling and reselling as greedy speculators sold to greedier speculators. The only sales going faster were those of plumes from the rookeries, where the birds seemed as inexhaustible as the land. No one bothered to study the environmental effects of canals, or even if they could "work." Some land was put into cultivation, but settlers on other land parcels were discouraged by hurricanes and continued flooding; land values dropped. The Audubon Society came in and began trying to protect the rookeries, which suddenly seemed doomed. Saltwater intruded from the sea. Fires flamed over parched sawgrass. Yet one project, the Tamiami Trail, the road connecting the east and west coasts of lower Florida, was built as envisioned. It took 12 years and a lot of lives, but the road was completed in 1928.

Also in 1928, another view of the Everglades was taking shape. A man named Ernest F. Coe saw the beauty and uniqueness of the Everglades in its natural state. He saw the varied landscapes as a vast national park, and he set out on a one-man crusade to share his vision. Others joined Coe, and on June 20, 1947, the Everglades National Park came to be.

Of course, controversies and challenges continued to come, especially concerning the lifeblood of the Everglades, water. And there will be more challenges as long as this national park and millions of citizens exist side by side in South Florida. Yet with increased awareness that the health of the Everglades is an indicator of South Florida's future, the River of Grass will endure.

Understanding the Climate

For the Everglades visitor, the paddling season coincides with one of the two seasons that dominate South Florida—the rainy season and the dry season. The rainy season lasts from May through October. During this time, days often start clear, then clouds build and local thunderstorms

These statistics for Everglades City, Florida, from the National Oceanic and Atmospheric Administration will help you know what weather to expect.

	Nov.	Dec.	Jan.	Feb.	March	April
Average Temp.	71	66	65	65	69	73
Average High	81	77	76	76	80	84
Average Low	61	55	54	55	59	63
Record High	90	88	88	89	91	95
Record Low	33	29	27	30	33	43
Average Monthly Precip.	1.26"	1.19"	1.56"	1.93"	1.95"	2.06"

drop heavy rains, then the skies clear and the cycle starts again. The result is nearly 7 inches or more rain per month, culminating in the hurricane season. Daytime highs reach 90 degrees, dropping to the low 70s at night.

The dry season, November through April, is the time when canoeists and kayakers enjoy the waters of the Everglades. It seems odd that the best time for paddlers is during the dry season, but days are usually clear, average highs range from the mid-70s to the low 80s, and lows drop to around 60 degrees. On average, there are fewer than 7 days per month of measurable rainfall.

Of course, those are all averages. Cold fronts can and do punch down from the north, bringing strong winds and nighttime lows into the 30s. Big thunderstorms can hit hard. Dreary rains can last for days. But overall, Everglades paddlers can expect good paddling weather from November through April, though the hurricane season can spill into November, and April can get really hot. Check ahead on the weather during the shoulder months. And carry a transistor or weather radio with you at all times while in the Everglades to get the latest weather information.

Navigating Your Way around the Everglades

Many first-time Everglades visitors are surprised by the park's landscapes. They are difficult to pigeonhole—there are eight different ecosystems within the preserve boundaries. But for the Everglades paddler, there are two primary environments: the coastal mangrove swamp and the Gulf of Mexico, also known as the "outside."

Lone mangrove at low tide. Photo by W. W. Armstrong

The Everglades is the ultimate water park, so it is no surprise that water is the major element of the coastal mangrove swamp, the "outside," and most other environments here. Freshwater from the sawgrass swaths flow south and west, subtly merging with tidal saltwater from the Gulf of Mexico. Here, the brackish water runs to the Gulf among the world's richest stands of mangrove trees, which seem at first like a continuous green shoreline that all looks the same. And there is a ceaseless nature to the mangrove, as it conspires with the flowing water in endless variations of creeks, ponds, bays, inlets, streams, lakes, rivers, undulating shorelines, and keys that confuse novice and experienced paddler alike.

Now add a horizon unbroken by elevated features to use as guideposts—no mountain peaks or river valleys by which to establish your position. This low profile does make for fantastic weather watching, as clouds move by in every shape and form, but it leaves navigators to find their position by discerning subtle changes in contours of a "more alike than not" shoreline. Canopied creeks corkscrew in apparent circles, and your view is only the 20 feet ahead of your craft.

Then add distance to the navigator's realm. On the far side of a bay, a group of mangrove islands looks like unbroken seashore. Coastal configurations lose their curves. Water, cloud, and sky meld into distorted mirages. The horizon is lost: Boats float in the air, birds fly underwater, and islands move imperceptibly.

Throw tidal variation into the mix. The tide is out, and what should be a group of keys is now connected by exposed land. A 100-foot-wide channel becomes a 20-foot-wide creek. Mud flats and oyster bars block your course, which is plainly shown as water on the charts.

And then there are marked channels: canoe trails where all you have to do is follow the numbered markers of PVC pipe; channels in Florida Bay, where arrows on wooden posts keep boaters in the deep waters; channels from Flamingo out to the Gulf through Whitewater Bay. And there is the Wilderness Waterway, the marked route from Flamingo to Everglades City.

So what is it like navigating your way around the Everglades? It depends on how you do it. A global positioning system (GPS) with a map showing your exact position eliminates the trouble and worry of figuring out where you are. It certainly is safer that way. But then so is staying locked in your house until the day you die. Having a GPS on you is a wise paddler's insurance. Call me old-fashioned, but I believe that using a nautical chart and a compass is an integral part of the Everglades experience. You study the landscape for known points that correlate with your estimated current position as you see it on the nautical chart in front of you. You fix your current position as certain, then move on to another position. In doing so, you must absorb every nuance of the setting around you. This strategy forces you to scrutinize the Everglades. After all, you have a major stake in knowing where you really are.

Navigating here ends up as something between paddling marked channels and negotiating a maze. You may start out on a marked trail, then branch off to unmarked routes. Or you may use portions of a marked route such as the Wilderness Waterway on your trip. A good thing about navigating in the Everglades is that there are enough certain fixed positions such as campsites, chickees, signs, and markers to periodically confirm your position, without so many markers that the backcountry becomes a sign-posted highway in the watery wilderness.

What You Need for Navigating

Your primary tools for navigation are a compass, a nautical chart, and a creative mind.

No other maps will substitute for proper nautical charts. The paddling backcountry of the Everglades is covered by three nautical charts published by National Oceanographic and Atmospheric Administration (NOAA). These charts are #11430 for the northern Everglades, #11432 for the central Everglades, and #11433 for the southern Everglades and Florida Bay. You can get them by calling NOAA at (301) 436-6990. But these charts are made of paper, don't last, and aren't practical for paddlers surrounded by water.

Much more preferable are the tear-proof, waterproof charts made by Waterproof Charts, out of Punta Gorda, Florida. They are based on NOAA charts and cost roughly the same, but they are compiled and numbered somewhat differently. Yet they include all the features you need to navigate the Everglades, such as channels, water depths, campsites, and markers.

For Everglades City to Lostmans River, you need waterproof chart #41 (Everglades and Ten Thousand Islands). For Lostmans River to Flamingo, you need waterproof chart #39 (Lostmans River to Whitewater Bay). For Florida Bay, you need chart #33E (Florida Bay).

These waterproof charts are available at most bait and tackle shops in the vicinity of the Everglades and at the Flamingo Marina, in the national park by Florida Bay. They can also be ordered by phone. Call Waterproof Charts at (800) 423-9026 from 8 A.M. to 5 P.M. Eastern Time. Or you can get them over the web at www.waterproofcharts.com. These charts are head and shoulders above the old NOAA charts. Not every tiny mangrove island and creek will be on them (nor are they on the NOAA charts), but there will be more than enough features to get you around.

Your second physical necessity for navigation is a compass. I prefer the Silva brand, myself. You can get as fancy as you want, but a simple one with a clear plastic base, moveable compass ring, cardinal points, and numerical degree calibrations will do. To find which direction you should go, point the direction-of-travel arrow on the plastic base toward your destination on your chart. Turn the compass housing ring until the north on the housing ring lines up with the north of the actual compass arrow. Line up the map north with the compass north. You are now oriented. Luckily, north in the Everglades is close enough to true north that you don't have to adjust your compass for magnetic declination.

The third element you need for navigating is a creative mind. Your view of the Glades with a nautical chart is from the top looking down; from the air looking down on the water, a vertical point of view. Your real-life view is from the water surface across the water, a horizontal outlook. Your mind must be able to turn your vertical view on its side, to a horizontal view. You must match the features in front of you with the features on the chart. This becomes easier over time and is a function of experience with maps.

Phases of the moon affect tidal cycles. Photo by W. W. Armstrong

When you're looking at the chart at home, it is a simple matter to make your way through the Ten Thousand Islands, down the North Harney River, and from Hells Bay to Lane Bay and so on. It is another matter in the field, but the slow pace of a paddler can be an advantage, because the setting changes slowly. Conversely, the slow pace makes mistakes less forgivable. In this book, the individual routes described are rated for navigational challenge. If you are inexperienced with map and compass, paddle some of the easier (lower-rated) routes or the marked canoe trails, then work your way up. More experienced navigators can paddle the more challenging routes.

Navigational Considerations

Just as there are no other Everglades on earth, there is no paddling experience like the Everglades. The Marjory Stoneman Douglas Wilderness comprises much of the paddling area of the park. Within the wilderness there are truly wild places, but the water column (that is, anywhere there is water within the wilderness) is excepted. That means, unlike areas usually designated wilderness, motorized craft are allowed in the water column. That means you will see motorboats on your trip.

Motorboats can be your navigational ally. Say you are crossing Blackwater Sound, trying to reach The Boggies, a channel leading into Florida Bay from Blackwater Sound. A motorboat is on the same route. The west end of Blackwater Sound looks like one continuous shore. You can watch the motorboat power to the channel, helping you figure out exactly where The Boggies are. Also, don't be afraid to flag down a boater and ask for directions. But this is as embarrassing as pulling into a filling station in a strange city and asking for directions, especially if you are a man.

Birds can be your navigational allies as well. Say you are paddling west across Snake Bight to Flamingo in Florida Bay. The tide is going out, but from where you are, the water stretches all the way across the bight. Then you see birds standing in sections of the watery bay. You know to avoid those shallows, as they may become impassable.

Distance and horizon can make things look other than they are. In paddling the keys of Florida Bay, for instance, distant islands you are paddling for may not be visible on the horizon. Get your position, set your direction, and trust your compass. Similarly, far-off features such as the creek leading past Darwin's Place, indistinguishable in the distance, become clearer as you approach them. Again, set your direction and trust your compass.

Tides can be a directional indicator as well. If you know the general times of tidal variation in a given area, you can tell which way the Gulf is and vice versa. I once spent the night lost, near the Roberts River. The next morning I knew the tide was outgoing and checked it, then followed a series of creeks out to the Roberts River and regained my position.

Numbered channel markers are very helpful for navigation. The Coast Guard maintains a marked route from Flamingo to the Gulf via Whitewater Bay and the Little Shark River. The numbers on the large red and green signs on metal posts get higher as you head north for the Gulf. There are also Coast Guard–maintained markers heading into Florida Bay from Flamingo and into the Gulf from Everglades City.

The Wilderness Waterway, maintained by the park service, starts in Flamingo and leads to Everglades City. Paddlers follow the Coast Guard markers to #48, just north of Whitewater Bay, then follow rectangular brown signs. These signs are numbered, getting higher the closer you get to Everglades City. The arrows on the signs *do not always* point you in the right direction. So double-check your chart and don't blindly follow the arrows of the Wilderness Waterway.

Paddling at night is a very viable option in the Everglades, especially on a full-moon night, and is a good way to use the tides or to avoid windy days. Don't expect to find your way around Hells Bay in the dark, but a less complex area, such as along the Gulf, can be paddled after the sun goes down. What helps are your two urban markers, Miami and Naples. The lights of Miami are visible no matter your position in the Glades. They can be your eastern beacon. The lights of the Naples area are much less bright, but in the northern reaches of the park, they are your northern signal. Lighted buoys mark the park's perimeter in the Gulf.

Obviously, the sun can be used through the day to help you figure out your position. Keep up with where you are at all times using these navigational helpers. Don't try either to paddle for an hour and then reposition yourself or to check your position only every now and then. The more you stay on top of your position, the less likely you will get lost.

Finally, do not—I repeat, do not—enter the backcountry without a nautical chart and compass, even if you have a GPS. Batteries can die.

Watching Out for Potential Hazards

Imagine a man-on-the-street interviewer asking passersby this question: "What do you think poses the biggest hazard in the Everglades?" Without a doubt the most popular answer would be "Alligators." In reality, wild alligators shy away from people. Food-habituated gators can pose something of a problem, but for the Everglades paddler there are several other hazards that may adversely impact a trip on a far more regular basis. A negative alligator encounter is very, very rare.

Wind can be the paddler's worst enemy, though a moderate tailwind can be a good thing. So can an insect-clearing breeze. But big blows can be dangerous. South Florida in the winter has fantastic weather more often than not—generally sunny and warm, but also regularly windy. The mornings are usually still, but the winds pick up as the morning moves along. And 10–15 knots is average. Days with wind speeds lower than this occur, but so do plenty of days with higher wind speeds. Small-craft advisories are common. Winds normally blow from the southeast, but when a winter cold front steamrolls down from the north, the temperature plummets and steady strong north winds of 15–20 knots can hold for days. Try to plan your trip to avoid strong winds, but when this is impossible, take smaller channels and use the lee sides of shores and islands to minimize the effect of the wind.

When the winds blow, the waves come right along with them. First-time Everglades trippers are often shocked at the vast amount of open water they traverse. And a good wind can blow a glassy bay into a choppy wave trap. Wind may slow your progress, but waves can capsize your craft—real trouble. Listen to weather reports—they usually forecast wind speed and direction. When big winds are expected, try to paddle early in the morning, when the wind and subsequent waves are generally lower. Consider paddling in the late afternoon or at night for the same reason.

In windy conditions, try to modify your route to stay in sheltered waters, or at least take sheltered breaks when you can, to avoid exhausting yourself. Don't try to fight through waves. Roll over a wave, riding the crest, then drop to the trough as gently as possible, then pull yourself up and over the next crest. Sea kayaks have the advantage in big waves. If you are kayaking, make sure any gear outside the craft is tied on very tightly, and consider using a wrist strap to connect yourself to your paddle.

Canoeists have to be more careful. First, try to avoid getting parallel to big waves. If you are heading in a direction parallel to the waves, paddle through them at an angle, going back and forth, not parallel to the waves. A wave crashing into the side of your canoe can be a quick capsizer. If water is splashing in, try to bail at intervals. Otherwise the water in your canoe will lower your waterline, allowing more water in faster, and eventually you will sink. Beware waves coming from behind; they can drop a lot of water in your boat when you are not looking.

In times of wind, bring rope to tie the corners of your tent to the posts of the chickee. Furthermore, wait until late in the day to erect your tent to avail yourself of more space on the chickee and not subject the tent to sun or wind damage. Follow this advice when camped on open beaches, as well.

Have a rope on both ends of your craft in order to securely tie it to a chickee, and pull your boat far above the high-tide line on beaches to make sure the boat will be there when you need it again.

When leaving a beach in your craft, aim your boat straight toward the waves and try to time your departure between wave surges, then paddle out at a slight angle to the waves. Do not allow your boat to get broadside to the waves, or it will fill with water and get pounded back to shore.

Tides can be your enemy or friend, much like the wind. Low tides can leave you stranded in the buggy Nightmare or expansive Florida Bay. Not only can tides cause discomfort or delay—sometimes they can do real damage. Be careful around manufactured canals; a strong pull will take you where you don't want to go, or ram you into a tree lying half submerged in the water. The biggest problem with tides comes when you are cutting corners in rivers, peninsulas, and straits. You will be paddling in one direction and the tide, flowing perpendicular to your direction, will catch the nose of your craft and turn you over before you know what happened. Watch for direction flow in the water ahead of you—ripples and currents—and adjust your speed and direction.

In the northern half of the Everglades paddling areas, especially closer to the Gulf, are oyster bars. These are huge clumps of oysters growing in a mass beneath the water. Their sharp shells are often exposed at low tides. Exercise caution with your craft and your feet. They can slice through your foot or a folding kayak before you realize it. Wear shoes when you get out of your boat, and carry duct tape for temporarily sealing tears in your boat.

One of the biggest potential problems is actually little. Mosquitoes and no-see-ums can dominate an outing. If you can't stand being bitten by bugs, don't come here! I have been on trips where I was bitten less than once a day, and I have been on trips where I was wearing full clothing and a head net whenever I was on land, and I was in the tent every night an hour before dark. Mosquitoes can take your breath away at ground sites, and no-see-ums can drive you to tears on the beach. Clothes are your best defense: shoes, socks, long pants, long-sleeved shirt, bandanna around your neck, and a hat. But by all means bring insect repellent, a good tent with fine mesh netting, and a head net. One thing about a head net: When you want one you really want one, and when you don't have one there is usually no means of obtaining one. Plan to have cooked your supper and cleaned your plates by sunset, or you'll be speed cooking in a mosquito-driven frenzy. Or wait an hour or so after dark to start cooking.

When erecting your tent, place it with the tent door facing the wind. Mosquitoes are less apt to stay on the windward side of a tent, so this way you will bring fewer mosquitoes with you when you go in and out of the tent.

There are two poisonous trees in the Everglades paddling area, man-chineel and poisonwood. You probably won't encounter manchineel—it is an uncommon coastal tree up to 30 feet high with leathery, light green, shallow-toothed leaves on long yellow stems. Its green to reddish fruits are deadly when eaten. The sap will burn you. The other tree is poisonwood. It is in the same family as poison ivy. Its shiny, dark green, compound leaves come in five leaflets, with irregular black spots on them. The sap of this tree is toxic, too. Be reasonably careful and covered when walking through tree hammocks.

Powerboaters are much like the winds and tides—they can either help you or hinder you, depending on the speed and direction they are going. Paddlers and powerboaters share the water, so let's share the best we can. *Powerboaters are not the enemy.* It is not us versus them. Powerboaters can aid in determining your direction and in an emergency. But they can also speed by without consideration. It all depends on the driver. Be a defensive paddler: Watch and listen for motorboats, then exercise the same courtesy toward powerboaters that you would expect from them.

Now, what about those alligators? And snakes? And scorpions? Alligators pose little problem except for the alligators that hang around campsites waiting for a handout of fish guts and other yummy leftovers. These food-habituated alligators will come toward anything thrown in the water. Keep out of the water in such situations. Never feed an alligator! You have nothing to fear from snakes. Consider yourself lucky if you see one—then you will have equaled the total number of snakes I've seen in the paddling country of the Everglades. Small scorpions can be inside dead wood. Be on the watch for these critters when breaking up firewood at beach sites.

Planning Your Trip

You want to paddle the Everglades, but where to begin? All the information you need is included in this book. But you can access official park information by calling (305) 242-7700 and asking for a Wilderness Trip Planner. Or go on the web at http://www.nps.gov/ever.

With the rules, routes, and campsite descriptions at your fingertips, you can plan a trip. But that is all you can do from home. **Wilderness permits, required for all overnight camping, are available only in person at Flamingo and Gulf Coast ranger stations. You can pick one up—in person—up to 24 hours in advance of a trip during the winter paddling season, November through April.** Phone permits are available for trips originating in the Florida Keys and for going to the following Florida Bay campsites: North Nest Key, Little Rabbit Key, and Carl Ross Key. During the off-season, May to November, you must register in person at Flamingo, Florida Bay, or Gulf Coast Ranger Station.

Head to the permit desk at Flamingo or Gulf Coast Ranger Station and make a backcountry trip request with park staff. Have alternate trips planned; this way, if campsites are already reserved, you have an alternate

Loading sea kayaks near Gulf Coast Ranger Station. Photo by W. W. Armstrong

ready. Once your permit is issued and park regulations have been explained to you, you must pay a modest permit-processing fee. The fee is $10 for parties up to 6; $20 for parties of 7–12; and $30 for parties of more than 12. Everglades National Park gets to keep 80 percent of the fees for reducing the backlog of park maintenance projects, including back-country campsites and chickees. The other 20 percent goes to parks that don't charge fees.

Heavy-Use Periods

The general paddling season in Everglades National Park runs from November through April. Insects, thunderstorms, and the possibility of hurricanes combine to keep the Everglades backcountry nearly deserted May through October. When the first north breezes cool and clear the air, reducing the insect population, paddlers turn their eye southward to the Everglades. A few campsites begin to fill on weekends. But the crowds really come around Christmas. The period between Christmas and New

Year's is the Everglades' busiest. Expect full campsites then and plan alternative trips. After January 1, weekends can be busy, yet you can nearly always get on the water and to a campsite in the general vicinity of where you want to go. Plan your trip during the week for the most solitude. The next big crowds come around Presidents' Day weekend in February. The last big hits come during mid-March, when college kids flock to the Glades for overnight trips. Again, get to the ranger stations early and you can get some campsites. As the weather warms up in April, visits taper off, dying by the end of the month.

Wilderness Waterway

For many paddlers, the only route to take in the Everglades is the Wilderness Waterway, which runs from Everglades City to Flamingo. This is a rewarding endeavor, though I believe there are better combinations of routes that result in a better experience for the tripper. But if you want to trace the Wilderness Waterway from beginning to end, use the routes I map out in the next paragraph. The campsites I mention are not necessarily the most appropriate places to stay, just points for reference.

To use the routes in this book to take the official Wilderness Waterway from the Gulf Coast Ranger Station in Everglades City: Take the Causeway Route to Lopez River Route to Hurddles Creek Route to Sunday Bay chickee. From Sunday Bay chickee, take Last Huston Bay Route to Darwin's Place Route to Lostmans Five campsite. From Lostmans Five campsite, take the Willy Willy Route to Rodgers River Bay Route to the Broad River Route to Broad River campsite. From the Broad River campsite, take The Nightmare Route to Harney River chickee to the Harney River Route. Paddle up the Harney River Route to Tarpon Bay and the Shark Cutoff Route. Take the Shark Cutoff Route to Oyster Bay chickee. From Oyster Bay chickee, briefly take the Cormorant Pass Route to Whitewater Bay Route to the Buttonwood Canal Route and on to Flamingo.

Paddlers' Waterway

If you want a route that goes from the north all the way to the south that is more friendly to self-propelled craft than the Wilderness Waterway, take what I call the Paddlers' Waterway. If you take the Paddlers' Waterway, you will minimize motorboat traffic and see the best of the Everglades, from the freshwater to the Gulf to shell mounds and on around fabulous Cape Sable.

To take the Paddlers' Waterway: Start on the Turner River Canoe Trail off the Tamiami Trail and paddle to the Hurddles Creek Route to Sunday Bay chickee. From Sunday Bay chickee, take the Last Huston Bay Route a short distance to the Huston River Route. Take the Huston River Route to Mormon Key in the Gulf. From Mormon Key, take the Turkey Key Route to Lostmans Ranger Station. From Lostmans Ranger Station, take the Lostmans River Route to Toms Creek Route. Take the Toms Creek Route to Rodgers River chickee. From Rodgers River chickee, take the Rodgers River Bay Route to Broad River. Take the Broad River Route up to Camp Lonesome. From Camp Lonesome, take the Wood River Route to the Broad River Campsite. From Broad River campsite, take The Nightmare Route to Harney River chickee. From Harney River chickee, take the Harney River Route a short distance east to the North Harney River Route. Take the North Harney River Route to Canepatch campsite. From Canepatch campsite, take the Harney River Route to the Shark Cutoff Route in Tarpon Bay. Take the Shark Cutoff Route to Oyster Bay chickee. From Oyster Bay chickee, take the Big Sable Route to Northwest Cape campsite. From Northwest Cape, take the Middle Cape Route to East Cape campsite. From East Cape take the East Cape Route to Flamingo.

Rules And Regulations

All plants, animals, and artifacts in the Everglades are protected; do not collect or disturb them. Unoccupied shells may be gathered—up to 1 quart per person.

Closed Areas—All keys (islands) in Florida Bay are closed to landing, except Bradley Key (sunrise to sunset) and those designated as campsites. In Florida Bay, the mainland from Terrapin Point to US 1 is closed to landing.

Fires are allowed only at beach sites along the Gulf Coast, below the storm-surge line, using only dead or downed wood. **No fires** are allowed at ground or chickee sites.

Search and Rescue—File a trip plan with a friend or relative before leaving. If you do not return home on time, that person should call Everglades National Park dispatch at (305) 242-7740, which operates 24 hours a day. If you are overdue, the park service is not going to look for you without being notified.

Trash must be packed out. Please help make everyone's wilderness experience enjoyable; leave campsites cleaner than you find them.

Human Waste—Use toilets where provided. At campsites without facilities, bury human waste in a hole at least 6 inches deep. Burn toilet paper in the hole or pack it out with your trash.

Food—Remove all food particles from dishes before washing. DO NOT dump food scraps in the water; pack them out with your trash.

Water—One gallon per person per day is the minimum recommendation.

Weather conditions change frequently and rapidly. Be prepared for intense sun, rain, strong winds, and cold.

Winds/Tides—Check the conditions before you depart and carry a weather or transistor radio. Current weather reports are indispensable for overnight Everglades trips.

Nautical Charts and Compass are necessary for most trips, even if you have a GPS.

Designated Site—You must stay at the site listed on the permit unless safety factors require otherwise.

Noise—Be considerate of other visitors, especially when in close proximity to other groups. Noise-producing machinery such as generators and bug sprayers is prohibited.

Weapons—Using or carrying weapons is prohibited.

Fishing—State fishing license regulations apply. You are responsible for adhering to the size and daily bag limits for Everglades National Park. **Pets** are not permitted.

Wildlife—DO NOT feed or harass alligators and other wildlife. Animals that are habituated to human food can be dangerous.

Equipment

Outdoor adventurers get to choose their own equipment. And they sink or swim with their choice. Just kidding. But good equipment choices can go a long way in making or breaking an Everglades trip.

Canoe or Sea Kayak?

The first choice for Everglades paddlers is which type of boat to take. Canoes have been the mainstay for years, but sea kayaks are really on the rise. Each type has its own advantages and disadvantages. Canoes can carry more equipment and allow more freedom of movement than kayaks, yet kayaks are faster and are safer in big waves. Canoes are easier to load and unload, but sea kayaks keep their loads stored away from the elements. Canoes are more maneuverable in tight quarters, but sea kayaks track better. And the comparisons can go on and on—choose the boat that works for you. I use both and enjoy each.

Sea Kayaks

So you have decided to use a sea kayak. Now, what type of sea kayak? There are numerous makes and models on the market. Sit-on-top kayaks are being used more and more in the Everglades, since staying dry is a less important issue here than in colder climates. The sit-on-tops are more comfortable and easier to get in and out of, but expect to get wet in waves. Folding kayaks are convenient for those flying to the Glades from far away, but I wouldn't want to be in one around the sharp oyster bars of the Ten Thousand Islands.

Touring kayaks are deservedly the most popular. These have ample room for storing camping gear, food, and water. They are stable and durable, but they can be hot on a sunny day, if you have the spray skirt on. I keep my spray skirt around my waist, ready to slip around the lip of the kayak if big waves come up.

I prefer models with a rudder. Tides, currents, and winds are easier to negotiate with a rudder. Be prepared to pop the rudder up in the shallow waters of the Glades. Two-person sea kayaks are catching on more and more. Sharing responsibility makes paddling and navigating easier for both parties. Someone unable or unwilling to navigate can travel with an experienced sea kayaker.

Paddles are a matter of personal choice. Kayakers almost always use double-bladed paddles. Each paddler must determine the right length and blade width for their needs. Most kayakers prefer a feathered paddle, which is a paddle with blades at 90-degree angles to one another. Consider buying a quality paddle, and always bring an extra paddle that breaks down, in case you lose your primary paddle. Bring a sponge to remove unwanted water from your cockpit and storage compartments.

Canoes

Among the many makes and models of canoes out there, which one is right for the Everglades paddler? I like to consider length, depth, volume, and durability when choosing a canoe. Tandem canoers want a boat at least 17 feet long for ample room. A canoe much longer than that can become a problem, getting through narrow Glades creeks. A canoe should have adequate depth and volume for gear storage and water displacement. The larger canoes are safer in the Gulf. Remember that paddlers here must carry all their own water, adding to the load.

Oyster bars, sandbars, and shell and beach landings can be rough on a boat. Old-time aluminum canoes solve the durability problem, but they are slower. If you use synthetic boat materials, your craft is going to wear the scars of travel here. This is no place to try to baby a canoe.

Solo paddlers should use a smaller boat. I have used a 14.5-foot Old Town Pathfinder in the Everglades for years. It is scarred on the bottom but has served me well. It has no keel, which makes for tracking problems but greater precision in paddling. There is a lot of open water in the

Glades—you may be better off with a keel, especially if you are a less experienced paddler.

I have never used a spray cover in the Everglades, but I have wished for one in big water on the Gulf. If you have one, bring it. A bailer made from a gallon milk jug can remove water from your canoe. Find the canoeing paddle you like and bring an extra for each person in the boat.

Life Vest

Not only is a personal floatation device sensible, but Coast Guard–approved life vests are required for Everglades paddlers. They can also keep you warm on cool days.

Storage

Quality rubber and plastic storage bags come in a dizzying array of sizes and strengths for sea kayaks and canoes. The sea kayak models are shaped to fit in the kayak. They can be a pain to load and unload, but they do the trick. Take the extra moment to close them properly after you put your gear inside.

A quality tent with no-see-um netting will spare you the misery of bugs and inclement weather. Photo by W. W. Armstrong

Other general waterproof bags can be strapped onto a sea kayak or set in a canoe. Strap your gear in a canoe if you are entering big water. If you capsize, your gear will stay with the boat. I trusted my laptop computer to dry bags when I was writing this book, and I didn't have a problem. Consider using several bags of medium size—that way you don't have all your eggs in one basket in case of a wetting. The models with shoulder straps can be handy for hauling your gear from the water to island campsites at low tide. These "Everglades portages" can be surprisingly long. Absolutely have a small waterproof bag close by for your personal items such as sunscreen, bug dope, lip balm, and so on. Even though your charts should be waterproof, I also use a waterproof map holder to keep my compass and map together.

Repairs

Keep duct tape on hand for temporarily repairing your boat and waterproof bags. Before you apply the tape, dry the item being repaired and brush away any sand and other debris, then apply the duct tape.

Shelter

The advantage of boat camping over backpacking is the increased equipment capacity paddlers have. You can bring a bigger shelter. For two campers, I prefer four-person tent models with a vestibule. When the bugs are bad and the January nights long, you will be happy for the extra room, though it will make chickees a little more cramped. Free-standing tents are a necessity for chickees. Make sure your tent has a bug screen with mesh tight enough to keep no-see-ums out. Also, make sure your packed tent will fit properly in a waterproof storage bag. Sand stakes are a good thing to have when you're camped on the beach on a windy day

By all means bring a tarp and rope. After paddling all day in the sun to a beach campsite, you are going to want some shade. Use paddles for poles and make a sun shelter.

Shade-producing hats are necessary for a safe and comfortable Everglades outing. Photo by W. W. Armstrong

Cooking Gear and Food

Campers in the Everglades must bring a portable stove, as fires are not allowed on chickees or ground campsites. Bring more than enough fuel for the duration of your trip. I like to grill over a fire, so a foldable, portable grill is part of my kit when I head to a beach campsite. With extra room, boaters can upgrade their cook kits somewhat. No matter how meticulous you are, expect to chew on a few grains of sand in your meal on the beaches. Many campers like to spread a sheet of plastic over their cooking area to minimize this unpleasant but regular Everglades experience. Bring more than enough matches and lighters—campers often drop items between the cracks in the boards of chickees and lose items in the sand of beaches. My best knife lies beneath the Sweetwater chickee.

Campers must bring not only all their food but their own water. *Bring 1 gallon of water per person per day.* There are few freshwater sources in the paddling area of the Everglades. Boaters can upgrade their food by using coolers, but don't expect ice to last more than a few days. You can convert your melted ice to drinking or cooking water. Consider using brackish water for cooking if you are low on freshwater. When bringing foods, keep in mind the potential sun and heat of the Everglades. They can spoil foods quicker than would be the case in cooler, more forested wilderness areas. Keep food out of the sun during the day and stored away in cooler areas. Many ground and beach campsites have persistent raccoons, so store your food and water in hard-sided containers and tie these shut with rope or bungee cords.

Clothing

When packing their clothing, Everglades novices often go heavy on shorts and T-shirts, light on cover-up clothes. They find they should have done the opposite. Though the weather is generally warm, shorts and T-shirts are bad for two Everglades situations: sun and bugs. Bring the summery clothes, but expect to wear long-sleeved shirts and long pants. They offer protection from both the sun and bugs. Bring light-colored clothing and make sure it is tightly woven. Salt marsh mosquitoes are very persistent and will bite through overly thin clothing. Thick socks and foot-covering shoes are important for protection from bugs and for cool weather. And cool weather can strike. Have several layers of clothing with you, culminating in a waterproof rain jacket and rain pants. These will keep you warm and dry. Gloves can provide blister and sun protection.

Hats are a must for the Everglades traveler. The sun shining in your eyes and off the water will burn and blind you. Consider wide-brimmed hats and flats fishing hats with neck protection. Bandannas will also protect your neck. Visors and ball caps are more comfortable but don't provide as much overall sun protection. By all means bring sunglasses—get a strap attachment for around your neck to prevent loss. And bring a spare pair. Your eyes will thank you. Invest in a head net. When the bugs are bad, you'll appreciate it, and there is no substitute for a head net if you don't have one. A bug suit can protect your body much as a head net protects your head.

Other Items

The three musts for navigators are a waterproof nautical chart, a compass, and a tide chart. Get the tide chart when you get your backcountry permit. Keep all three items handy at all times. You will need them. Bring a

Fishing is a popular Everglades pastime. Photo by W. W. Armstrong

spare compass stowed away. Binoculars will help you find markers and discern shorelines. A first-aid kit, knife, rope, flashlight, timepiece, and weather radio or transistor radio will aid in your day-to-day existence. (Cellular and digital phones offer hit-or-miss coverage in the Everglades.) A timepiece will help you calculate the tides. A first-aid kit will help until you can flag down aid. Flares will help you flag down aid. Bring a light strong enough to shine brightly at night. Radios can provide vital weather information.

Do not enter the Everglades without sunscreen and bug dope. I've seen campers so sunburned they could hardly paddle. Use sunscreen! Bug dope will make life much more bearable when the swamp angels are singing. Bring creams for your skin and sprays for your clothing to keep the bugs at bay. Don't forget personal items such as your toothbrush. Also, bring toilet paper and a trowel for human waste. Not all campsites provide toilets—dispose of your waste properly.

Backcountry Pastimes

Once in the backcountry, there are things to do besides paddle. Most folks don't want to navigate and stroke the blade all day, then fall into camp, eat some grub, and immediately hit the bag. Fishing, birding, and beachcombing are among the most popular activities Everglades explorers undertake.

Anglers will have a hard time finding more varied waters to fish than in the Everglades. To fish in Everglades National Park, you must have a valid Florida state license for fresh- and/or saltwater species. Check for the latest size and bag limits. Get more salt-tolerant and heavier tackle than you would normally use from a self-propelled craft.

Freshwater bass and bluegill ply many of the interior creeks, such as the upper North River, near the beginning of the Hells Bay Canoe Trail, and upper Lostmans Creek. Some of the richest waters for fish occur where freshwater meets saltwater. Snook, Jack Crevalle, ladyfish, and mangrove snapper will take a well-presented lure. Paddlers will be in for a big fight if they hook a tarpon. It's happened to me. I was almost thankful the giant got off the lure—I didn't know what I was going to do if I got it to the boat! Sea trout, reds, and other fish inhabit the rivers and coastlines of the Everglades. Many anglers like to use live bait, though it is harder to keep for paddlers than for most other anglers. Consider trolling with lures on long paddling days. It breaks up the stroking, and you just may catch dinner.

Birders flock to the Everglades like birds once flocked to the park. Birds are still around the Glades, just not in the numbers they once were. Day to day, birds are the most prevalent wildlife you'll see. Many times you can quietly stay in one location and let the birds come to you. Invest in one of the birding books available in park visitor centers. Otherwise it will be an endless guessing game. Binoculars are a big help in identifying the avians.

One of my personal interests is trees. Though most of the Everglades paddling area is mangrove or water, there are many trees to identify. Years ago, before I became well-acquainted with Florida, I was amazed at the numerous species of palm trees. Plant and tree identification is especially challenging here, where differing environments subtly blend into one another. Also in the visitor centers are good tree-identification books to help you.

Beachcombing is fun on Everglades beaches and keys. You can gather up to 1 quart per person of unoccupied shells. Remember that all keys in Florida Bay are closed to landing, except Bradley Key and those designated as campsites. In Florida Bay, the mainland from Terrapin Point to US 1 is closed to landing.

The Routes

Florida Bay

Dildo Key Bank Route

Begin: Little Rabbit Key

End: Flamingo

Distance: 12.5 miles

Time: 7 hours

Potential Tidal Influence: 5

Potential Wind Influence: 5

Navigational Challenge: 3

Highlights: Wildlife in Florida Bay

Hazards: Motorboat traffic, big winds and strong tides in Florida Bay

Campsites: Little Rabbit Key

Connections: Man of War Route, Shark Point Route, East Cape Route, Buttonwood Canal Route

This route is the third leg of the Florida Bay loop. This loop has its downside: It is a total of 36 miles of paddling, and if the winds and tides are against you, it can be downright exhausting and possibly dangerous. The long distances and open water favor sea kayakers, though canoers can make it when the weather is right. No matter which craft you choose, be sure you have a favorable weather forecast before embarking on this jour-

Cockpit view of sea kayaking in Florida Bay. Photo by author

ney. This leg of the loop passes several islands and shallows where there will be birds aplenty and fish swimming all around, too.

Leave the dock at Little Rabbit Key campsite and paddle north around the west side of Big Rabbit Key, then set your compass for Cluett Key—the waters vary in depth but are generally shallow, with a grassy ocean bottom. Tides have an east-west direction to them between the Rabbit Keys and Cluett Key. Approach and pass Cluett Key on the east at 4 miles, then split the difference between Dildo Key and the Pelican Keys. Dildo Key is named for a cactus native to South Florida that has long thorny three-angled stems. The twin Pelican Keys are easy to spot; the channel between them makes them more identifiable from a distance as you pass by them.

If the tide is on the rise, there should be no trouble traversing the shallows of Dildo Key Bank. If you are finding the waters too shallow here, veer closer to the Pelican Keys. The man-made structures of Flamingo will start to become visible in the distance.

You can take an interesting side trip at this point by swinging northwest around relatively small Catfish Key and past Dave Foy Bank, where bird life is often abundant. Otherwise, take the pass between Frank Key and Palm Key, then enter the busy boating area around Flamingo. The water will often be somewhat murky here. Watch for motorboats, and parallel the channel markers leading to the Flamingo Marina cut, arriving at Flamingo Marina at 12.5 miles. The Catfish Key detour will add about 1.5 miles to your paddle.

East Cape Route

Begin: Flamingo
End: East Cape Campsite
Distance: 10 miles
Time: 5 hours
Potential Tidal Influence: 5
Potential Wind Influence: 5
Navigational Challenge: 2
Highlights: Lots of beach camping
Hazards: Motorboat traffic, big winds, and strong tides in Florida Bay
Campsites: East Clubhouse Beach, Clubhouse Beach, East Cape
Connections: First National Bank Route, Middle Cape Route, Snake Bight Route, Buttonwood Canal Route, Dildo Key Route, Bear Lake Canoe Trail

This route runs by the most southerly piece of mainland real estate in the country. You'll leave Flamingo Marina and civilization behind for a mangrove shoreline that becomes more sandy, as in beaches. You will have your pick on this route of one of three quality campsites to do some serious beach camping. How close you stay to shore will depend on water levels, which change dramatically out here with the winds and tides. This is the open water of Florida Bay, on the "outside" of the Everglades, so keep apprised of any changes in the weather.

East Clubhouse Beach. Photo by author

Leave the Flamingo marina and head west, hugging the shoreline. Look for the osprey nest on channel marker #15. Continue to trace the shoreline, passing park housing and the Flamingo Campground. Stay on the outside of the narrow island that parallels the campground. If the tide is up, take the route between Bradley Key and the coast. The tall mangrove forest will provide an interesting contrast to the bay. Also, you can mark your progress better. If the tide is out, stay outside Bradley Key and several hundred yards offshore, as the waters can be boat stoppingly shallow.

Pass diminutive Curry Key at mile 2.5. Continue west and come to East Clubhouse Beach campsite at mile 4. This is a good place to stop and camp or just stretch your legs. East Cape Sable appears on the horizon just after you pass the first point beyond East Clubhouse Beach campsite. Sandy Key and Carl Ross Key are visible to your left, way out in Florida Bay. The Middle Ground Buoy is visible as well.

Pass Slagle Ditch at mile 6. Back in the early 20th century, Model Land Company dug this ditch as part of an effort to drain Cape Sable to make it more fertile and appealing to potential land buyers. The intermittent beach continues until you come to the Clubhouse Beach campsite at mile 7. This marked campsite has a longer stretch of beach than average for this section and is backed by a sizable marl prairie.

Beyond Clubhouse Beach, stay the course west, passing House Ditch, then East Cape Canal, which runs to Lake Ingraham. This is the southwesterly terminus of the Bear Lake Canoe Trail. The canal is more than 100 feet wide and very straight. This can be an emergency only alternate return route if the waves are too big in Florida Bay. Check with Flamingo Ranger Station about water levels in the Bear Lake Canoe Trail before considering this alternate route.

Pass a mangrove creek, then a second shortly thereafter. The second creek marks the beginning of the East Cape campsite. End your route at the rounded East Cape, which curves northwesterly at mile 10. Middle Cape is visible just as you swing around East Cape. The Middle Cape Route leads north 9.5 miles to Northwest Cape.

First National Bank Route

Begin: Flamingo

End: Carl Ross Key

Distance: 10 miles

Time: 5 hours

Potential Tidal Influence: 5

Potential Wind Influence: 5

Navigational Challenge: 3

Highlights: Solitude, second half of trip

Hazards: Motorboat traffic, big winds, and strong tides in Florida Bay

Campsites: Flamingo Campground, Carl Ross Key

Connections: Dildo Key Bank Route, East Cape Route, Snake Bight Route, Buttonwood Canal Route

---

This route is the first leg of the Florida Bay loop. The Florida Bay loop is a minimum two-night, three-day loop paddle that traverses west and central parts of Florida Bay, from the shallows of several banks that are havens for birds at low tide to deep basins where the grassy sea floor can be seen several feet down. It heads for Carl Ross Key, then Little Rabbit Key, to circle back to the mainland. This first leg leaves the busy Flamingo Marina and heads west on the First National Bank Route, paralleling Club-house Beach before turning south to the lonely and set-apart Carl Ross and Sandy Keys. Sandy Key is a preserved bird-nesting area; there are often hundreds of birds all over the island. Carl Ross Key is a beach camper's paradise, with fantastic views in all directions. You may want to consider a layover day here, as two consecutive nights of camping are allowed.

Paddle out of the cut at Flamingo and veer southwest for the southern tip of Bradley Key. The water will be shallow, but at least motorboats will be out of your path. At the tip of Bradley Key, paddle toward channel marker #8, in the vicinity of the Oyster Keys. Sandy Key is barely visible on the horizon. Stay west past marker #8 toward channel marker #6. Pass between channel marker #6 and the marked Conchie Channel at mile 4, keeping west. The water has long since deepened, and you can now see both Carl Ross Key and Sandy Key on the horizon.

Stay west a little longer. East Clubhouse Beach is visible on your right. Begin to veer south and look for the marked Rocky Channel. If the tide

Campsite at Carl Ross Key. Photo by author

is low or out, you may have to use Rocky Channel to cross First National Bank. Approach Carl Ross Key from the south, avoiding the shallows. A few large black mangrove grow on the northwest tip of the island. This is your deepest approach. Paddle in to this beautiful camp at mile 10. It really seems like an island paradise out here. Sandy Key and Carl Ross Key are the most westerly keys in Florida Bay. Sandy Key is a protected bird-nesting area. The Florida Bay loop continues to Little Rabbit Key via the Man of War Route.

Man of War Route

Begin: Carl Ross Key

End: Little Rabbit Key

Distance: 13.5 miles

Time: 7.5 hours

Potential Tidal Influence: 5

Potential Wind Influence: 5

Navigational Challenge: 3

Highlights: Wide-open ocean paddling

Hazards: Big winds and strong tides in Florida Bay

Campsites: Little Rabbit Key, Carl Ross Key

Connections: Dildo Key Bank Route, First National Bank Route

This route is the second leg of the Florida Bay loop. Paddlers will head across a wide open stretch of Florida Bay past Man of War Key. Once past Man of War Key, the route traverses the Rabbit Key Basin to Little Rabbit Key and another backcountry campsite. Be aware that making a beeline for Man of War Key from Carl Ross Key may leave you stranded high and dry on First National Bank if the tide is going out.

This is the best route for this trip because you are aiming for fixed objects on the horizon rather than repeatedly looking down to follow an exact compass direction, which is harder to do in a slow-moving, self-propelled craft. The overall navigation is easy despite the daunting open water. This route *does* take you across some of the most wide-open water described in this entire guidebook.

Looking out on Florida Bay from the dock at Little Rabbit Key. Photo by author

Leave Carl Ross Key and paddle south of Sandy Key, then head east for Man of War Key. Man of War Key will be the most southerly of the keys on the eastern horizon. Stay generally south of the shallow First National Bank, unless the tide is incoming. If you strike out early, the sun will be in your face.

Pass the marked Man of War Channel at 6 miles. Be prepared for strong tidal currents running through the channel. Man of War Key will be on your left, but stay well south of the island, because the waters near it are very shallow. Once past Man of War Key, you can see the Rabbit Keys. They will be the most southeasterly keys on the horizon. The two islands are very distinguishable. The much larger Big Rabbit Key will be on the left and your destination, Little Rabbit Key, will be on the right.

The waters will deepen as you paddle across Rabbit Key Basin. The water here can be exceptionally clear, with the grassy floor several feet below you. There will be a water-monitoring station on your right as you near Little Rabbit Key. There is also a water-monitoring station on the north shore of the key by the campsite. The dock of Little Rabbit Key will be facing you on the west as you paddle in at mile 13.5. This rustic island is a literal "get away from it all." The clarity of the water around Little Rabbit Key will stun you. The Florida Bay loop continues via the Dildo Key Bank Route, which leads 12.5 miles to Flamingo.

North Nest Key Loop

Begin: Key Largo   End: Key Largo

Distance: 16 miles   Time: 8 hours

Potential Tidal Influence: 4   Potential Wind Influence: 5

Navigational Challenge: 3

Highlights: Colorful ocean waters, camping on a key on Florida Bay

Hazards: Motorboats near Key Largo, open water in Florida Bay

Campsites: North Nest Key

Connections: None

This loop offers some of the best paddling in Florida Bay and the Florida Keys. It begins at Key Largo, passing through the colorful waters for which the Keys are known. You'll paddle across large sounds, small creeks, and open bay waters to North Nest Key, where a swim beach and campsite await. Here, you can while away the day or spend the night. Camping is recommended, as the entire loop is a long one-day paddle, though it is more do-able on long summer days. The return route is more sheltered, part of the Intracoastal Waterway. The civilized Keys are never far away, and motorboats will be with you the entire route, yet the scenery in Florida Bay is hard to beat.

Your jumping-off point is Florida Bay Outfitters, (305) 451-3018. They are located at mile marker #104 on the bay side of US 1. This is your headquarters for canoeing and sea kayaking the keys. The outfitters offer everything from guided tours to gear for rent or sale. Start your paddle here, at the rear of the outfitters. Head west into Blackwater Sound between channel marker #40 and Bush Point; this paddle is part of the

Intracoastal Waterway. Once past marker #40, you have entered Everglades National Park waters.

Continue through the clear waters of the sound, bearing toward The Boggies, which is marked with a buoy. Enter The Boggies, traverse the 20-foot-wide creek lined with mangroves, and emerge into wide-open Florida Bay at mile 4. Bear west for the island nearest you, Duck Key. Once in the bay, begin to bear more southwesterly past a sandy shoal, marked with PVC pipe. The Nest Keys will appear as two long, low islands on the horizon. The sea beneath you has taken on that aquamarine green characteristic of the Keys. The ocean bottom is easy to see. The waters change to other attractive hues with the changing depths, distances, and shades.

Aim for the northern point of North Nest Key, then swing around the west side of the island. A low-slung shore of mangroves parallels the sandy shoreline. Pass a swim beach marked with buoys before rounding another point of the island and coming to the island's campsite at mile 7.5. Here lie a dock, beach, and shaded camping area. Pull up your craft to eat lunch or to spend the night.

Continue your loop by circling North Nest Key past a few other small beach and mangrove areas to split the channel between the Nest Keys. You are now paddling southeast, back toward Key Largo. Shoot for Porjoe Key, an island in the making, and arrive at the isle at mile 11. Small mangrove trees are growing on the edges of the island, attempting to mature, then to enlarge the key. Keep southeasterly, entering Little Buttonwood Sound via some small islands that form a broken southern border of the sound. Find the short channel leading to Grouper Creek and channel marker #52 at mile 13. You are now on the Intracoastal Waterway. Keep appropriate watch for motorboats using the waterway.

This waterway marks the border of the Everglades National Park. Follow the markers northeast; the numbers will be declining as you enter Dusenberry Creek. This deep, warm creek is a wintering area for manatee. You may see one of these gentle giants in the Dusenberry. Leave the stream and head into Blackwater Sound. Bear east for the populated shoreline of Key Largo and return to Florida Bay Outfitters at mile 16.

Snake Bight Route

Begin: Alligator Creek campsite   End: Flamingo

Distance: 12 miles   Time: 6 hours

Potential Tidal Influence: 4   Potential Wind Influence: 5

Navigational Challenge: 2

Highlights: Paddling in Florida Bay

Hazards: Shallow water and big winds on Florida Bay

Campsites: Alligator Creek, Shark Point

Connections: West Lake Canoe Trail, Dildo Key Bank Route, First National
Bank Route, East Cape Route, Buttonwood Canal Route

Wide-open Florida Bay can be a place of exceptional beauty, but if the
wind and tides turn on you, paddling can be very tough. This route leaves
the quiet and remote Alligator Creek to enter shallow Garfield Bight,
then heads south to skirt Shark Point, where there is a backcountry campsite. Depending on the tides, you can take the route across Snake Bight
either via the shallows or via the Tin Can Channel back to Flamingo.

Roseate spoonbills in formation over Snake Bight. Photo by author

Combine this route with the West Lake Canoe Trail for a little-used one-way overnight trip encompassing myriad Everglades environments.

Depart the Alligator Creek campsite and paddle south, following the left (east) bank of Garfield Bight. The mud bottom of the bay gives the shallow water a brownish tint. Pass a water-monitoring station. Soon you will be able to see the Flamingo tower to your west around Porpoise Point. Continue along the shore to Shark Point and the Shark Point campsite. A tiny "beach" on the southwest end of the point allows you to land your craft along the otherwise heavily wooded shoreline at this very seldom used camp. This is your only convenient stopping point along this route.

From here you have two choices for crossing Snake Bight. If the tide is rising or up, it is possible to shoot directly west for Flamingo. But if the winds shift (water depths in Florida Bay are heavily influenced by wind as well as tide) or the tide heads out, you could be slogging through the mud or worse. Not only is this a literal drag, it is ecologically unsound for the bay.

Your other choice is to head southwest from Shark Point toward Buoy Key and the Tin Can Channel. The water will be plenty deep here, and if the tide is going out it will be flowing in the direction you want—west. Make the northern tip of Buoy Key at mile 4.5. Pick up the marked Tin Can Channel heading west. Watch out for motorboats.

Proceed across the open waters of Florida Bay, passing Cormorant Key and Palm Key to the south. As you near Flamingo, make sure to go around the outside of Joe Kemp Key, avoiding shallow waters. Veer north and cross Joe Kemp Channel. The visitor center will be visible as you near Flamingo. Stay west of the marked bird-nesting island to enter the cut to Flamingo Marina and the end of your route at mile 12.

Cape Sable, Whitewater Bay, and the South

Bear Lake Canoe Trail

Begin: Buttonwood Canal	End: Florida Bay
Distance: 10.5 miles	Time: 6.5 hours
Potential Tidal Influence: 3	Potential Wind Influence: 2
Navigational Challenge: 1	

Highlights: Paddlers-only trail

Hazards: Shallow water, overgrown trail, potentially excessive mosquitoes

Campsites: None

Connections: Buttonwood Canal Route, East Cape Route

Check with the Flamingo Ranger Station before paddling Bear Lake Canoe Trail. This route traces the old Homestead Canal, built in the 1920s as a means of draining Cape Sable in order to develop the cape. As with many Everglades land schemes, the land failed to drain properly and the only thing left is the canal. And there is not much left of it. Through the years it has become silted and overgrown, making passage more and more difficult. Time has also allowed the regrowth of mangrove here, and in

Beneath the mangrove tunnel on the Bear Lake Canoe Trail. Photo by author

places the path is barely passable at best. The mosquitoes along here can be among the worst an Everglades paddler will face. A plug at the East Cape Canal prevents the tides from scouring the Homestead Canal, so water depth is dependent on rain and inflow from the freshwater Glades between the canoe trail and Whitewater Bay, which in winter are historically low. If the water is low, the Bear Lake Canoe Trail can be too shallow to paddle and too mucky to walk. Once out of Homestead Canal, paddlers may find extremely strong tides in the East Cape Canal. Incoming tides can be powerful enough to effectively prevent an exit to the Gulf. The tides on the Homestead Canal are insignificant.

Also be advised that there are two portages on this route. The first is a 160-yard carry from Buttonwood Canal to the beginning of the Bear Lake Canoe Trail. The second is a shorter carry over the plug between the Homestead and East Cape Canals.

Considering all of this, I do not recommend the Bear Lake Canoe Trail in its entirety. But if strong winds prevent you from returning to Flamingo via Florida Bay on the East Cape Route, consider making the complete paddle.

Unload yourself and your gear onto a small wooden dock on the west side of the Buttonwood Canal 2 miles from Flamingo; here, a sign reads "Bear Lake Canoe Trail." Carry your canoe and gear along the small foot trail, which turns onto a road. Stay right onto another short road to a gravel landing and a dock at the beginning of the Bear Lake Canoe Trail.

Load your gear, and paddle west beneath the shady canopy of mangrove down the shallow, constricted tunnel. You are now on the Homestead Canal. The first 2 miles of this route, from Buttonwood Canal to Bear Lake, are shallow but cleared of impassable obstructions. Mangrove roots crowd the waterway until it is sometimes only canoe width. A foot trail parallels the canal to Bear Lake. Come to the unmarked north turn to Mud Lake, shortly before coming out to Bear Lake. The lake here will seem quite open after the canoe trail.

Continue in a direct westerly line until you reach Gator Lake. The trail is marked with PVC pipe. Turn south, then west, passing through a very shallow lake scattered with islands until the Homestead Canal turns south again, coming to the dam at the East Cape Canal at mile 9.5. Carry over the dam, then hope for an outgoing tide; otherwise you may be waiting for the tide to turn.

The East Cape Canal is much wider than Bear Lake Canoe Trail. The 100-foot-wide waterway is arrow straight and leads south in a beeline to the Gulf of Mexico at Florida Bay. To the west, it is 1 mile to the East Cape campsite on the East Cape Route. Back to the east it is 9 miles to Flamingo.

Big Sable Route

Begin: Northwest Cape Campsite   End: Oyster Bay chickee
Distance: 13 miles   Time: 8 hours
Potential Tidal Influence: 5   Potential Wind Influence: 5
Navigational Challenge: 2

Highlights: Diverse waterways on route
Hazards: Big waves in the Gulf of Mexico, strong tides in Little Shark River
Campsites: Northwest Cape, Oyster Bay chickee
Connections: Middle Cape Route, Cormorant Pass, Wilderness Waterway, Shark River Chickee Route

---

Big Sable is a long but do-able route. No matter which direction you paddle this waterway, you will most likely end up fighting the winds or the tides or both. Expect a little bit of everything: wide-open ocean, a river, and an inland bay. Start early and plan for a full day at the outdoor office. Also, there are virtually no convenient locations at which to stop and get out of your boat. Plan on tying up to some mangrove roots to eat lunch or relieve yourself. So why traverse this route? Because it provides an important and scenic connection between the "inside" and the "outside." The "outside" is the Gulf of Mexico and the "inside" is everything else paddleable in the Everglades National Park. Why this route? Because it's challenging!

Leave Northwest Cape and its white beaches behind and head north. Parallel the shoreline and soon pass Little Sable Creek, once the only way in and out of Lake Ingraham. The second creek you pass connects to Little Sable Creek. The point in the northern distance is the south tip of the Big Sable Creek inlet. Look closely at the mangrove seacoast here. The forest of spindly trees grows tightly together in competition for light and space. A maze of tangled prop roots holds the whole affair up.

Come to the south end of the Big Sable Creek inlet at mile 3. The inlet here extends nearly a mile across. Once you are at the bay of the inlet, the tip of Shark River Island is visible, as is the balance of the Everglades coast extending northwesterly. The tall mangrove shoreline continues north of Big Sable Creek. The seashore is more jagged due to numerous tidal creeks forming small coves of their own.

The bay between Shark River Island and the main coast narrows to the Little Shark River channel. Continuing north at mile 7, pass the elaborate light marker at the mouth of the Little Shark River and enter the river. If you continue north up the Gulf coast, it is 4 miles across Ponce De Leon

Sea kayaker lands a sea trout. Photo by W. W. Armstrong

Bay to the Graveyard Creek campsite via the Ponce De Leon Bay Route. From this point forward the Big Sable Route is blazed with the customary green and red Coast Guard markers all the way to Oyster Bay, making navigation easy. Make your way around a sharp curve and continue easterly up the Little Shark River.

A lot of water moves up and down the Little Shark River channel, so be prepared for a strong tide. The river is a couple of hundred feet wide and is bisected by several small creeks that run perpendicular to it. There are no more channel markers until the Little Shark River splits off to the northeast by channel marker #69. Stay with the Little Shark; the channel is much narrower here; watch for motorboats. This channel continues for a quarter mile until it connects to the multiple channels that are part of the Shark River complex, which drains much of the freshwater Everglades. But the water is all brackish to salt this close to the Gulf.

Stay with the channel markers, and don't let yourself get confused. Leave the Little Shark River at marker #65 and head southeast toward Oyster Bay, still following the markers as their numbers decrease. Come to the west end of Oyster Bay at marker #53, 12 miles from Northwest Cape. Head east across Oyster Bay, passing one lone island, into a group of islands on the opposite shore. The Oyster Bay chickee is backed against the far (east) side of one of these islands. Paddle into these islands and come to the chickee in a little lagoon, ending your route at mile 13. The channel markers continue on another half mile to the Wilderness Waterway. From Oyster Bay chickee it is 3 miles north to Shark River chickee via the Shark Cutoff Route. It is 4 miles south to Joe River chickee and 8 miles east to Watson River chickee via the Cormorant Pass Route.

Buttonwood Canal Route

Begin: Flamingo

Distance: 5 miles

Potential Tidal Influence: 2

Navigational Challenge: 1

End: Coast Guard Marker #10 at Whitewater Bay

Time: 2.5 hours

Potential Wind Influence: 2

Highlights: Important route connecting Whitewater Bay and Florida Bay

Hazards: Motorboats and tour boats on whole route

Campsites: None

Connections: Snake Bight Route, East Cape Route, First National Bank Route, Dildo Key Bank Route, Joe River Route, East River Route, Whitewater Bay Route

---

There are two primary departure points for Everglades paddlers, Flamingo and Everglades City. The Buttonwood Canal Route is the primary route departing the Flamingo area. And even if you don't use the canal to leave Flamingo, you will likely use it to get back to Flamingo. This is also the last segment of the Wilderness Waterway, which links Flamingo and Everglades City. It is the necessary pathway for boaters to get to Whitewater Bay and all points north. And this means all types of boats, from sea kayaks to skiffs to houseboats. Tour boats also use this route. So expect a lot of company. And expect your picture to get taken by tourists on the tour boats as they pass your gear-laden craft.

Load up at the Flamingo boat ramp, then head north from the marina on the Buttonwood Canal. This waterway was dug in 1956 and 1957 by the park service so boaters could access Whitewater Bay without having to go via the Gulf. Here, the shores of the canal are primarily mangrove, but also mahogany, gumbo-limbo, Jamaica dogwood, Brazilian pepper, cactus, and—of course—buttonwood. Paddle under the bridge that is Main Park Road. Look left to observe the limestone rocks and cement placed to keep the canal banks solid. Running parallel to the canal is Bear Lake Road.

The forest shoreline resumes, and the canal continues its southerly course until more limestone rock appears on your left just as you come to the Bear Lake Canoe Trail at 2 miles. There is a dock here, and a portage trail goes to the beginning of the old canal route that heads west to Bear Lake and beyond.

You and the Buttonwood Canal then turn northeasterly toward Coot Bay, arriving there at 3 miles. Coot Bay is the only place on this route where there may be wind problems. Follow the channel markers northwest across Coot Bay to Tarpon Creek. Upon entering Tarpon Creek, there is a "Please Watch for Manatees" sign; watch also for boaters, even though Tarpon Creek is a no-wake zone. The creek is about 50 feet wide, banked with mangrove and a challenging paddle if the tide is going against you. It meanders north for about half a mile to Whitewater Bay, which you will probably hear before you see it. Just ahead is the wide-open bay and the end of the Buttonwood Canal at Coast Guard marker #10, at 5 miles. From here, it is 6 miles to Hells Bay chickee via the East River Route. It is 12 miles to Coast Guard marker #40 at Cormorant Pass via the Whitewater Bay Route. It is 6 miles to the South Joe chickee via the Joe River Route.

Cormorant Pass Route

Begin: Joe River chickee	End: Watson River chickee
Distance: 12 miles	Time: 6 hours
Potential Tidal Influence: 3	Potential Wind Influence: 4
Navigational Challenge: 3	

Highlights: The narrows of Cormorant Pass
Hazards: Motorboats through Cormorant Pass

Campsites: Joe River chickee, Oyster Bay chickee, Watson River chickee

Connections: The Labyrinth Route, Joe River Route, Big Sable Route, Whitewater Bay Route, The Cutoff Route

---

The Joe River Route leaves the narrows of Joe River and enters Oyster Bay, then crosses a key portion of the Wilderness Waterway, Cormorant Pass. This part of the route is marked, but beyond Cormorant Pass you must leave the channel markers and skirt northeastern Whitewater Bay to arrive at Watson River chickee. Unfortunately, there is the possibility of motorboat traffic most of the way, except near Watson River chickee. The paddle path provides vital connections to the Gulf of Mexico, the east side of Whitewater Bay, and all points north in the Glades. The cormorant, prevalent throughout the park, is a black ducklike bird.

Leave the cove of Joe River chickee and paddle the final northerly section of Joe River. As you leave Joe River, there will be a "Please Watch for Manatees" sign on your right. Mud Bay will be on your left. Enter the ever-widening Oyster Bay and continue north, keeping a set of islands to your east.

Two miles beyond Joe River chickee, Oyster Bay widens and the islands to your east have petered out. Almost due north in the middle of the open bay is a conspicuous lone island. Oyster Bay chickee is set in a group of islands on an east-west line parallel to the lone island. Head northeast in the open bay toward a seemingly continuous shoreline. The individual islands will show themselves as you paddle closer. Oyster Bay chickee faces east in a lagoon among these islands. Arrive at this chickee at 4 miles. From Oyster Bay chickee it is 6 miles to the Gulf at Shark River Island via the Big Sable Route. It is 3 miles to Shark River chickee via the Shark Cutoff Route—if you run into some channel markers you have paddled too far north beyond the chickee.

Leave Oyster Bay chickee and paddle north past Shark River chickee, heading for the markers north of it. Spot marker #50, then veer southeast to follow the channel markers of Cormorant Pass through the many pint-sized islands. Make sure the channel marker numbers are decreasing; if they are increasing, you have gone the wrong way and are heading north on the Wilderness Waterway.

Make a southerly traverse through Cormorant Pass to Coast Guard marker #40. From this marker it is 12 miles southeast to Tarpon Creek at the south end of Whitewater Bay via the Whitewater Bay Route. On the Cormorant Pass Route, leave the Wilderness Waterway to skirt the northeastern edge of Whitewater Bay, passing a few very large mangrove islands. Follow a clear but unmarked open course toward Watson River chickee. After swinging around the largest mangrove island between Cormorant Pass and Watson River chickee, you will see Watson River chickee. It faces north between two keys at mile 12 of your route. From here, it is 6 miles southeast to Roberts River chickee on The Cutoff Route. It is 6 miles to Shark River chickee via The Labyrinth Route.

The Cutoff Route

Begin: Roberts River chickee	End: Watson River chickee
Distance: 6 miles	Time: 4 hours
Potential Tidal Influence: 3	Potential Wind Influence: 4
Navigational Challenge: 3	

Highlights: Some solitude, good camping

Hazards: Big water on Whitewater Bay

Campsites: Roberts River, North River, Watson River

Connections: Roberts River Route, North River Route, The Labyrinth Route, Cormorant Pass Route

The Cutoff is a route that provides a necessary connection for traversing the wild rivers east of Whitewater Bay. The route connects three backcountry chickees for some good camping. Powerboat traffic is minimal until you get to Whitewater Bay. On the rivers here, you really get a sense of the untamed Everglades. And one short section of this route reveals three Everglades environments within a stone's throw of one another.

Whitewater Bay is an environment all its own, and depending on wind conditions you can skirt your way through mangrove keys or take to the open water north to Watson River chickee. The chickee seems really small in all that water, even though it is tucked away among a few mangrove keys.

From Roberts River chickee turn right and head north up the Roberts River. The low mangrove banks of the river resume beyond the chickee, then get taller on river right, approaching The Cutoff proper, which connects the Roberts River and the North River. These days it is not possible to cross watersheds above The Cutoff, as mangrove have blocked the creeks connecting the two rivers.

The Roberts River has narrowed considerably by the time you see a confluence of two streams; bear left (northwest) on the stream with the lower banks. You are now on The Cutoff. (There is another Cutoff connecting Lostmans and Rodgers Rivers farther north from here.) On river right just before the confluence is an old shell mound grown into a hammock. This used to be a camping ground for Everglades travelers.

Beyond the hammock on The Cutoff, look over the low mangrove to your right to see the sawgrass prairie that makes up so much of the Everglades interior. Continue on The Cutoff for a mile. The route has widened from stream inflow until it ends at the North River. When leaving The Cutoff, pay undivided attention to your position. Do not take the natural course down the North River. The correct route will end up heading due west in a channel much wider than the North River proper. This unnamed channel has irregular jagged banks of low mangrove that funnel southwest to North River chickee, which isn't actually on the North River. It should be called the river north of the North River chickee. As if the place isn't confusing enough without adding confusing names!

Anyway, this unnamed channel narrows and runs directly into the North River chickee, which is backed up against the east side of a small mangrove island. It is a single chickee of older make and oozes solitude. This is a good spot to take a break or to camp.

Swing south around the tiny island against which North River chickee is set and paddle southwest on this 50–90-foot waterway. The deep channel meanders down to the first and only island beyond the chickee. Past this island, the channel widens as it enters Whitewater Bay. A key of high mangrove, running north-south, lies between you and the bulk of Whitewater Bay.

Make your decision about which way to go around the key based on wind and experience—if a manageable wind is blowing from the south, head into the big water and catch a ride alongside the scattered keys to Watson River chickee. In Whitewater Bay, look north for a white manatee-warning sign at the mouth of the Watson River to help guide you toward Watson River chickee. This sign is actually north of the chickee. Alternatively, if the wind is not favorable or you like a more intimate setting, zig-zag through the channels on the east side of the bay to Watson River chickee.

No matter what your path is, Whitewater Bay will offer wide-open water and accompanying wide-open views of mangrove islands and shores that undulate on the horizon. From Watson River chickee it is 12 miles to Oyster Bay chickee via the Cormorant Pass Route. It is 6 miles to Shark River chickee via The Labyrinth Route.

East River Route

Begin: Coast Guard marker #10 at Whitewater Bay

End: Hells Bay chickee

Distance: 5.5 miles   Time: 3 hours

Potential Tidal Influence: 2   Potential Wind Influence: 4

Navigational Challenge: 3

Highlights: Varied waters

Hazards: Big water on Whitewater Bay

Campsites: Hells Bay chickee

Connections: Buttonwood Canal Route, Whitewater Bay Route, Joe River Route, Hells Bay Canoe Trail

This route is easier to trace from Whitewater Bay to Hells Bay than vice versa, because getting on the right channel leading to the East River from Hells Bay can be tricky.

Start at Coast Guard marker #10 at the south end of Whitewater Bay. Paddle northeasterly from this marker along the southeast shoreline of Whitewater Bay. The water is fairly open here, subjecting the paddler to some potential wind problems. Generally hug the shoreline; you will see more wildlife, be safer, and not get turned around.

At 3 miles, the route shoots between the southeast shore of Whitewater Bay and a key running north-south that shields the headwaters of the No Mans and East Rivers. Watch for the blue-and-white sign that reads "Please Watch for Manatees, Operate with Care," which marks the entrance to the East River, and head easterly up the East River, with mangrove banks of varying height on both sides. Here, potential wind influence diminishes and potential tidal influence increases. This river stays

Hells Bay chickee. Photo by author

generally true to its name for about a mile, with little bays and creeks splintering off it.

Then the East River veers generally north and stays about 60 feet wide before coming to a diminutive bay with two distinct narrow outlets. The smaller outlet is to the left (north). Take the outlet to the right and head east northeast for about a quarter mile, where the channel splits once more. Both channels immediately lead into Hells Bay. Veer southeast in Hells Bay, entering the Gates of Hell, which is a pass between two peninsular mangrove fingers. Beyond the Gates about 200 yards is a white PVC pipe, which is the last marker of the Hells Bay Canoe Trail. The canoe trail runs 6 miles between this point and its beginning at Main Park Road. Head east for the PVC pipe, and the Hells Bay chickee will be on your right just before you come to the pipe marker. From here it is 2.5 miles to Lane Bay chickee via the Lane River Route.

Hells Bay Canoe Trail

Begin: Main Park Road   End: Hells Bay chickee
Distance: 6 miles   Time: 3.5 hours
Potential Tidal Influence: 1 Potential Wind Influence: 2
Navigational Challenge: 1
Highlights: Marked canoe trail leading through headwaters of East River
Hazards: Completely confusing landscape
Campsites: Lard Can, Pearl Bay, Hells Bay
Connections: East River Route, Lane River Route

In my early days of exploring the Everglades, I used to think I could find my way to Hells Bay from the Main Park Road even if the paddle path wasn't marked. Now, I laugh at my ignorance and thank the park service for placing the numbered PVC pipe markers to guide the way. This place is confusing even for very experienced navigators! The area is not on the nautical charts, although you could theoretically use USGS quadrangle maps to get around. The quads of the Everglades are photographic, which helps in a place with little elevation variation.

The Hells Bay Canoe Trail, according to old-timer and *Gladesmen* author Glen Simmons, "twisted and turned worser than any snake." He is right. The trail doubles back and curves generally northwesterly through countless small streams that connect ponds, and it eventually leads to Hells Bay, which got its name because it is hell to get into and hell to get out of.

The park service cut out and marked this trail in the 1960s. It traces an old trail that rough-and-tumble alligator-hunting gladesmen such as Simmons used to explore the headwaters of the East River, which connects Hells Bay to Whitewater Bay. Back then, this trail was reopened each year by following the flow of water between the mangrove and looking for previous signs of trail clearing, such as sawn limbs.

Leave the dock and Main Park Road behind as you follow the markers (the marker numbers will be increasing). Travel is slow with all the turning, especially in a loaded boat. The trail is especially tortured past marker #40. Sounds of the road will still be with you at first, but those may be the last engines you hear, as no boat motors are allowed on the trail until Lard Can campsite.

Touch your paddle down where you can see the whitish creek bottom. The hard surface is limestone marl, which underlies much of the Everglades. On drier clumps of land, there are patches of wax myrtle and coco plum. There is a dry landing at marker #80, where you can stand up for a minute. At marker #114 is a patch of paurotis palm. Notice how the stream can be as deep as 5 feet, but the shallow bays are made more shallow by hydrilla, vegetation growing below the water surface.

At marker #154, the trail leaves a stream and enters the biggest bay yet. Look to your right (east) between marker #155 and #156 across a small bay for the Lard Can backcountry campsite. It is 120 yards distant and is marked by two PVC poles by the shoreline. Stop here for a break and enjoy the tropical hammock with large ferns, palms, coco plums, and other hammock vegetation. The word "hammock" is derived from the Indian word "hamas," meaning "shady place." Since Lard Can is natural

Lard Can campsite. Photo by author

ground, it has been camped on for hundreds of years, first by Calusa Indians, then gladesmen, and now ecotourists. You are now 3 miles and 2 hours from the Main Park Road.

Continue following the sequentially marked poles beyond Lard Can. Begin trying to correlate your position with the nautical chart, even though the trail is marked—this will help you learn to navigate when there are no markers to rely on. The direction stays northwest as the poles lead you through a small creek to Pearl Bay. The Pearl Bay chickee comes into view to your left at the north end of the bay. This is a two-party, handicapped accessible chickee. The distance to Pearl Bay chickee is 1 mile and is about a half hour paddle from Lard Can.

Head southwest from Pearl Bay chickee, then enter another intimate creek. This one is longer and emerges into an unnamed bay surrounded by low mangrove. Another, shorter, small creek connects the unnamed bay with Hells Bay. As the waterway widens at marker #177, look to your right and you can see Hells Bay chickee just beyond a few tiny islands.

This two-party chickee is your destination. It takes a little over an hour to get here from Pearl Bay. From here it is 6 miles to Coast Guard marker #10 at lower Whitewater Bay on the East River Route. It is 5 miles to the Roberts River via the Lane River Route.

Joe River Route

Begin: Coast Guard marker #10 in Whitewater Bay
End: Joe River chickee
Distance: 12 miles　　　　　　　Time: 6 hours
Potential Tidal Influence: 3　　　Potential Wind Influence: 3
Navigational Challenge: 2
Highlights: Good starter paddle for Everglades novice
Hazards: Motorboats on Joe River
Campsites: South Joe River chickee, Joe River chickee
Connections: Buttonwood Canal Route, Cormorant Pass Route, East River Route, Whitewater Bay Route

---

In pre-park days, Flamingo residents called this the South River instead of the Joe River. Some of these Flamingoites used to come up here to hunt, fish, and camp. Nowadays, this route is used as a good way to head north from Flamingo without getting into too much big water in Whitewater Bay along the Wilderness Waterway. The fishing and camping are still good. The Joe River varies in width, seeming at first like a bay until it settles down and becomes more riverine. There are two good chickees along the river, and this route makes up part of two good overnight loops, one around Whitewater Bay and the other around Cape Sable.

Enter Whitewater Bay from Tarpon Creek at Coast Guard marker #10. Paddle west, staying with the western shore of the big bay. This leads you into the Joe River. And if you stay with the shore to your left, you will have no problem navigating up the Joe River. There will be big views of Whitewater Bay. As you continue west, the bay begins to shrink. Finally, on a north turn at mile 5, the Joe River narrows to riverlike proportions, around 200 feet wide. Here, on river right, there is a "Please Watch for Manatees" sign.

Stay with the southwest shore and watch for a meandering channel leading left. Take this channel into the bay of the South Joe chickee, which will be dead ahead as you enter the bay at mile 6. This is a double chickee that makes for a good first day's paddle from Flamingo or just a good resting spot.

Leave the South Joe chickee and swing around the corner, taking the other creek out of the bay. This creek leads north back into the Joe River. Continue northwest up the river, passing around a large island that splits the Joe. After the island, the Joe resumes a 200-foot width and a north-westerly course. The mangrove shorelines vary from 4 to 40 feet in height. The depth of the river is fine for all craft, which makes it an easy route for motorboaters.

As the Joe takes on a more northerly direction, pass three channels leading off to your right into Whitewater Bay as you continue upriver, The first and third of these channels offer views into the big bay. You will find yourself cutting point to point across the river's meanders. At mile 12, come to the small cove on your right and end your route at the Joe River chickee. From here it is 4 miles to Oyster Bay chickee via the Cormorant Pass Route.

The Labyrinth Route

Begin: Shark River chickee

End: Watson River chickee

Distance: 6 miles

Time: 4 hours

Potential Tidal Influence: 2

Potential Wind Influence: 1

Navigational Challenge: 5

Highlights: Intricate navigating challenge, solitude, no motorboats

Hazards: Getting lost in The Labyrinth

Campsites: Shark River chickee, Watson River chickee

Connections: The Cutoff Route, Cormorant Pass Route, Graveyard Creek Route

The Labyrinth is one of the most challenging routes in the Everglades. It is also one of the most rewarding. You must paddle your way through a literal maze of small streams connecting the Shark River to northern Whitewater Bay, choosing the right streams to get through. There are no markers to point the way, and no motorboaters are going to be passing by to help guide you. You'll need experienced map-reading skills and a steely nerve to make the hours-long trek without knowing for certain that you are where you think you are. And that is the trick: While passing through The Labyrinth you must eyeball the nautical chart and keep fixing your position on the chart. Only when you reach Whitewater Bay will you breathe a sigh of relief, knowing that your chart reading got you through.

So why traverse The Labyrinth? For the navigational challenge, for solitude—there will be no roaring motors here—and for the shortest route between Shark River chickee and Watson River chickee. I paddled The Labyrinth for the first time when I had gotten off my route due to untenable high seas in the Gulf. I was behind schedule and trying to catch up. Sitting at the Shark River chickee, I traced the route on the chart with my finger and dared myself to try it. Then I took the plunge into The Labyrinth (not knowing at the time it was called The Labyrinth) and made it. I was one happy paddler upon seeing Whitewater Bay!

There are no directions for getting through The Labyrinth, only hints. Check the tidal flow at the chickee and the tide charts. If the tide is just turning, then tidal direction will remain the same throughout your paddle. Make certain of where you are as you paddle. There is more than one way through the maze. If you aren't sure where you are, don't just plunge ahead and hope. Take your time. Look back every now and then as you paddle. This may help you if you have to backtrack. Good luck. This is paddling the Everglades at its finest.

After you reach Whitewater Bay, keep southeast past some large keys to your southwest. The north-facing Watson River chickee will appear in the distance, backed up against some other islands. Once at Watson River chickee, it is 6 miles to Roberts River chickee via The Cutoff Route.

Lane River Route

Begin: Hells Bay chickee

End: Confluence of Lane River and Roberts River

Distance: 5 miles

Time: 3 hours

Potential Tidal Influence: 2

Potential Wind Influence: 3

Navigational Challenge: 3

Highlights: Bird life on Lane River

Hazards: Confusing section between Hells Bay and Lane Bay chickees

Campsites: Hells Bay chickee, Lane Bay chickee

Connections: Roberts River Route, Hells Bay Canoe Trail, East River Route

---

The Lane River Route stays in the intimate east side of Whitewater Bay, forming a dogleg connection between Hells Bay and the Roberts River. Leave Hells Bay and head north to Lane Bay, passing the single-occupancy Lane Bay chickee, then veer southwest and enter the Lane River proper. The low mangrove allows sweeping vistas, yet the size of the river never overwhelms you. This general area is where small ponds, bays, and rivers form a complex of paddle routes that are preferable when the brawny winds are blowing on Whitewater Bay. The commanding form of plant life in the Everglades paddler's realm, the mangrove and its attendant fish and bird life, is all around you.

Head north from Hells Bay chickee, noting that there are more tiny islands than are shown on the navigational charts in northern Hells Bay. Here you must fight the urge to head to the largest section of open water. Instead, catch the 40–50-foot-wide creek connecting Hells Bay to a small, island-studded, unnamed bay. Continue northwest through the unnamed bay, then merge into The Funnel, which is a slightly wider creek that leads into Lane Bay. Continue north through Lane Bay, taking time to inspect some of the islands for West Indies mahogany. Identify this tropical tree by its compound leaves and its giveaway hard, brown fruit about the size of a pear.

Osprey on an island in Lane Bay. Photo by author

Up ahead is Lane Bay chickee, backed up against a tall wooded hammock on the north side of Lane Bay. Arrive at this older chickee at 2.5 miles. Take the opportunity to stretch your legs here.

The trickiest navigational section of this route comes when you leave Lane Bay chickee and dogleg southwest into the Lane River. Pay close attention to the chart and keep westerly. The mangrove on the Lane River is low, sometimes only 3 feet in height, with bleached skeletal trees emerging from the greenery that make for ideal avian roosts. The mud-bottomed river is deeper than your paddle and runs clear with a tannish tint. The width averages around 80 feet but narrows to as little as 50 feet, such as when it splits around an island to your left about a mile from Lane River chickee. Bird life can be abundant.

On down, the river widens considerably as a fair-sized creek merges from the north. Downriver, you can see the high tops of healthy mangrove in Whitewater Bay. Just before its confluence with the Roberts River and the Roberts River Route, Lane River veers southwest and narrows again, ending at a sign warning about manatees in the area. To your left, it is 2.5 miles to the Wilderness Waterway and the Whitewater Bay Route at marker #18. To your right (northeast), it is 2.5 miles up the Roberts River to the Roberts River chickee.

Middle Cape Route

Begin: East Cape campsite   End: Northwest Cape campsite

Distance: 9.5 miles   Time: 5 hours

Potential Tidal Influence: 5   Potential Wind Influence: 5

Navigational Challenge: 2

Highlights: Lots of beach camping, natural beach

Hazards: Big waves and strong tides in the Gulf of Mexico

Campsites: East Cape, Middle Cape, Northwest Cape

Connections: East Cape Route, Big Sable Route

The Middle Cape Route connects the three points of Cape Sable: East Cape, Middle Cape, and Northwest Cape. Cape Sable has been called one of the finest pieces of real estate in North America. I have to agree. This is a preserved piece of natural Florida coastline that will leave you coming back for more—miles of shell-laden beach backed by natural native vegetation. No glaring high-rises or phony landscaping here. And the camping on the cape is superb. Come see it for yourself.

Start your route by heading northwest in the Gulf from the East Cape campsite. Middle Cape is the point visible to your left as you round East Cape. The beach narrows somewhat beyond East Cape, but the shoreline of sand, grass, and varied trees, as opposed to uninterrupted mangrove, continues. The beach lines the water's edge all the way to Middle Cape. Overall, the shoreline is very attractive, with gumbo-limbo and cabbage palm increasing as you near Middle Cape. This landscape gives way to a grassy prairie studded with palm and cactus and the beginning of the Middle Cape campsite.

The shore turns almost due west before coming at mile 4.5 to the Middle Cape itself, which culminates in a very sharp point, especially in contrast to the more rounded East Cape. The point was once the site of Fort Cross, established in the 1850s as a base for U.S. soldiers attempting to eradicate Seminoles far back in the Glades. Past Middle Cape, the shore resumes a more north-south orientation.

Around Middle Cape, a coconut farm was established in the 1880s, the Waddell Plantation. The owners soon left it to caretakers, and the place

Prickly pear cactus near the beach. Photo by W. W. Armstrong

Palms, grass, and beach at Northwest Cape. Photo by author

never had much of a plantationlike appearance. Coconuts were harvested off and on through the years, until the palms were blown away by a hurricane in 1935.

Pass the Middle Cape Canal at mile 6. Most signs of civilization in the area have been obliterated by time and the elements, but this canal that connects Lake Ingraham with the Gulf keeps growing with the incessant action of the tides. Be careful when paddling by, as the tides are very strong at the mouth of the canal. A friend and I once got sucked in by the strong tides and were stuck in there for several hours before we finally pulled ourselves and our canoe out by grabbing mangrove roots on the shore, one after another, until we were back in the Gulf.

Beyond the canal, the shore is sporadic mangrove growing out of the sand. But as the land turns more northwest, a palm prairie begins. This large prairie goes back from the sea a good half mile or more. Some Jamaica dogwood, cactus, and a few wooded hammocks break up the grass and palm field that extends to Northwest Cape and beyond. End your route at 9.5 miles at the gently curved Northwest Cape, which is an attractive camping area of its own. From here, it is 6 miles north to Shark River Island via the Big Sable Route.

When the winds kick up, the Middle Cape Route can become impassable. Should this happen, there is a "backdoor" route connecting East Cape and Northwest Cape. This backdoor route is tidally influenced and can be nearly impassable in its own right, unless the tides are in your favor. You can also use part of this route as a birding excursion into Lake Ingraham.

This is the backdoor route: Leave East Cape and paddle east a short distance to the East Cape Canal. Paddle north into the canal, a nearly impossible task if the tide is going out, and head toward the dam and the old Homestead Canal, part of the Bear Lake Canoe Trail. Just before the dam, bear northwest through a canal into Lake Ingraham and follow the markers across the shallow lake. There can be much bird life back here. Head northwest across Lake Ingraham to the Middle Cape Canal, if you want to go to Middle Cape. Time your exit with a slack or outgoing tide, otherwise you are stuck in Lake Ingraham. If you see a motorboat coming at high speed on Lake Ingraham, don't expect it to slow down. Powerboats must stay on plane to make it through the shallow waters here; if they come off plane they may get stuck.

To access Northwest Cape, keep north along Little Sable Creek from Lake Ingraham, an overgrown but passable waterway. This creek reenters the Gulf just north of the Northwest Cape campsite. This alternative may save you from big waves in the Gulf. Just remember to consider the tides if you plan to use this route.

Mud Lake Loop

Begin: Main Park Road	End: Main Park Road
Distance: 7 miles	Time: 4 hours
Potential Tidal Influence: 2	Potential Wind Influence: 3
Navigational Challenge: 2	

Highlights: Paddling in no-motor zone

Hazards: Insects on Bear Lake Canoe Trail and portage to Buttonwood Canal

Campsites: None

Connections: Buttonwood Canal Route, Bear Lake Canoe Trail

Paddling the Mud Lake Loop gives you a good taste of some open water, some confined water, and—more important—quiet water. A 4-mile stretch of this loop is for hand-propelled craft only. There is a price to pay for this solitude, however: A leg of your loop requires a portage between waterways. The first portion of this route can be used as a shortcut to Whitewater Bay. I recommend Mud Lake Loop for canoers only—the narrow creeks, downed trees, and portage make sea kayaking downright troublesome.

The paddle starts on Coot Bay Pond, then passes beneath a mangrove tunnel to Coot Bay. It connects briefly to the Wilderness Waterway and the Buttonwood Canal Route before following a small creek to Mud Lake, which is a more appealing place than its name suggests. You can enjoy the quiet of Mud Lake, then take another creek to the Bear Lake Canoe Trail and trace an old drainage canal to the newer Buttonwood Canal—getting to Buttonwood Canal requires the portage, 160 yards. The loop route heads back to Coot Bay Pond via the Buttonwood Canal and Coot Bay.

Set out from one of the small landings on Coot Bay Pond, paddling north to a small tunnel-like opening. From a distance, it seems there is no passage, but this man-made cut barely wide enough for a canoe will lead you to Coot Bay. The spoils of the cut create land areas upon which drier plant species grow, such as palm. Open up into Coot Bay and paddle west for Coast Guard marker #3 and the Buttonwood Canal Route. Continue to follow the channel markers north for the shortcut to Whitewater Bay, but for this loop stay with the south shore of Coot Bay to a PVC pipe marker at 2 miles, signaling the creek that leads to Mud Lake.

Enter this shady slender waterway, which is made even more narrow by hundreds of fallen trees sawn off just enough for your passage. Expect to slide over a few logs. Live mangrove hovers over you until you emerge onto Mud Lake in a group of small circular islands. Follow the PVC pipe markers south and west across this pretty lake. Its copper-colored waters contrast well with the green shores. The markers lead to the lake's most southwesterly corner and a short creek connecting to the Bear Lake Canoe Trail. Follow this creek to the Bear Lake Canoe Trail.

Once on the canoe trail, make sure to turn left (east). The pungent waters here are rich with the smell of decaying vegetation. It is a couple of hundred yards east to Bear Lake. The Bear Lake Canoe Trail traces the old Homestead Canal, built in the 1920s alongside a road meant to connect Florida City to Cape Sable. The road has reverted to a trail, and the canal is silting in, making for very shallow paddling. Roots of mangrove grow into the water and branches hang overhead. Insects can be bothersome on the nearly 2 miles of paddling that take you to the dock and ground landing at the portage.

Once at the portage, take your canoe on the foot trail to your left, then left again toward two wooden posts to a landing on the Buttonwood Canal. Head left (north) up the waterway, which will seem like the Mississippi River after the Bear Lake Canoe Trail. Come to Coot Bay at mile 6 and paddle east toward a PVC pipe marker to the small channel to Coot Bay Pond. Head back through the tunnel to Coot Bay Pond, completing your loop at mile 7.

Nine Mile Pond Loop

Begin: Main Park Road	End: Main Park Road
Distance: 5.2 miles	Time: 3.5 hours
Potential Tidal Influence: 1	Potential Wind Influence: 3
Navigational Challenge: 1	

Highlights: Marked trail through diverse flora, no motorboats
Hazards: Confusing landscape, sawgrass
Campsites: None
Connections: None

The name Nine Mile Pond may lead you to believe this paddle is 9 miles. This day trip is actually 5 miles of multiple Everglades environments packed into one loop. It received its name because the pond was 9 miles from the original park visitor center at Coot Bay Pond. This trail is marked with sequentially numbered poles to help you navigate among the mangrove islands, prairies, and tree islands of the region. Prairies here are vastly different than those in the Midwest. Everglades prairies are open treeless wetlands, with sawgrass emerging from the water. The water levels of these prairies change, depending on the season, and the prairies can dry up completely at times. The water here is clear and very shallow; check with the park visitor center to see if there is enough water to float your boat. In some areas you will be paddling through sawgrass that can slow your craft down a bit. Be advised there is no easily accessible dry land upon which to stretch your legs.

From the Flamingo Visitor Center, drive east on Main Park Road to Nine Mile Pond parking area at 11.2 miles. Start your trip at Nine Mile Pond, which can be a little cloudy, and head directly across the water from

PVC pipe marks the Nine Mile Pond Loop. Photo by author

the parking area to the farthest inlet of the pond. This inlet lies east, between two sawgrass stands. Here the sequentially numbered poles begin. Keep your eyes peeled, because Nine Mile Pond is a good place to see alligators. Pass through a mangrove tunnel and emerge onto a small prairie. The mud bottom gives a brownish tint to the otherwise clear water, where you can see small fish and minnows darting from your path.

The mangrove and sawgrass environments alternate. Here, the sawgrass on the trail is sparse and doesn't affect your travel. Enter a wide-open prairie of sawgrass just beyond marker #42. Sawgrass is the most common plant in the Everglades; to many people sawgrass *is* the Everglades. Across the prairie are palm-topped tree islands, also known as bayheads.

Just after you enter the prairie, follow the numbered poles sharply to the right into a mangrove tunnel to continue the entire loop. If you want to shorten your loop, do not take the sharp right turn but rather continue forward past marker #44 to #44A and across the prairie to marker #82. Then turn left and complete your shortened loop.

The full trail opens into another prairie where the sawgrass is thicker and can slow you down. Take time to examine the microcosm of life that flourishes below you. Your direction has been primarily east and north until marker # 73. Here the trail turns sharply to the left and begins heading westward back toward Nine Mile Pond. Tall hammocks dotted with palm extend beyond the sawgrass on both sides of the trail, though you pass close to a few palms at marker #80. Leave the sawgrass behind and enter small mangrove islands leading to a few dense palm patches.

Emerge onto a murky alligator pond and veer left through an opening in a line of sawgrass onto another pond. Beyond this pond is yet another opening in the sawgrass, through which you can see the parking area. Paddle through this opening and the parking area is on your right across Nine Mile Pond, completing your loop.

Noble Hammock Loop

Begin: Main Park Road   End: Main Park Road

Distance: 2 miles   Time: 2 hours

Potential Tidal Influence: 1   Potential Wind Influence: 2

Navigational Challenge: 1

Highlights: Sheltered, often shaded, marked canoe trail, tree hammock

Hazards: Completely confusing landscape

Campsites: None

Connections: None

The marked Noble Hammock Loop offers quiet quality once you leave Main Park Road behind. An intimate narrow canoe path winds through a mangrove maze, looping past Noble Hammock, a haven for moonshiners in the early 20th century. Many fish will stir the waters upon your arrival. Take this trail if the wind is howling, or if you have time for only a short trip. And paddle slowly here—the sudden twists and turns of the trail demand it. Full-sized sea kayaks are not maneuverable enough to enjoy this trail. A canoe and maximum cooperation between bow and stern paddlers will bring you the greatest pleasure here. Bring insect repellent along with you in these covered waters.

From Flamingo, drive east on Main Park Road for 10.2 miles to the Noble Hammock put in, on the right-hand side of the road. Depart the small dock away from the Main Park Road and shortly turn right, following the first of 124 sequentially numbered poles. Don't let these markers detract from the scenery, for you would soon be lost in that scenery if it weren't for the upright white PVC pipes. The waters of the Noble Hammock Loop have a coffee-colored tint due to the decomposition of plant matter on the bottom.

Passageways barely wide enough for a canoe give way to tiny bays, where openings draw you toward them—but don't go. Follow the poles. Just as quickly, the trail leads into tiny creeks over which hangs shade-rendering mangrove. And so it goes. After marker #45, at a clump of paurotis palms you can get out and stand for a moment. There is very little dry land around here.

Continue on through the dense growth. Soon, on your right, there is a sign marking Noble Hammock. You can get out at the small landing, but exploring Noble Hammock and finding the remains of Bill Noble's Prohibition-era moonshining brick furnace requires some serious bush-whacking. It was this very growth and available buttonwood for burning that led to this tree island's becoming a moonshiner's asylum, along with many others.

Don't be surprised when the water stirs as you round a corner on this trail. Many fish ply these waters, including such native species as bluegill, largemouth bass, and the distinctive, long-snouted Florida gar. Unfortunately, you will also see tilapia, a non-native breamlike fish that is success-fully reproducing here.

The moving cars along the park road will signal the end of the trip. Surprisingly, you will end your paddle at a small dock beside the park road about 100 yards away from where you started. Walk onto the road and your vehicle will be up the road to your right (east).

North River Route

Begin: Coast Guard marker #30 in Whitewater Bay
End: The Cutoff at North River

Distance: 4.5 miles	Time: 2.5 hours
Potential Tidal Influence: 2	Potential Wind Influence: 3

Navigational Challenge: 2
Highlights: Good connector route
Hazards: Big water on Whitewater Bay
Campsites: None
Connections: The Cutoff Route, Whitewater Bay Route

The North River Route is primarily used by travelers in the Whitewater Bay area to make loop paddles. Paddlers often stay at some of the chickees on the perimeter of Whitewater Bay and return toward Flamingo via the North River. This route was part of my first trip into the Everglades. The navigation is easy, but the waves can get big in Whitewater Bay. Once in North River proper, you need concern yourself only with the direction of the tides.

From Coast Guard marker #30 in the middle of Whitewater Bay, make your way easterly through a couple of lonely keys, then enter a wide channel, which marks the beginning of the North River. This channel shrinks to a couple of hundred feet, then seems to be blocked by a wall of mangrove. However, it is actually an island that splits the mouth of the North River. Directly in front of this island on the side facing Whitewater Bay is a "Warning, Manatee Area" sign.

At 3 miles, proceed either way around the island on the North River to yet another sizable island that splits the river. Beyond this second island, it is clear sailing down an easily recognizable deep channel banked by mangrove. The river widens to more than 300 feet at points but narrows to as little as 100 feet while meandering northeasterly for another 1.75 miles to intersect The Cutoff Route. The Cutoff proper is a quarter mile to your right (northeast). To your left on The Cutoff route (west) the unnamed river north of the North River leads 1 mile to the North River chickee. The actual North River continues for another three-quarters of a mile before it splits off into smaller branches and melds into the sawgrass of the Everglades in a freshwater network of feeder streams.

Roberts River Route

Begin: Coast Guard Marker # 18 in Whitewater Bay

End: Roberts River chickee

Distance: 5.5 miles   Time: 3 hours

Potential Tidal Influence: 2   Potential Wind Influence: 4

Navigational Challenge: 2

Highlights: Solitude on Roberts River, hammock right by Roberts River chickee

Hazards: Wind on Whitewater Bay

Campsites: Roberts River

Connections: Whitewater Bay Route, Lane River Route, The Cutoff Route

---

The Roberts River Route encompasses multiple environments, leaving the Wilderness Waterway and wide open Whitewater Bay for a somewhat calmer channel heading northeast. This channel narrows further as it gets upriver from Lane River. The actual Roberts River begins here and continues northeasterly as a very intimate waterway with little navigational hazard. It widens a bit before ending at Roberts River chickee, one of the best camping spots in the southern Everglades paddling region.

Head northeasterly from Coast Guard marker #18 for a strait between a series of keys that forms a channel leading to the mouth of the Roberts River, passing a couple of isles at the mouth of the channel. The passageway that you have paddled northeasterly continues to narrow until it jogs right and bottlenecks to about 50 feet in width just past the Lane River, marked by a manatee-area warning sign. The Lane River Route leads east 5 miles to the Hells Bay chickee. You have now paddled 2.5 miles.

On the Roberts River Route, continue up the deep channel, now the Roberts River in name and body, where you will experience solitude more often than not. Shortly, come to a confluence of two creeks, nearly the same in size. Stay left (north), and now the river is less than 50 feet wide and mostly remains that width for around a mile. Then the Roberts widens into an elongated bay with finger peninsulas jutting into the bay, between smaller creeks meandering into the mangrove. At the head of this elongated bay is the Roberts River chickee. It is backed up against a tall hammock and is on your right in a small cove, well protected from the elements. This hammock, just a few feet north of the chickee, has some dry ground and freshwater plants and ferns. From the Roberts River chickee, it is 1.5 miles to the North River proper via The Cutoff Route and 3 miles to the North River chickee via The Cutoff Route.

West Lake Canoe Trail

Begin: Main Park Road Florida Bay	End: Alligator Creek campsite at
Distance: 8.5 miles	Time: 4.5 hours
Potential Tidal Influence: 2	Potential Wind Influence: 2

Navigational Challenge: 3

Highlights: Less-used trail, no motorboats allowed on last 5 miles of trail

Hazards: Extremely shallow water, excessive mosquito potential

Campsites: Alligator Creek

Connections: Snake Bight Route

The West Lake Canoe Trail trail uses a mix of lakes and small creeks to take you to some of the Everglades' least used backcountry. Past West Lake, you will see no motorboats as you work your way in winding fashion to Florida Bay. West Lake was the site of a hunting and fishing camp from 1916 to the 1930s. Both before and after this time, alligator and plume hunters used this very canoe trail to access these creeks and adjoin-

Crocodile on West Lake Canoe Trail. Photo by Mike Audette

ing lakes for their rich wildlife. Be prepared for mosquitoes on all the creeks of this trail. Day paddlers can turn around at any point in the round-trip route of 17 miles. Overnight campers can enjoy the little-used Alligator Creek campsite and return to West Lake or head into Florida Bay to Flamingo and beyond.

Leave the dock on an arm of West Lake and head south into the main lake, where there are many downed trees in the borders of the lake. The official canoe trail follows the right bank south, then east. It is marked by very occasional plastic PVC pipes. Otherwise you can just paddle for the extreme southeastern corner of the lake, where a creek links West Lake to Long Lake. There is a marker and buoy at the entrance to this creek at mile 3.5. No motors are allowed beyond this point.

Head south into this canopied creek that is only 10–15 feet wide and interspersed with branches. Open into shallow Long Lake after a short distance. Keep east through small islands, ending up in the most south-easterly portion of this lake, where marked Mangrove Creek begins.

Mangrove Creek is broken up by two small ponds that open up the otherwise shady creek, where prop roots of red mangrove drop into the water, along with their branches. Thousands of aerial roots of black mangrove line the shore. The final of three sections of Mangrove Creek feeds into The Lungs, which is a lake shaped vaguely like human lungs. Keep south through this slender cove of The Lungs and emerge into the main part of the lake. The marked beginning of Alligator Creek will be on the west shore.

Alligator Creek, about 20 feet wide, does have alligators. Their flattened-mud lounging locations can be seen along the creek's edge. A couple of ponds break this creek up, too. Mangrove lines the creek, but in the final section, shrubby prairies open up behind the tree-lined bank. Scattered black mangrove and the bleached skeletons of trees past offer an eerie contrast to these prairies.

Pass some old pilings of a road bridge, which was built in the 1930s. The road was used by government employees who were trying to eradicate tree cotton. This cotton, native to the Everglades, was thought to be blighted, which could threaten commercial cotton operations to the north. Soon after the bridge pilings, come to the Alligator Creek campsite on your right and Garfield Bight, a part of Florida Bay, at mile 8.5, and the end of the canoe trail. From here it is 2.5 miles to Shark Point campsite via the Snake Bight Route.

Whitewater Bay Route

Begin: Coast Guard marker #10 in Whitewater Bay

End: Coast Guard marker #40 at Cormorant Pass

Distance: 12 miles   Time: 6 hours

Potential Tidal Influence: 2   Potential Wind Influence: 5

Navigational Challenge: 1

Highlights: Marked route for less experienced navigators, multiple route connections

Hazards: Big waves and motorboats

Campsites: None

Connections: Joe River Route, East River Route, Roberts River Route, North River Route, Cormorant Pass Route, Shark Cutoff Route

---

This is the shortest and most direct route north through Whitewater Bay. It encompasses a significant leg of the Wilderness Waterway, but this segment is little used by paddlers on the waterway because there are no campsites in Whitewater Bay. The route is used in its entirety primarily by powerboaters navigating their way north through Whitewater Bay.

There is a reason for the name Whitewater Bay. This is by far the most open stretch of water on the "inside." The waves can become high here, and powerboaters will make more waves. But inexperienced navigators can benefit from the marked route, especially in accessing the rivers east of Whitewater Bay and making other route connections. Keep an eye out for powerboats at all times while paddling this route. I have paralleled the route, staying off to one side a bit, giving powerboaters the main route right beside the markers. If the winds are high, get behind some of the scattered islands in the bay to rest along the way.

Leave Tarpon Creek and come to Coast Guard marker #10 and the open bay. Paddle north, looking ahead from marker to marker. Pass between a couple of islands, turning northwesterly, and come to marker #18 at 3 miles. Northeast from here is the Roberts River Route. Proceed up Whitewater Bay through the Midway Keys to marker #30 at 6.5 miles. Northeast from here is the North River Route.

Now, enter the most open stretch of water. It is 3 miles northeast to the Watson River chickee from marker # 34, at 8 miles. Ahead of you are myriad islands that look like one continuous shoreline, but as you paddle closer the individual islands begin to stand out. The marked path leads through Cormorant Pass, which slices through these islands. The current can be strong going in and out of the pass. The pass begins at marker #40, at 12 miles, the end of the Whitewater Bay Route. Intersect the Cormorant Pass Route here. The Watson River chickee is 3 miles east from marker #40. Oyster Bay chickee is 1 mile distant through Cormorant Pass. You can continue on the Wilderness Waterway via the Shark Cutoff Route.

The Central Rivers Area

Broad River Route

Begin: Gulf of Mexico	End: Camp Lonesome
Length: 11.5 miles	Time: 6 hours
Potential Tidal Influence: 4	Potential Wind Influence: 3
Navigational Challenge: 2	

Highlights: Varied Everglades environments

Hazards: Motorboat traffic in Broad River

Campsites: Highland Beach, Broad River, Camp Lonesome

Connections: Highland Beach Route, Wood River Route, The Nightmare Route, Cabbage Island Shortcut, Rodgers River Bay Route

The Broad River Route traces Everglades waters from the salty Gulf to the freshwater near Camp Lonesome. The varied water and changing vegetation keep the scenery interesting. Along the way you'll pass from beach to bay to an old shell mound along the upper Broad River. Part of this route is on the Wilderness Waterway. These are popular fishing waters, so expect to hear motorboat engines roar. The deep and wide river makes for strong tidal flow upstream and down.

Leave the Gulf, following the marked channel into the Broad to avoid the many oyster bars that crop up at low tide. There will be no problem for hand-propelled craft that enter the island-studded bay on a rising tide. Work your way east among the islands, being careful not to erroneously enter the Rodgers River. The Broad River stays true to its name, stretching nearly 250 feet across as it intersects the Wilderness Waterway at marker #25. Here the Wood River and The Nightmare converge into the Broad. From here, the Wood River Route leads east 10 miles to Camp Lonesome on the upper Broad River. The Nightmare Route leads 8.5 miles south to Harney River chickee. Just east of marker #25, on the south bank of the Broad River, is the Broad River campsite at mile 2. This ground campsite has a dock and is a convenient stopping point.

Continue up the Broad, which has settled down to around 200 feet in width. Pass a water-monitoring station on the south bank about a mile past the campsite. There is much more than mangrove on the shoreline. Palms, poisonwood, and gumbo-limbo indicate drier land. Unfortunately, there is also an excessive amount of Brazilian pepper, an exotic invasive bush with red berries that birds spread and that the park service simultaneously tries to eradicate. It's disheartening to see the pepper literally line the Broad. In other places there are copses of palms.

At 6 miles, come to The Cutoff at a particularly sharp bend in the river. This channel is at the northern outer edge of the bend and connects the Broad River to the Rodgers River. This should not be confused with the other Cutoff that connects the Roberts River with the North River, down south near Whitewater Bay. East of The Cutoff 150 yards, on the same north bank, is the Cabbage Island Shortcut, which leads to Rodgers River Bay. This channel is only half as wide as The Cutoff.

A half-mile east of The Cutoff, the Broad River pinches in just before entering Broad River Bay. The shoreline is nearly all mangrove and buttonwood. As you paddle up the bay, you can use its undulations and points to mark distance paddled. Come to Wilderness Waterway marker #26 at mile 8.5. Here, the Wilderness Waterway turns north for Rodgers River Bay. The Rodgers River chickee is 4 miles north via the Rodgers River Bay Route. The Broad River Route, however, continues easterly

Dock at Camp Lonesome. Photo by author

toward Camp Lonesome. Broad River Bay constricts, passing a conspicuous island in the middle of the channel, and then the riverine characteristics of the Broad resume. Just beyond this island, come to a water-monitoring station on the north bank.

The waters now are clear and usually fresh, depending on rainfall and
tides. The bottom is very visible and the river varies between 50 and 60
feet in width. An occasional palm and wax myrtle pop out of the now
lower mangrove edges. Come to the confluence of four waterways, including the one you are on. The Wood River flows in from the right. Dead
ahead is an unnamed channel, and to your left is the continuation of the
Broad River. Take the Broad River left; above the mangrove line are tall
Jamaica dogwood and gumbo-limbo. Follow the left shoreline to reach
the Camp Lonesome dock, tucked away amid some trees and brush at
mile 11.5. This is an old shell mound that has been occupied, going back
untold centuries, by the Calusa, the Seminoles—and now you. From
here, the Wood River Route leads 10 miles west back to the Broad River
at The Nightmare.

Cabbage Island Shortcut

Begin: Rodgers River chickee

End: Broad River just west of Broad River Bay

Length: 3.5 miles

Time: 2 hours

Potential Tidal Influence: 2

Potential Wind Influence: 2

Navigational Challenge: 3

Highlights: Quality creek paddling

Hazards: Choosing wrong creek from Broad River

Campsites: Rodgers River chickee

Connections: Rodgers River Route, Broad River Route, Rodgers River Bay Route

---

The Cabbage Island Shortcut offers the best in Everglades creek paddling. The waterway is small but not enclosed; it is grown up but not overgrown. There are just enough twists and turns and tree limbs to wind around to keep the paddle lively without becoming tiresome. There is only one channel, so the route doesn't become a guessing game as to which way to go. Logistically speaking, it is the quickest way to the Broad River from the Rodgers River chickee.

Start your route by paddling southeast from the Rodgers River chickee toward Cabbage Island. Aim for the channel along the west side of Cabbage Island. There is a conspicuous palm tree at the point for which you should aim. Take this slender channel and head for the extreme southwest corner of a small bay southwest of Cabbage Island. Where the bay splits at its end, take the south creek, which is about 20 feet wide and plenty deep. Begin your southwesterly course toward the Broad River. There is a preponderance of buttonwood on this creek.

Every now and then you'll have to sneak past some roots and limbs, but the paddling never becomes an ordeal. Keep south and west before coming out at a big bend in the Broad River at mile 3.5. Just 100 yards west is the entrance to The Cutoff, which also connects Broad River to Rodgers River. This is not to be confused with The Cutoff that connects North River and Roberts River near Whitewater Bay.

If you are paddling this route from Broad River to Rodgers River Bay, make sure not to take The Cutoff. The Cabbage Island Shortcut is *east* of The Cutoff from the Broad River. Once on Broad River, it is half a mile east to Broad River Bay. Southwest 4 miles down Broad River is the Broad River campsite via the Broad River Route.

Graveyard Creek Route

Begin: Shark River chickee	End: Graveyard Creek campsite
Distance: 7 miles	Time: 3.5 hours
Potential Tidal Influence: 4	Potential Wind Influence: 3
Navigational Challenge: 3	

Highlights: Mature mangrove forest, good camping at Graveyard Creek

Hazards: Strong tidal flows up and down river

Campsites: Shark River chickee, Graveyard Creek

Connections: Highland Beach Route, Shark Cutoff Route, The Labyrinth Route

The Graveyard Creek Route gets you from the "inside" to the "outside," or vice versa. Start at the Shark River chickee, which is on the Little Shark River, and paddle a short distance to the Shark River, then head west toward Ponce De Leon Bay. From the Shark River, there are several connecting tributaries that you can use to make your way toward the bay. Paddle among some of the tallest mangrove in the park while winding through these channels to end up in the northern end of Ponce De Leon Bay. From here it is but a short paddle in the Gulf to the Graveyard Creek campsite, which has characteristics of both beach and ground campsites, though it is officially classified as a ground campsite

Leave Shark River chickee and make a few strokes north to the Little Shark River. Turn right (northeast) up the Little Shark River just a short distance to Wilderness Waterway marker #6. At this point, you can see far up the waterway above the confluence of the Shark and Little Shark rivers. Take the north channel by marker #6, which shortcuts to the Shark River.

Turn up this channel and shortly connect to the Shark River. Turn left (west) on the Shark and make your way downriver. The mangrove shoreline here rises from the waterway with the trees growing taller beyond the bank, creating the illusion of hills rising from the Shark.

The waterway is generally about 150 feet wide as it flows into the central part of Ponce De Leon Bay. But before continuing too far down the river, consider taking some of the many interconnecting channels that run parallel to the Shark. Paddling the Shark into the Ponce De Leon Bay will necessitate a paddle across big water to reach Graveyard Creek, which may be an undesirable paddle on windy days. Also, more powerboats will be using the Shark than the interconnecting channels north of the Shark, which run east-west. These channels also offer a more intimate view of the mature mangrove woodland, and they empty into the northern part of Ponce De Leon Bay closer to the Graveyard Creek campsite. I recommend using these channels. And if the wind is really fierce, you can use these channels and side creeks to avoid the bay altogether, arriving at the campsite via Graveyard Creek.

Be advised that tides run very strong in the Shark and its tributaries. Paddling against the tide here can be slow and exhausting. Try to time your paddle with the flow of the tides. Also, pay strict attention to the nautical charts, as the interconnecting nature of these channels can be confusing, though their east-west orientation and their common destination, Ponce De Leon Bay, make mistakes more forgivable.

After you choose your exact route among the channels of the Shark, hug the northern shore of Ponce De Leon Bay. Beach and mangrove intermingle as the coast turns north and overlooks the Gulf of Mexico. Come to the small inlet of Graveyard Creek at mile 7. The Graveyard Creek campsite is on the north side of the inlet, with the best landing up Graveyard Creek, where a small beach and some relatively deep water allow paddlers their best access to the campsite, which can be hard to reach at low tide.

Harney River Route

Begin: Canepatch campsite End: Gulf of Mexico

Distance: 13.5 miles   Time: 7 hours

Potential Tidal Influence: 4 Potential Wind Influence: 3

Navigational Challenge: 2

Highlights: Route extends from freshwater to saltwater

Hazards: Strong tides both upriver and down

Campsites: Harney River chickee, Canepatch campsite

Connections: Highland Beach Route, Shark Cutoff Route, The Nightmare

---

The Harney River connects the freshwater Glades to the salty Gulf on its east-west course. The river was named for Colonel William Harney, who used the river for passage to the Gulf in 1840, after crossing the Everglades westward from the Miami River. This Gulf passage took place after Harney pursued and killed the Indian Chekika, who had conducted his own deadly raid on some white residents at Indian Key during the Seminole Wars. Your passage on the Harney River Route will be less dangerous. The route passes from the freshwater creeks and Tarpon Bay to enter the Harney. The river splits and widens, then reaches the Gulf beyond an island-dotted bay just north of Ponce De Leon Bay.

Leave the Canepatch campsite and paddle south a short distance to Avocado Creek, passing a "No Wake" sign. Proceed westerly down Avocado Creek. Though this creek is narrow, you will have no problems getting through. It is deep enough—and the vegetation is kept clear enough—for small motorboat passage. The upper creek was opened by Hurricane Andrew in 1992. Broken and low trees, punctuated by surprising amounts of sawgrass and other freshwater vegetation, occupy the shoreline, while the creek varies in width from 15 to 40 feet. Wider views than normal are available for a creek of this diminutive size. The shore crowds right in on your sea kayak closer to Tarpon Bay, though there are few canopied sections.

Pass an "End No Wake" sign and enter the arm of Tarpon Bay created by Avocado Creek at mile 1. Continue westerly in the arm along a shore of mangrove with scattered sawgrass and palms, traveling into the south arm of Tarpon Bay and then into the heart of Tarpon Bay. Tarpon Bay is several hundred feet wide at this point. Stay along the south shore, coming to Wilderness Waterway marker #9 at 4 miles. To your south is the commencement of the Shark River and the Shark Cutoff Route, which follows the Wilderness Waterway south. The Harney River Route, however, picks up the Wilderness Waterway as it heads northwest along the beginning of the Harney River.

Paddle west along the Harney River, where the passage settles down to around 120 feet. Watch for a feeder stream to the North Harney River at mile 5.5, then a water-monitoring station on river north. Merge with the North Harney River by Wilderness Waterway marker # 11, at mile 9. Northeast from marker #11, the North Harney River Route heads 10.5 miles back toward Canepatch. The Harney River is a good 200 feet wide here. Continue westward one-half mile to Wilderness Waterway marker #11, passing a partly concealed water-monitoring station on the south bank. In the center of the river are an island and Harney River chickee at mile 9.5. To your north, the Wilderness Waterway heads to Broad River via The Nightmare Route. Harney River chickee is an important staging area for paddling The Nightmare Route because of tidal considerations.

To continue the Harney River Route, leave the island of Harney River chickee and paddle the river almost due west, leaving the Wilderness Waterway behind. Continue west, staying with the south bank as the river turns south, passing by a channel on the right that also heads to the Gulf. A second, smaller channel splitting the south bank leads back to the Harney River chickee. The river resumes a westerly course, more than 100 feet wide and several feet deep.

Beyond the split in the river, watch the south bank for high ground with perpendicular banks that are high enough to support salt-intolerant species such as palm. Part of this was once a farming area known as Ellis Fields. The river continues to widen as it nears the Gulf, becoming more than 200 feet across when it enters a bay enlarged by a merging river

Mouth of the Harney River at low tide. Photo by author

coming in from the south. The Gulf side of this bay seems to be blocked by multiple islands, but as you get closer there are three distinct channels to choose from to enter the Gulf at mile 13.5. From here it is 7 miles north to Highland Beach and 2 miles south to Graveyard Creek campsite via the Highland Beach Route.

Highland Beach Route

Begin: Lostmans Ranger Station at Lostmans River

End: Graveyard Creek campsite

Distance: 13 miles

Time: 7 hours

Potential Tidal Influence: 4

Potential Wind Influence: 5

Navigational Challenge: 2

Highlights: Highland Beach, many river mouths

Hazards: Big Gulf water and winds, being stranded at low tide

Campsites: Highland Beach, Graveyard Creek

Connections: Lostmans River Route, Rodgers River Route, Broad River Route, Harney River Route, Shark River Route, Ponce De Leon Bay Route, Turkey Key Route

---

The shoreline of the Highland Beach Route is as wild as the Florida coast gets in this era. This route covers the less traversed central Everglades Gulf Coast. Getting here takes more paddling than the time constraints of most trips allow. The Gulf paddle is varied and scenic, with mangrove and beach coastline. Both campsites on this route offer quality experiences. In

Walking the shell mound at the mouth of Lostmans River. Photo by Ellen Connally

pre-park days, much of this land was settled, first by the Calusa and later by a family of Hamiltons and other settlers. Out here, it is just the mainland and the wide-open Gulf. There are no islands to hide behind or slip between. The Gulf feels big out here, and when the waves come up, these waters can be downright treacherous.

This paddle starts at the mouth of the Lostmans River, where the high shell mound of Lostmans Ranger Station overlooks the landscape. The route passes Lostmans Key, then Little Creek, and swings around Highland Point to come to Highland Beach. The beach here is airy and impressive—it stretches for 2 miles. Then the route takes you to the river mouths, cycling through the daily flow of the tides. The paddle ends at Graveyard Creek, just south of Shark Point, and an excellent campsite.

Leave the Lostmans Ranger Station and paddle south, crossing the channel that enters Lostmans River, then paddling parallel to Lostmans Key. Notice the sloping beaches on Lostmans Key as you pass the island and the south entrance to Lostmans River.

Come to the inlet of Little Creek, then make your way around Highland Point and at 4 miles come to the long and attractive Highland Beach, which has returned to its wild state. Palm trees grow atop the tall sand bluff formed by waves, which slopes back to a grass prairie studded with cabbage palm, Spanish bayonet, and cactus. In pre-park days, this high land was farmed by the Rewis family. This is a great campsite, but be aware that low tide will leave you stranded on the beach until the water rises later.

Continue south, passing the wide bay of the Broad and Rodgers Rivers. The Broad River and Rodgers River Routes lead into the interior Everglades from here. The channel markers in this bay, at mile 6, guide boaters from the Gulf into the Broad River between the sand and mud bars so numerous here. Pass the mouth of Broad Creek and head toward Harney River. In this section between Broad River and Harney River, you may have to paddle a mile or more from shore to avoid the numerous sand, mud, and oyster bars that extend into the Gulf here. Come to the Harney River and the Harney River Route at 11 miles.

Past the Harney River, the Gulf gets deeper closer to shore. Pass around

Shark Point, and the shoreline veers southeasterly at the northern end of Ponce De Leon Bay. Come to Graveyard Creek campsite, at mile 13, in the small inlet where Graveyard Creek enters the Gulf. Your best campsite access is up Graveyard Creek and to the beach area on the north side of the inlet. From here it is 4 miles across Ponce De Leon Bay to Shark River Island and the Big Sable Route on the Ponce De Leon Bay Route. It is 7 miles to Shark River chickee on the Graveyard Creek Route.

Lostmans River Route

Begin: Wilderness Waterway marker # 52 near Second Bay in Lostmans River

End: Lostmans Ranger Station at Lostmans River

Distance: 6 miles

Time: 3.5 hours

Potential Tidal Influence: 4

Potential Wind Influence: 3

Navigational Challenge: 2

Highlights: Shell mound at Lostmans Ranger Station

Hazards: Strong tides in Lostmans River

Campsites: None

Connections: Willy Willy Route, Turkey Key Route, Highland Beach Route, Toms Creek Route

---

The Lostmans River Route connects the Wilderness Waterway to the Gulf on the history-laden Lostmans River. Modern farmers, homesteaders, hunters, and fishermen followed the Calusa, who enjoyed the bounties of nature from this river and the Gulf. The upper Lostmans is made up of bays; the middle Lostmans is more riverine in character. Another bay opens up by the Gulf, near Lostmans Key. The Calusa reaped the natural harvest here, before white settlers, as is evidenced by the impressive shell mound at the mouth of the Lostmans, where the Lostmans Ranger Station sits. The Lostmans Ranger Station is boarded up, locked, and no longer maintained on a regular basis. There are no means of seek-

Lostmans River Ranger Station. Photo by author

ing help here. As a paddler, you will use the ranger station merely as a marker or a place to stop for lunch and stretch your legs.

Leave the Wilderness Waterway and the Willy Willy Route at Wilderness Waterway marker #52. Paddle southwest into wide Second Bay, keeping in the main flow of the current to avoid mud bars. Pass the mouth of Toms Creek to the east at mile 1.5. This is the terminus of Toms Creek Route, which heads east to the Rodgers River chickee.

Enter the riverine portion of Lostmans River, which now flows west. The mangrove shoreline is impressive here, rising high along the shore. The tidal flow can be strong in the 200 feet between the streambanks. This river section lasts a little shy of 2 miles. The depth of the river is way over your head here—10 or more feet. This is one of the few places in the Everglades with this kind of depth, thus the strong tides.

Pass a water-monitoring station on the south bank, half a mile west of Toms Creek. There are pilings from an old dock on the north bank across from the water-monitoring station. The dry land behind the pilings is the old homesite of Walter Hamilton, who lived here in the early 1900s. Stay with the north bank as you enter First Bay. The water becomes shallow farther westward. Lostmans Key blocks most of First Bay, but there are Gulf access channels north and south of the key. Head for the north channel, which is marked for boaters. Other markers lead into the Gulf beyond Lostmans Key.

There used to be a campsite on the sandy south shore of Lostmans Key, but it was blown away in a storm. Pass the north side of Lostmans Key through the north channel and soon come to the Lostmans Ranger Station at a point on the north shore. Look for the remains of a dock and the end of your route at 6 miles.

The Lostmans Ranger Station sits on a high and extensive Calusa shell mound, which was also built up by storm surges from the Gulf. Note the sea grape, coconut palms, and extensive grasses on this high sand perch. This site was also once a fish house and small community of palmetto shacks. To the north it is 3 miles to Hog Key on the Turkey Key route. To the south it is 4 miles to the Highland Beach on the Highland Beach Route.

The Nightmare Route

Begin: Broad River campsite End: Harney River chickee
Distance: 8.5 miles Time: 4 hours
Potential Tidal Influence: 2 Potential Wind Influence: 2
Navigational Challenge: 4
Highlights: Canopied creeks, bird life
Hazards: Fallen and overgrown trees, low tide
Campsites: Broad River, Harney River chickee
Connections: Harney River Route, North Harney River Route, Broad River Route, Wood River Route

---

The Nightmare is the stuff of Everglades legends. This is the only paddling route not on the Gulf to connect the northern and southern Everglades. This makes it an essential link for those traveling the Wilderness

Alligator along The Nightmare near Wood River. Photo by author

Waterway from end to end, especially if the wind and waves are high on the ocean. Many of the linked creeks, pungent with decaying vegetation, are overgrown with mangrove in places. And if the tide is low, this route can be risky and become too shallow to paddle for a time. But you only have to wait for the tide to rise, then resume your course. Otherwise, you can always paddle out the Broad River to the Gulf and rejoin the Wilderness Waterway up Broad Creek. There is much bird life along the route's quiet creeks, where a paddler rarely if ever sees a motorboat. I presume this segment of the Everglades is so named for the disagreeable possibility of being stuck here at low tide, especially when the mosquitoes are buzzing.

Leave the Broad River campsite and paddle west down the Broad River a few hundred feet to Wilderness Waterway marker #24 and the Wood River. Turn left (south) on the Wood River and trace it a short distance to Wilderness Waterway marker #23. From here, the Wood River Route heads left (east) 10 miles to Camp Lonesome on the upper Broad River.

Turn right (southwest) at marker #23 and begin a convoluted paddle that will take you in all compass directions. This route is partly canopied and partly open overhead. There is much downed and dead wood in the water, and live trees, limbs, and roots to paddle around. There are also a few open shrubby areas. Other creeks spin off here and there, but the main channel is usually obvious. If you are in doubt, look for limbs sawn and branches broken by other paddlers to keep The Nightmare passable. The creeks here are also a little deeper than indicated on the chart. You can run them not only at high tide, but also on a rising tide or a high falling tide from the Broad River campsite. Just don't run the route at absolute low tide. The tides flowing in and out of here scour the creek bed and keep The Nightmare runnable.

Come to Wilderness Waterway marker #23 at mile 2.5. To your right is a channel to the Gulf. Stay left. Here, the creek opens up somewhat. Stay left again at marker #21, which is off to the right in another channel leading to the Gulf. Coming from Broad River, you may miss this marker and see marker #19 next. Here, the creek is no longer canopied. Merge with Broad Creek at marker #17. This is where the low-water Gulf alternative rejoins the Wilderness Waterway.

Paddle east up the rich waters of Broad Creek, which remains broad for about a mile until it seems to dead-end in mangrove; the creek is just overgrown here. At this point, stow your gear and fishing rods below the gunwales of your canoe and batten down any gear strapped on your sea kayak. Through this section of Broad Creek, expect to be ducking and darting amid the growth of some large red mangrove. Be prepared for a few spider webs, too. Water depth is no problem here. Often, water extends far into the mangrove beyond the main channel, creating a swamp effect.

Emerge from the tangle of Broad Creek just before reaching marker #16, 7 miles into the route. Leave Broad Creek and head southwest down a much more paddler-friendly creek to marker #14. Here, you pick up a mud-bottomed stream winding southeasterly to merge with the Harney River at Wilderness Waterway marker #12. Harney River chickee is dead ahead at mile 8.5, the end of the route. To the west it is 4 miles to the Gulf on the Harney River Route. To the east, the Harney River Route leads 5.5 miles to Tarpon Bay and the Shark Cutoff Route. The North Harney River Route starts half a mile east on the Harney River.

North Harney River Route

Begin: Wilderness Waterway marker #11 at Harney River
End: Canepatch campsite
Distance: 10.5 miles   Time: 6 hours
Potential Tidal Influence: 4   Potential Wind Influence: 3
Navigational Challenge: 4
Highlights: Many types of waters
Hazards: Tiny creek near Canepatch
Campsites: Harney River, Canepatch
Connections: Harney River Route, The Nightmare Route

Are you looking for the route less traveled? Are you looking for a route that encompasses bays, rivers, streams, and creeks, with a little navigational uncertainty thrown in for good measure? Then paddle the North Harney River Route. It starts innocuously enough as it splinters off the Harney River, traveling east and getting a little smaller as time goes on, until it is but 20 feet wide just before meeting big Tarpon Bay and its mixture of fresh and saltwater flora. Then comes the finale—a trip through tiny, deep creeks where you have to trust your chart and your compass, especially at the end when these freshwater streams seem overgrown—but they are passable to your destination, Canepatch campsite. This campsite is a historic shell mound that is still growing the descendants of its final farming incarnation. Don't expect to see any motorboats, except, maybe, on Tarpon Bay.

Start your route at Wilderness Waterway marker #11, a half mile east of Harney River chickee. Paddle north from the marker, then east to get on the North Harney River, which veers east to parallel the much more heavily traveled (by boaters of all stripes) Harney. The North Harney is a good 150 feet wide but soon shrinks to just under 100 feet. Tributary streams splinter off the north bank. Occasional fern patches dot the shore.

At mile 3.5, come to your first navigational challenge. About 120 yards after the river has made a sharp southeasterly jog, come to a small inlet and creek on the south bank, then a split in the river into two channels of roughly equal size. The southerly channel meets the Harney, while the easterly channel is the continuation of the North Harney. Take the east channel.

Although the river is now only 40 feet wide, the effective paddling area is only 15–30 feet. There is no canopy, but the shores are lush with mangrove. Always inclined toward the east, the North Harney winds in all directions. This is great paddling—a clear meandering stream with no serious obstructions and few if any motorboats. The mangrove shore lowers and is punctuated with fern patches and bare mud spots where alligators sun themselves.

Leave the serpentine stream and enter a series of tapered bays that continues easterly and finally opens into Tarpon Bay at mile 8. Here the appearance of sawgrass, mahogany, palm, and wax myrtle indicates fresher water and bits of higher land.

Stay on the primary northeast arm of the bay until it veers southeast toward the Canepatch campsite. Paddle to the very end of the bay, staying with the south shore to keep on the correct track.

Do not take the tiny creek at the very end of the bay—it is overgrown. Take instead the 10-foot-wide creek leaving northeast just a few paddle strokes away. The correct creek is plenty deep, with fingerlike roots of trees floating in the water. Follow this uncanopied waterway until it appears to dead-end. Two very small creeks split off here. Take the overgrown, canoe-width creek flowing in from the south. The mangrove brush is very low, but the water is deep and passable. Look for saw marks on bigger branches.

You will be paddling southerly against the current here, because this creek is above the normal tidal cycles and naturally flows toward the Gulf. This freshwater also brings about more vegetational changes, including coco plum and fig. From here, the creek is alternately open and overgrown. Merge into a tiny bay with a creek flowing in from the east, with a water-monitoring station in view. You, however, paddle south through a slender channel, immediately coming to the dock of the Canepatch campsite on your right at mile 10.5.

This campsite is an old shell mound in use as long as there has been an Everglades. The Harney River Route has come into Canepatch via Avocado Creek to the southwest, where you see a "No Wake" sign.

Ponce De Leon Bay Route

Begin: Shark River Island   End: Graveyard Creek campsite

Distance: 4 miles   Time: 2 hours

Potential Tidal Influence: 4   Potential Wind Influence: 5

Navigational Challenge: 2

Highlights: Open Gulf paddle

Hazards: Big water, strong tides

Campsites: Graveyard Creek

Connections: Highland Beach Route, Big Sable Route, Graveyard Creek Route

---

Ponce de Leon Bay Route is a short connector route for travelers paddling north and south along the Gulf coast of the Everglades, on the "outside." Ponce De Leon Bay is the single largest bay on the Everglades Gulf coast. This significant stretch of water divides Cape Sable to the south from the central Glades and the Ten Thousand Islands to the north. The tides will be felt as they push in and out of the bay, which drains the Shark River and Whitewater Bay. The relatively deep water of the bay means big waves if the wind is blowing. In that case, you will have to circumvent Ponce De Leon Bay via the many channels of the Shark River system.

Start your route at the oversized flashing buoy just southwest of Shark River Island at the mouth of the Little Shark River. South of you is the continuation of the Big Sable Route, which swings around Cape Sable. For the Ponce De Leon Bay Route, paddle north around Shark River Island almost due north across the bay. The water becomes more shallow on the last half of the bay. Graveyard Creek flows into the north end of the bay. The campsite is marked by a couple of coconut palms. Your best bet for accessing the campsite is to paddle into Graveyard Creek about 50 yards and land on the sandy north side of the creek. Here, the water is deep and access is possible regardless of the tides, which can leave the Gulf side of the campsite high and dry. From Graveyard Creek, the Highland Beach Route heads north up the Gulf 13 miles to Lostmans River.

If the winds are high, you can alter the Ponce De Leon Bay Route. Paddle up the mouth of the Little Shark River, following the Coast Guard markers to marker # 64. Then veer north into the system of channels and islands of the Shark River, circumventing Ponce De Leon Bay. You can even work your way around to enter Graveyard Creek campsite via Graveyard Creek. This will obviously add time and mileage to your paddle, but I was very glad the option was available for me one blustery day when it was dangerous to cross the bay in an open canoe.

Rodgers River Route

Begin: Gulf of Mexico

End: Rodgers River chickee

Distance: 10.5 miles

Time: 6 hours

Potential Tidal Influence: 3

Potential Wind Influence: 3

Navigational Challenge: 3

Highlights: Old homesites, solitude

Hazards: Oyster and mud bars at mouth of river

Campsites: Highland Beach, Rodgers River chickee

Connections: Highland Beach Route, Broad River Route, Cabbage Island Shortcut, Rodgers River Bay Route

---

The Rogers River Route is a good connector, and much quieter than the nearby Broad River, for those heading for Rodgers River chickee and the "inside" from the Gulf. The Rodgers River is seldom used by motorboaters. It is challenging to enter from the Gulf, and the many mud bars at the river's west end make navigation difficult unless you are in a shallow-draft hand-propelled craft. Once past the many islands at the river's entrance, the route passes a surprising amount of high ground and accompanying vegetation and an old homesite before the river narrows and

Raccoon on the bank of the Rodgers River. Photo by author

changes course. The upper half of the Rodgers is slender and winding before opening up into Rodgers River Bay, where the route ends at Rodgers River chickee.

Leave the Gulf of Mexico near Highland Beach and enter a maze of islands inhabiting a large bay formed by the confluence of the Rodgers and Broad Rivers. This area can be confusing. Use the flow of the tides to help you through the islands, making sure you are paddling northerly into the Rodgers River and not easterly into the Broad River.

Leave the bay and islands behind as the Rodgers River turns easterly. Note the mud bars on the inside bends of the waterway at lower tides. The Rodgers constricts to less than 100 feet wide as high ground appears on both sides of the river, harboring a palm or two. About 2 miles from the Gulf, note the proliferation of hammock species such as fig, gumbo-limbo, and tamarind on the north bank. Tamarinds, with their spreading branches of tiny compound leaves, are indicators of old home sites. This is most likely the home site of Shelton Atwell. On this property in the late 1800s, Atwell sold sugarcane he grew in cleared fields behind his home along with assorted vegetables for sustenance. As you paddle upriver, look for other palm-studded lands. They are ordinarily on the outside bends of the Rodgers, which has further compressed to about 80 feet and is more uniformly deep. Also watch for alligators, which seem to inhabit the river in inordinately large numbers.

Come to The Cutoff at 6 miles. This waterway connects the Rodgers to the Broad River. The Cutoff is not to be confused with another Cutoff that connects Roberts River to the North River near Whitewater Bay. The Rodgers River turns sharply southwest at The Cutoff and heads in that direction for three-quarters of a mile before resuming a northeasterly bearing. The dry land is all but gone here, and the shoreline is mostly mangrove, buttonwood, and occasional fern patches. The waterway maintains a 40-foot width before widening and twisting around to arrive at Rodgers River Bay at mile 9.5.

Paddle east through a narrow neck of the bay, which opens up. Begin to look for Rodgers River chickee in an inlet on the north side of the bay, coming to the chickee at mile 10.5. The Rodgers River Bay Route and the Wilderness Waterway are 1 mile east. The Cabbage Island Shortcut leads southwest 3.5 miles to Broad River. The Toms Creek and Lostmans routes lead 11.5 miles to the Gulf at Lostmans Ranger Station.

Rodgers River Bay Route

Begin: Willy Willy Campsite   End: Wilderness Waterway marker # 26 at Broad River Bay

Distance: 7 miles   Time: 3.5 hours

Potential Tidal Influence: 2   Potential Wind Influence: 3

Navigational Challenge: 3

Highlights: Nearby freshwater creeks

Hazards: Motor boats on Wilderness Waterway

Campsites: Willy Willy, Rodgers River chickee

Connections: Willy Willy Route, Toms Creek Route, Rodgers River Route, Cabbage Island Shortcut, Broad River Route

The Rogers River Bay Route leaves the shell mound of Willy Willy and heads south on Rocky Creek to Lostmans Creek, to rejoin the Wilderness Waterway through Rodgers River Bay, making a side trip to Rodgers River chickee. Paddlers come back to the Wilderness Waterway and skirt Cabbage Island to enter a twisting channel that emerges onto Broad River Bay. This is one of three routes heading south from Rodgers River Bay, and it is the preferred route if you are heading for Camp Lonesome on the upper Broad River. Freshwater creeks flow into the bays from the marshy glades to the east and make for good side explorations.

Leave Willy Willy campsite and paddle a scant 50 yards east up Rocky Creek Bay to Rocky Creek. Turn south on Rocky Creek and punch the dark objects below the clear water with your paddle. These rocks gave the creek its name. The shore here is fraught with hammock tree species— palm is the most easy to identify. Rocky Creek widens. Turn right at the first side creek. It comes into Rocky Creek at an acute angle from the northwest. This is not Rocky Creek, but it too has a rocky bottom. The stream quickly circles southwest, opening into a bay that runs north-south.

Paddle to the south end of the bay into Lostmans Creek, which at this point is an east-west arm of Big Lostmans Bay. Steer toward the distant western shore of the bay. Dead ahead is Wilderness Waterway marker #39. Join the Wilderness Waterway, but instead of doubling back around the slender island in front of you, take the south channel before the marker and paddle south to marker #37. This marker is not shown on current charts.

Enter Rodgers River Bay and paddle southeast from marker #37 to marker #36. This area can be confusing, because the Wilderness Waterway was rerouted away from the most open part of Rodgers River Bay. Stay south past marker #35 into an 80-foot-wide channel with mangrove and buttonwood banks. Marker #34 is gone, though it is still on the charts. Keep south and come to marker #32, at 4 miles. To your west 1 mile, not visible from here, is Rodgers River chickee. To reach this chickee, paddle west along the north shore until you come to a shallow inlet. There is the chickee, perched about 10 feet from the north shore. From here it is 3.5 miles to Broad River Bay on the Cabbage Island Short-cut. It is 11.5 miles to the Gulf on the Rodgers River Route, and it is 11.5 miles to the Gulf on the Toms Creek and Lostmans River Routes.

Return to Wilderness Waterway marker #32 on the Rodgers River Bay Route. Stroke south, skirting the east side of Cabbage Island and marker #31. East of marker #31 is Indian Camp Creek, another good freshwater paddle. For the Rodgers River Route, stay south past marker #29 into a winding channel that leads to Broad River Bay. Come to Broad River Bay and Wilderness Waterway marker #26 at 7 miles. To the east, it is 3 miles to Camp Lonesome on the Broad River Route. To the west, it is 6.5 miles to the Broad River campsite on the Broad River Route.

Shark Cutoff Route

Begin: Wilderness Waterway marker #9 at Tarpon Bay
End: Oyster Bay chickee

Distance: 7.5 miles	Time: 3.5 hours
Potential Tidal Influence: 4	Potential Wind Influence: 2

Navigational Challenge: 2
Highlights: Big trees on Shark River
Hazards: Tidal flow on Shark River
Campsites: Oyster Bay chickee, Shark River chickee
Connections: Big Sable Route, Shark River Route, The Labyrinth Route, Whitewater Bay Route, Harney River Route, Cormorant Pass Route

---

The Shark Cutoff Route forms part of the primary "inside" connector for north-south Everglades paddlers using the Wilderness Waterway. The route follows the Shark River from its beginning at Tarpon Bay down to its confluence with the Little Shark River, coming to the Shark River chickee. Then, following the Little Shark River, the route turns south at the Shark Cutoff, entering the northern reaches of Oyster Bay. It leaves the Wilderness Waterway and enters a small group of mangrove islands, coming to the Oyster Bay chickee in a lagoon among the islands.

Start your route at Wilderness Waterway marker #9, 4 miles west of Canepatch campsite, and 5.5 miles east of Harney River campsite. Paddle south on the Shark River, bordered by young, small mangrove and buttonwood. Larger, taller patches of mangrove look like hills off in the distance. Arrive at Wilderness Waterway marker #9 at mile 2. On your left is an unnamed channel coming from the eastern end of Tarpon Bay. This channel is an alternative, windy-day route for those paddling to Cane-patch campsite.

Here, the Shark River widens and turns more westerly. The straight nature of the waterway allows for distant views downriver. Pass Gunboat Island at mile 3.5. Someone accurately imagined that this island looked like a warship steaming up the Shark River. Just north of the island is a water-monitoring station. The great mangrove forest of the Shark is evident below this island. Not far downstream is the confluence of the Shark and Little Shark Rivers and another unnamed channel. The southerly channel leads into The Labyrinth. The westerly channel is the Shark River. Straight ahead, southwesterly, is your route, the Little Shark River.

Dead ahead is Wilderness Waterway marker #6. To your north, the Graveyard Creek Route leads 7 westerly miles to Graveyard Creek. Stay southwesterly on the much narrower Little Shark River. On the next channel south of you is the Shark River chickee and the beginning of The Labyrinth Route. The Shark River chickee, about 50 yards up the channel at mile 4.5, is a good place to camp or stop and stretch your legs. There is no dry ground on this route.

Return to the Little Shark River and paddle southwesterly on the Wilderness Waterway for another 1.5 miles, coming to Wilderness Waterway marker #5 and the Shark Cutoff. Turn south on the Wilderness Waterway, traversing the winding shortcut into the northern fringe of Oyster Bay, passing Wilderness Waterway marker #3. The waterway penetrates the bay, heading southeasterly toward a passage between some mangrove islands. Trust your compass; these islands look like one continuous shore-line from afar. Make the passage among the islands and look for Wilderness Waterway marker #2.

Leave the Wilderness Waterway at marker #2 and bear southwest toward Coast Guard marker #50. Do not head for Coast Guard marker #48—it leads to Whitewater Bay and points south through Cormorant Pass, on the Cormorant Pass and Whitewater Bay Routes. Paddle south from marker #50 into a small group of islands. Inside a lagoon amid the islands is the Oyster Bay chickee at mile 7.5. From the Oyster Bay chickee, it is 4 miles south to the Joe River on the Cormorant Pass Route. It is 6 miles west on the Big Sable Route to the Gulf of Mexico at Shark River Island.

Toms Creek Route

Begin: Rodgers River chickee   End: Lostmans River at Second Bay

Distance: 7 miles   Time: 3.5 hours

Potential Tidal Influence: 3   Potential Wind Influence: 3

Navigational Challenge: 3

Highlights: Shortcut between Rodgers River chickee and Gulf

Hazards: Winds on Rodgers River Bay

Campsites: Rodgers River chickee

Connections: Cabbage Island Shortcut, Willy Willy Route, Rodgers River Route, Lostmans River Route

---

The fastest and best way to access Lostmans River from Rodgers River chickee is the Toms Creek Route. And it is off the motorboaters' beaten path. The route runs west out of the Rodgers River Bay into a very shallow bay and then into Toms Creek. Both sections of this little-used waterway, which exudes a feeling of the wild Everglades, meet the east end of the Lostmans River and the Lostmans River Route.

Leave Rodgers River chickee and paddle west on the south Rodgers River Bay through a neck in the bay to the wider north Rodgers River Bay. Turn north, passing the beginning of the Rodgers River to the southwest at 1 mile. From here the Rodgers River Route heads west 10.5 miles to the Gulf.

Stay northwest, aiming for the peninsula that extends out from the west shore of Rodgers River Bay. Once around this point, continue your paddle path west through three bays. The west end of the last bay funnels into Toms Creek. This final bay is very shallow, as is evidenced by numerous snags in the water. This is what discourages motorboats from using this route. Palms grace the shore at the origin of Toms Creek, at mile 4.5.

The stream, about 40 feet wide, is kept deep enough by tidal action, which can be surprisingly swift. Toms Creek starts west but then meanders north for a little short of a mile, where it widens before opening into the Lostmans River. Stay with the west shore of the river and swing around a point, paddling back south into the continuation of Toms Creek. At low tide, watch for and avoid a big mud flat on the point as you swing around it.

Now paddle southerly on the wider, second portion of Toms Creek. The mangrove shore is much taller on this winding stretch. You will find yourself shortcutting the bends here, where the tides are less pronounced. Shy gators will slip into the water upon your approach.

Toms Creek opens up near an island on Lostmans River. Stay on the north side of this island and end your route at the south end of Second Bay on the Lostmans River. To your west, it is 4.5 miles to the Lostmans Ranger Station on the Gulf via the Lostmans River Route. It is 1.5 miles to Wilderness Waterway marker #52 and the Willy Willy Route via the Lostmans River Route.

Wood River Route

Begin: Camp Lonesome	End: Wilderness Waterway marker #24 at The Nightmare
Distance: 10 miles	Time: 5 hours
Potential Tidal Influence: 2	Potential Wind Influence: 2
Navigational Challenge: 2	

Highlights: Much of route is paddler only
Hazards: Overhanging limbs and brush in river
Campsites: Broad River, Camp Lonesome
Connections: Broad River Route, The Nightmare Route

The creeklike Wood River Route encompasses a variety of Everglades settings, then throws in an added bonus: Much of the route is for paddlers only. Bird life is abundant. The price to be paid is the added effort required to squeeze through some tight spots. But these tight squeezes are what keeps motorboaters off this route.

Leave Camp Lonesome and head southeast, immediately coming to the confluence of four waterways, one of which you are on. Paddle west into the smallest waterway among the four. The river seems blocked until you paddle into it and find that it jogs north. The channel is about 30 feet wide, but the effective paddling area is 5–20 feet in width, due to the thick mangrove bank. Come to Wood River Bay at 1 mile, soon passing a creek on your left that leads back toward Camp Lonesome. Pass this skinny bay's only island, dotted with palm, before coming to a split in the bay. Take the western channel; the eastern channel leads deep into the Glades.

The Wood River gently tapers beyond the bay until it is but a slender ribbon of mangrove-lined water snaking westerly through the surrounding marsh. This mangrove-ribbon shoreline is very irregular, with small bushy trees near the water backed by tall trees. With the myriad skeletal trees that lie above and beneath the pristine creek, this stretch is a mosaic of life and death in a mangrove wood.

At mile 4, come to the channel leading to the Mud Lakes. This creek meanders north to these shallow lakes. Continue southwesterly on the Wood, which can be alive with birds in this section. Patches of cattails appear irregularly.

Around mile 7, the river becomes more junglelike in both appearance and fact, as the waterway has narrowed, the mangrove shoreline has risen, and the mangrove now canopies over and into the Wood, mixing with the already ample fallen trees in the water. The paddling here can be challenging. Also, the lower the tide, the more obstacles you will encounter in the water. This lesser depth, however, can add wiggle room for sneaking beneath overhanging trees. The waters down here become thick and pungent with the smell of salt and decay, much like those of Broad Creek, which parallels the Wood one watershed south. Just when you're about tired of the tangled stretch, the waterway opens first to 40 then to more than 60 feet in width, with little to impede your paddling. Occasional shrubby patches break up the mangrove.

Intersect the Wilderness Waterway at marker #24. You have paddled 10 miles. To your left is The Nightmare Route, which leads south toward the Harney River chickee. The Wood River continues north a short distance to meet the Broad River. The Broad River campsite is just a couple of hundred yards east up the Broad River. The Gulf of Mexico is 2 miles west down the Broad River on the Broad River Route.

Ten Thousand Islands

Causeway Route

Begin: Chokoloskee

End: Gulf Coast Ranger Station

Distance: 3 miles

Time: 1.5 hours

Potential Tidal Influence: 4

Potential Wind Influence: 3

Navigational Challenge: 2

Highlights: Connector between Chokoloskee and Gulf Coast Ranger Station

Hazards: Low water and strong tides under Halfway Creek bridge

Campsites: None

Connections: Hurddles Creek Route, Lopez River Route, Turner River Canoe Trail, Rabbit Key Pass Route, West Pass Route, Indian Key Pass Route, Sandfly Island Route, Halfway Creek Canoe Trail

---

The Causeway is a connector route in its purest sense. There is nothing scenic about this paddle. Much of it parallels the road connecting Chokoloskee Island to the mainland. What you can accomplish with this paddle is getting back to your car at Gulf Coast Ranger Station from Chokoloskee or vice versa. Making this connection can be tough at low

Canoe launch at Gulf Coast Ranger Station. Photo by W. W. Armstrong

tide, because the main channel along the causeway can be shallow and the canoe launch at Gulf Coast Ranger Station can be nothing but mud. Time your paddle not to pass through here at dead low tide.

Leave the park service landing at Chokoloskee and paddle north into a slender channel at one-half mile. The channel parallels the causeway. Keep northwest until the channel opens up. Halfway Creek is off to the east and leads 7.5 miles to the Tamiami Trail on the Halfway Creek Canoe Trail. Stay with the road until it opens up at the Halfway Creek bridge. Paddle southwest under the bridge and open into Chokoloskee Bay at mile 2. Be careful—tides can power through here. Resume a northwesterly direction, passing a tour boat landing and two brown park service buildings before coming to the canoe launch at Gulf Coast Ranger Station at mile 3, ending the route.

Chatham River Route

Begin: Mormon Key

Distance: 7.5 miles

Potential Tidal Influence: 4

Navigational Challenge: 3

End: Sweetwater chickee

Time: 4 hours

Potential Wind Influence: 3

Highlights: Old homesite, quiet chickee

Hazards: Ghosts at Watson's Place

Campsites: Mormon Key, Watson's Place, Sweetwater chickee

Connections: Pavilion Key Route, Turkey Key Route, Last Huston Bay Route, Huston River Route, Darwin's Place Route

---

The Chatham River Route leaves the lower Ten Thousand Islands at Mormon Key and heads into the interior Glades via the Chatham River. This river, with its numerous and shifting sandbars and mud bars, can be tricky to navigate, but it is much less dangerous for self-propelled craft than for the motorboats you will see. Once beyond the mouth of the Chatham, the route weaves its way up to Watson's Place, home of the infamous Ed Watson, who murdered his way into Everglades lore at this very locale. His homesite is now a campsite, and you can explore the ruins of Chatham Bend, as the now overgrown farm was called. But be aware that the bodies of several Watson victims were never found . . . The route continues up the Chatham from Watson's Place to intersect the Wilderness Waterway near Last Huston Bay, then up the hard-to-find but rewarding Sweetwater Creek to Sweetwater chickee, which is off the main traveling routes.

Leave Mormon Key and paddle north into the mouth of the Chatham, passing close to a point of the mainland to your east. Do not go too far west, which would take you up the Huston River and the Huston River Route. The correct route will take you past some shallows into a deep channel flanked by a set of finger islands. Keep northeast between mud flats and oyster bars on this 70-foot-wide channel, surprisingly slim for a river of this volume.

Work your way northeast among the islands until there is nothing but wide-open river in front of you. A continuous mangrove shoreline is broken only by one or two marl flats covered with pickerel weed and scattered mangrove, and by an occasional feeder stream entering the river.

If the tide or winds are against you, the bends in the Chatham, forming breaks in the current, make it easier to paddle up the river. Pass some pilings and concrete of a former dock on the south shore of one such bend. It is obvious by the vegetation that this is dry land. Around this bend on the north bank is a water-monitoring station, then the dock of Watson's Place campsite, at mile 4. Notice the tall gumbo-limbo trees extending above the forest at the old home place.

This cleared area once extended for 35 acres and was a full-fledged cane and vegetable farm. Nowadays, you see a cistern, old farm implements, and a kettle encased in brick for boiling cane juice into syrup. Other remaining artifacts are scattered about the dense woods. Watson's Place is a popular camping spot for paddlers and motorboaters alike.

The story of Ed Watson has been told time and again. He came to the Everglades in the 1890s with a troubled past, then settled at Chatham Bend, but he had a few scrapes in which one man was wounded and two others wound up dead. Neighbors kept an eye on Watson. Other ruffians and drifters joined him from time to time and worked on his farm. In 1910, some of Watson's workers were seen in the Chatham River—floating, with weights attached to their bodies. The ire of residents on nearby Chokoloskee Island was raised. Some of them gunned Watson down when he landed on their island and attempted to explain the deaths of his workers.

Leave Watson's Place, noting the sheared shell shore just beyond the dock near a tamarind tree. The gumbo-limbo trees continue up the north riverbank. The Chatham widens as it joins an unnamed channel leading to Huston Bay. Here, the Chatham River continues east, then northerly, passing a few more islands and coming to the Wilderness Waterway at marker #99, at mile 5.5.

To the northwest, the Last Huston Bay Route leads 7 miles to the Sunday Bay chickee. To the southeast, it is 3 miles to Darwin's Place via the Darwin's Place Route. The Chatham River Route, however, continues almost due east from marker #99, up an 80-foot-wide channel leading toward Sweetwater Creek, Sweetwater Bay, and the Sweetwater chickee. Paddle up this channel and come to an arm of Last Huston Bay.

You cannot access Sweetwater chickee via Last Huston Bay. Do not get sucked into the open-water trap by paddling into Last Huston Bay. Instead, from the end of the channel, paddle northeast no more than 200

Sweetwater chickee at dawn. Photo by W. W. Armstrong

feet across the arm of Last Huston Bay to an opening in the shoreline, which is the mouth of Sweetwater Creek. The creek immediately turns north, then northeast again, as it widens to more than 40 feet. Pass Sweetwater Bay on your right (east). Stay north into the second segment of Sweetwater Creek. Come to a conspicuous island topped with a few palm trees. Sweetwater chickee, the end of your route, is on the far side of the island, 2 miles from Wilderness Waterway marker #99 and 7.5 miles from Mormon Key.

Darwin's Place Route

Begin: Wilderness Waterway marker #99 at Chatham River	End: Lostmans Five campsite
Distance: 9.5 miles	Time: 5 hours
Potential Tidal Influence: 2	Potential Wind Influence: 4
Navigational Challenge: 2	
Highlights: Historic shell mounds, varied vegetation	
Hazards: Motorboats on Wilderness Waterway	
Campsites: Darwin's Place, Plate Creek chickee, Lostmans Five	

Connections: Last Huston Bay Route, Chatham River Route, Gopher Key
Route, Willy Willy Route

The Darwin's Place Route passes through a few historic settings while it
alternately traverses spacious bays and slender creeks. It traces the Wilderness Waterway through Chevelier Bay, named for an early Everglades
plume hunter and naturalist, then comes to Darwin's Place. This is a park
service campsite on a shell mound that has been occupied off and on since
the time of the Calusa. The route slips past Cannon Bay and Tarpon Bay
into narrow Alligator Creek, which contrasts well with the big water of
Alligator and Dads Bays. Another intimate paddle follows, on Plate
Creek. Then the route opens up on Plate Creek Bay, only to repeat the
small-water paddle one more time before arriving at Lostmans Five campsite, another bit of ground that has played host to humanity for a long
time here in the Glades.

Start your route at Wilderness Waterway marker #99, where the Chatham River intersects the Wilderness Waterway. Paddle east toward Chevelier Bay. The water is very shallow among the islands as you swing
around Chevelier Point and marker #97. This point and bay are named
for Frenchman Jean Chevelier. He was a contradictory man: In the late
1800s, his naturalist's bent led him to collect and stuff birds, while at the
same time he depleted bird stocks by pluming throughout the area from
his home base on Opossum Key. He was thought to have buried a fortune
somewhere in the Everglades, and folks have searched nearby islands for
his stash ever since. Of course, if Chevelier did bury loot, it must remain
where it is as a park artifact, just like any settlers' or Calusa artifacts.

Stay along the south bank of shallow Chevelier Bay, bordered by low
mangrove, turning almost due south from Wilderness Waterway marker
#93 toward a pass between a lone island and a point on the south shore at
marker #89. To avoid confusion, stay with this shoreline to marker #88.
Here, you enter a creek and shortly veer south to marker #87, where there
is a "No Wake" sign. Soon you'll come to the Darwin's Place campsite at
mile 3. This is a good resting and camping spot. Arthur Darwin, the park's
last living resident, was also the last in a long line of people to live here,

dating back to the Calusa. This shell mound has had huts, houses, and crops on it for a long time. It is much more grown over since it has become a campsite.

Leave Darwin's Place and paddle southeast past marker #86 and another "No Wake" sign toward marker #85, barely visible between two islands off in the distance. The bulk of Cannon Bay opens up to the east. To the southwest is the mouth of Gopher Key Creek, part of the Gopher Key Creek Route.

Soon, squeeze into a tapered channel south to Tarpon Bay, much smaller than the other Tarpon Bay by the Harney River. This Tarpon Bay is also the smallest bay on this route. Paddle the length of Tarpon Bay, tracing the markers, until you reach Alligator Creek, at marker #77. It would stand to reason that there would be more than one Alligator Creek in the Everglades, and there are. Do not confuse this Alligator Creek with the Alligator Creek on the West Lake Canoe Trail near Flamingo.

On this Alligator Creek, pass a "No Wake" sign as you enter the 20-foot-wide stream. The shoreline rises high with mangrove but is cleared enough to allow an average skiff to pass. There is no canopy to speak of, and the water is plenty deep. A few palm and buttonwood trees accompany the mangrove at first. The creek widens to a "No Wake" buoy, then narrows again, passing a clump of land on creek left, just before emerging onto Alligator Bay at Wilderness Waterway marker #75.

Keep southeast across the big water, aiming for the channel that connects Alligator Bay to Dads Bay. The shoreline here has much palm and wax myrtle. Stroke it a full mile across Alligator Bay. Southwest lies the bulk of the bay. Pass a north-facing point and gain entry to Dads Bay at mile 6. The bulk of Dads Bay is also to the southwest. Keep along the east shore of the bay and notice the Gator Bay Canal, which was likely a feeble drainage effort by land developers. Stay in Dads Bay to a 10-foot-wide channel at marker #68. Turn east toward the "No Wake" sign and enter Plate Creek. Way back, Gregorio Lopez dropped a plate in this creek, giving the creek its name. Buttonwoods reach over the water. The south bank almost passes for land. It certainly features palm, coco plum, and poisonwood on its shore.

Ellen Connally at Plate Creek chickee. Photo by author

Enter Plate Creek Bay at marker #65. Another canal leaves the bay from the north bank. It is possible to paddle up this canal for awhile before it becomes overgrown. In the bay, the Plate Creek chickee is visible, backed up against an island, at mile 8.5. This chickee is built on the pilings of an old land office complex. The larger pilings of the chickee shelter were parts of the water tower for the series of floating buildings. Plate Creek Bay is an especially pretty place, with towering palms swaying over the varied mangrove forest below.

Come to an inlet and another modest creek at marker #63. There are clumps of land along this creek, too. It is but a short distance to Lostmans Five Bay. Look southeast across the bay to spot the Lostmans Five campsite at the mouth of Lostmans Five Creek, at mile 9.5. From here it is 8 miles to the Gulf on the Willy Willy and Lostmans River Routes. It is 10 miles to Willy Willy campsite via the Willy Willy Route, using a portion of the Wilderness Waterway.

Gopher Key Route

Begin: Darwins Place Campsite   End: Gopher Key Mound

Distance: 3 miles each way   Time: 2 hours each way

Potential Tidal Influence: 2   Potential Wind Influence: 2

Navigational Challenge: 3

Highlights: Bird life, storm devastation, historic shell mound

Hazards: Bugs on Gopher Key, shallow water

Campsites: None

Connections: Darwin's Place Route

The Gopher Key Route is a there-and-back paddle to an old Calusa mound. The route leaves Cannon Bay near the Darwin's Place campsite and heads down Gopher Key Creek to Gopher Key. The key was named after the boat that archaeologist Clarence B. Moore used in his early 1900s explorations of Calusa cultural sites. Once at Gopher Key, you can walk around, exploring the hilly shell mound. If you like quiet creeks and less-paddled routes, go for this one. There are numerous birds back here. The trees on Gopher Key are larger than those on most shell mounds, and the storm-altered landscape on the way to Gopher Key is very different from nearby Cannon Bay's. *Remember, mounds like this are protected: No digging. Leave anything you happen to find. These are special treasures we should preserve for all to enjoy.*

Depart the Darwin's Place campsite, paddling south into Cannon Bay. If you look back toward Darwin's Place, on the horizon you will see the gumbo-limbo trees towering over the mangrove. Look back periodically on this entire route to make sure you can get back to Darwin's Place. To find Gopher Creek, hug the west shoreline of Cannon Bay, passing between the shore and several islands in Cannon Bay. The mouth of Gopher Creek, at one-half mile, lies almost due south as you paddle. Pass a small teaser creek before coming to Gopher Key Creek. Gopher Key Creek's mouth is about 50 fifty feet wide, soon tapering to about 30 feet. The banks here are forested with red and black mangrove. The water is plenty deep. Fallen trees pose no obstacle to the paddler.

Snags along Gopher Key Creek. Photo by author

After awhile, the forested banks give way to a shoreline of sea purslane and pickleweed, backed by younger mangrove. But the most striking features of the landscape are the gangly skeleton trees standing along the shoreline and beyond. Other, fallen trees are piled along the creek. Come to the northeastern arm of Gopher Key Bay. Continue paddling southwest through this shallow bay into the main body of Gopher Key Bay at mile 1.5. Birds are found here, as they are all along the creek.

Traverse the wide heart of the bay, keeping a southwesterly course to the continuation of Gopher Key Creek. At more than 40 feet, this second half of the stream is much wider than the first. It is also very shallow in spots. Open into a small lagoon, and keep your eyes peeled to the southwest. The taller vegetation of Gopher Key will be visible in the distance, especially the red-trunked gumbo-limbo trees.

Just before you come to Gopher Key, the lagoon splits—take the very shallow east channel and follow the right bank closely. Look for a canoe-width clamshell landing between two mangrove trees. This is where you leave your craft to explore Gopher Key. Get your bug dope ready. On foot, cross the open area of sea purslane and head northwest for the mound. Previous explorers have made small "trails" that wind around the mound—it is grown over, so keep your compass with you just in case. Check out the fig trees and other vegetation that cloak the numerous hills here. As I did, try to imagine the time it took for this mound to come to be, shell by shell.

Halfway Creek Canoe Trail

Begin: Tamiami Trail   End: Gulf Coast Ranger Station
Distance: 7.5 miles   Time: 4 hours
Potential Tidal Influence: 3   Potential Wind Influence: 2
Navigational Challenge: 2
Highlights: Diverse habitat, mangrove tunnels
Hazards: Low water, strong tides under Halfway Creek bridge
Campsites: None
Connections: Turner River Canoe Trail, West Pass Route, Indian Key Pass Route, Sandfly Island Route

---

The Halfway Creek Canoe Trail is a microcosm of South Florida in many ways. It reveals man's hand on the landscape and offers a good view of the beauty left under park protection. First, paddle down a man-made canal, a landscape feature that is definitely a part of South Florida today. Next comes an attractive habitat of sawgrass, cattails, and tree islands. Then the route passes through a strange and wonderful mangrove tunnel that turns to a brackish stream beneath a taller shady forest. The paddle leaves the park boundary, passes by houses, then goes under the bridge of an artificial causeway to emerge in the wide-open, busy Chokoloskee Bay, ending at Gulf Coast Ranger Station. Consider paying for a shuttle from an outfitter to make this a one-way day paddle. This creek is not on the waterproof charts, but the route is marked most of the way and the Big Cypress National Preserve Visitor Center produces a fine map of this trail for your use.

Start your trip on the Tamiami Trail, US 41. To get there from Everglades City, drive north on State Road 29 for 3 miles to US 41. Turn right (east) on US 41 and drive 2 miles to Sea Grape Drive. Turn right on Sea Grape Drive and follow it a short distance to the Halfway Creek landing.

Put into the canal and begin paddling southwesterly. Note the limestone banks here. The water is crystal clear, bordered by sawgrass, cattails, and occasional mangrove. Other freshwater plants adorn the higher dry land of the south bank. Soon, pass the markers of an airboat trail crossing the canal. Leave the 40-foot-wide canal and come to the first lake at mile 1. Keep southwest. Numerous palms grace the shore.

Pass marker #1 toward the end of the lake, which meanders, and keep west past marker #2. A beautiful variety of South Florida vegetation is all around; here you'll enjoy some of the most scenic paddling of all the routes in this guidebook. The white PVC pipe with no numbers helps guide you in the right direction. Paddlers headed toward the Gulf will be looking at the green side of these markers. Paddlers heading away from the Gulf will be seeing the red side of the same markers.

The trail alternates between small lakes and narrower creeks, keeping a generally southwesterly direction. Stay with the markers. Past marker #6, limbs of trees crowd the slender creek until the trees eventually form a tunnel that continues for a good distance. Keep a reasonable pace, not going too fast among the twists and turns of the tunnel. The water here is plenty deep, but at times you have to duck your head under vegetation. Watch for a bit of land on creek right where you can get out and take a break.

Farther down the tunnel, Halfway Creek becomes murky and pungent. More fallen trees and brush lie in the water. The canopy rises as you proceed downstream. Tidal influence increases. Come to a major split in the creek at 5.5 miles. To your left (east), a creek leads toward Turner Lake and Left Hand Turner River. To your right (west), Halfway Creek widens and continues toward Chokoloskee Bay. Stay with Halfway Creek.

Leave the Everglades National Park boundary and pass a few houses on your right. Notice the Australian pine, Brazilian pepper, and other exotic vegetation. The Plantation Island community is on your right, before the creek opens into a bay. The Causeway Route leads southeast 2 miles to Chokoloskee Island. Keep southwest on the Halfway Creek Canoe Trail under the Halfway Creek bridge. Watch for strong tides flowing through here. Once through the bridge, turn northwest, passing a tour boat landing and two brown park service buildings to the Gulf Coast Ranger Station, ending your route.

Hurddles Creek Route

Begin: Chokoloskee	End: Sunday Bay chickee
Distance: 7 miles	Time: 3.5 hours
Potential Tidal Influence: 3	Potential Wind Influence: 2
Navigational Challenge: 3	

Highlights: Calusa shell mound

Hazards: Motorboats in Chokoloskee Bay

Campsites: Sunday Bay chickee

Connections: Turner River Canoe Trail, Lopez River Route, Last Huston Bay Route, Huston River Route

Hurddles Creek is the preferred route for southbound paddlers from Chokoloskee using the "inside" routes. There are fewer motorboats on this route than on the Lopez River Route, and it traverses more varied and sheltered waters and passes a Calusa shell mound on the way. The route begins with a paddle up the Turner River, passing the shell mound, to Hurddles Creek with its tall mangrove. Then it traverses the Cross Bays to intersect the Wilderness Waterway at Crooked Creek. It traces the Wilderness Waterway a short distance before splitting off to Sunday Bay chickee.

Start your route at the park service boat ramp on the north end of Chokoloskee Island, near the Outdoor Resort. Leave the ramp and paddle easterly toward the Turner River. Pass a few minuscule mangrove islands just before coming to Wilderness Waterway marker #129, at the mouth of the Turner River.

Cross the Wilderness Waterway and enter the Turner River, hugging the south bank. Mixed mangrove of varying sizes crowd the river. About half a mile up the south side of the river is an old Calusa shell mound. Look for the nearly vertical bank of shell, on top of which grow hammock species such as gumbo-limbo. Parts of this mound reach 19 feet in elevation, a dizzying height by South Florida standards.

Keep paddling up the deep river, passing Left Hand Turner River, on the north, at mile 1.5. The Turner River veers east and diverges into two channels. The now smaller Turner River splits easterly, while the wider Hurddles Creek goes southeast. Take Hurddles Creek. Soon, pass a small watercourse coming in from the east. This creek heads east into Hells Half Acre, which is a maze of ponds and channels in which paddlers get lost. Stay away. Hurddles Creek, meanwhile, about 50 feet wide and bordered by tall mangrove, meanders southeasterly to Mud Bay.

Enter shallow Mud Bay, passing a little island on your right. Veer easterly into the creek that exits Mud Bay. This is the continuation of Hurddles Creek, wider than before. It makes a sharp U-turn south before coming to the first of the Cross Bays at mile 4. The shallow nature of these bays discourages motorboat traffic, especially at low tide. Keep southeast across the bay, then traverse a channel to the second of the Cross Bays. Stay southeast across this bay, which narrows into yet another creek. In the creek, stay with the left (northeast) bank, pass an island, then come to Wilderness Waterway marker #125. Chokoloskee is 7 miles by the Lopez River Route and the Wilderness Waterway.

It is another mile to Wilderness Waterway marker #123 in Sunday Bay, at 6.5 miles. At this marker, paddle in the direction the arrow on the marker points, easterly, toward what looks like one island but is actually two. Come to a slight split between the two islands. Look north between the two islands, and there will be the Sunday Bay chickee, which is perched against the mangrove in a small bay of its own at mile 7. The Last Huston Bay Route continues southeast via the Wilderness Waterway. The Huston River Route starts 1.5 miles south of the chickee at Wilderness Waterway marker #119.

Huston River Route

Begin: Wilderness Waterway marker #119 at Sunday Bay
End: Mormon Key
Distance: 9 miles   Time: 5 hours
Potential Tidal Influence: 4   Potential Wind Influence: 4
Navigational Challenge: 2
Highlights: Solitude
Hazards: Shoals in Huston River
Campsites: Mormon Key
Connections: Last Huston Bay Route, Chatham River Route, Pavilion Key Route, Turkey Key Route

---

The Huston River Route is one of the best lesser-used connectors between the Gulf and the interior bays of the Wilderness Waterway. From its obscure beginning near Sunday Bay to the shallows of House Hammock Bay to the shifting shoals and numerous oyster bars of the Huston River, this paddle path has reasons for lesser use. The shallows need not deter paddlers. The sole navigationally challenging section is among the many isles just before the Gulf. The only busy segment is out in the Gulf, from Gun Rock Point to Mormon Key. From Sunday Bay, the route is southerly to House Hammock Bay. Beyond the bay, it follows the Huston River southwest into island-dotted Storter Bay, where the Chatham and Huston Rivers meet and flow into the Gulf at Chatham Bend. From the Gulf it is not far to the beach campsite at Mormon Key.

Start your route at Wilderness Waterway Marker #119 in the southeastern corner of Sunday Bay. Paddle southerly past some tiny isles into the channel, which leads to House Hammock Bay. This channel flows 1.5 miles before opening into the bay. This body of water was named for Dan House, who along with his family homesteaded an old shell mound in the vicinity. Keep southeast across the bay, entering the Huston River at mile 3. To your left (east), the Huston leads half a mile to Huston Bay. To your right (southwest), the Huston leads to the Gulf. Head southwest.

The river is more than 200 feet wide here, with an occasional solitary island growing on shallow oyster and mud bars. The preponderance of these bars keeps all but the most intrepid motorboaters from using this river. Stay along the northwest bank and look for Brazilian pepper bushes that ring a peninsula jutting out from shore. Here is another shell mound built by Calusas and later known as Camp Huston by local white settlers.

The river widens and turns southeast, still with myriad shoals. The islands increase in size and number as you enter Storter Bay. It is possible to cut easterly to the Chatham River here, then to Mormon Key, to avoid open Gulf water if the winds are high. Otherwise, follow the deep channel cut by strong tides among these islands on the Huston River, coming to the Gulf at mile 7.5. The peninsula of Gun Rock Point will be to your right. The beach of Mormon Key will be visible to your left (south), across Chatham Bend. Aim south for the beach at Mormon Key, arriving there at 9 miles. This is an agreeable campsite and a good location for heading in either direction on the Gulf. From here it is 8 miles south to Hog Key via the Turkey Key Route. It is 8.5 miles to Rabbit Key on the Pavilion Key Route.

Indian Key Pass Route

Begin: Gulf Coast Ranger Station   End: Picnic Key

Distance: 7 miles   Time: 4 hours

Potential Tidal Influence: 5   Potential Wind Influence: 3

Navigational Challenge: 2

Highlights: Local culture, fastest route to outer Ten Thousand Islands

Hazards: Commercial fishing boats and recreation boats

Campsites: Tiger Key, Picnic Key, Kingston Key chickee

Connections: West Pass Route, Pavilion Key Route, Sandfly Island Route, Rabbit Key Pass Route, Halfway Creek Canoe Trail, Causeway Route

---

Sometimes, to get to a scenic destination, you travel the shortest distance between two points, even though the route may not be quite so appealing.

Such is the case with the Indian Key Pass Route. It connects the Gulf Coast Ranger Station with the superior camping destinations of Picnic Key and Tiger Key, but the marked route is a veritable highway full of tour boats, recreational motorboats, and commercial fishing vessels. It is engaging to see all the watercraft, but it may not be the natural experience you desire. Think of Indian Key Pass as your highway to the Gulf, only this highway has some brawny tides that should be worked to your advantage, if that is possible. Your first task is to span Chokoloskee Bay to enter marked Indian Key Pass, cruising between the islands while sidestepping boats. Eventually, the route opens into the Gulf, with Indian Key guarding the mouth of the pass. Slicing through a few mangrove islands, the route ends at Picnic Key, where there is a beach and a campsite.

Start your paddle from the canoe landing at Gulf Coast Ranger Station. Try not to leave here at dead low tide; it's hard paddling in the mud that can be exposed when the water is down. Paddle westerly across Chokoloskee Bay, immediately passing a couple of channel markers connecting Barron River to Sandfly Pass. Stay westerly, aiming for Indian Key Pass. Look for boats coming out of the pass across Chokoloskee Bay toward the Barron River; its mouth is near the ranger station. A few islands will be off to your right, between you and the marked channel of Indian Key Pass. At 1.5 miles, intersect the pass at channel marker #24. A sign here states, "Welcome to Everglades National Park."

Enter the channel of Indian Key Pass. Around you, there are numerous small mangrove islands; it's easy to see how this area was dubbed Ten Thousand Islands. The dry ground on a few islands represents the spoils from dredging the channel of Indian Key Pass to make it deep enough for some of the big boats that travel this way. Continue westerly, as low mangrove islands give way to a taller shoreline with bays splitting off the pass. The channel widens and turns southwesterly at marker #15. Watch for tour boats, pleasure boats, fishing boats, and any other boats you can imagine, as well as a few sea kayaks and canoes.

A little beyond marker #10, at 3.5 miles, the Gulf opens up before you. Keep your craft aimed for channel marker #6. If the winds are strong, consider splitting some of the mangrove islands due west of marker #6

Pelicans at low tide. Photo by W. W. Armstrong

and maneuvering the waters to emerge on Gaskin Bay and the east side of Picnic Key. Otherwise, stay with the pass toward Indian Key, swinging northwesterly after the Stop Keys, avoiding their shallows. If you are heading for Kingston Key chickee, paddle to marker #4. See the chickee to your south, and come to the platform at 6 miles. If the chickee is not your goal, look for the sandy, Gulf-facing, southwest side of Picnic Key at 7 miles. Here, a long beach backed by coastal vegetation makes for a good campsite. The beach at Tiger Key is 1 mile distant around the far side of Tiger Key. From Picnic Key, it is 7 miles to Rabbit Key via the Pavilion Key Route. It is 8.5 miles back to Gulf Coast Ranger Station via West Pass Route.

Last Huston Bay Route

Begin. Sunday Bay chickee	End: Wilderness Waterway marker #99 at Chatham River
Distance: 7 miles	Time: 3.5 hours
Potential Tidal Influence: 2	Potential Wind Influence: 4
Navigational Challenge: 2	

Highlights: Paddling Wilderness Waterway

Hazards: Motor boats on channels of Wilderness Waterway

Campsites: Sunday Bay chickee

Connections: Hurddles Creek Route, Huston River Route, Chatham River Route, Darwin's Place Route

---

The Last Huston Bay Route traces the Wilderness Waterway as it travels southeasterly through a series of broad bays broken by brief channels. The entire paddle path is periodically marked at strategic points by small, brown park service signs. Even though this route is on the "inside," the open bays can get bumpy in big winds, though tidal influence will only be felt in the channels between bays. Motorboats frequent this route while fishing the Glades, so stay alert in the channels.

Leave Sunday Bay chickee and return to the Wilderness Waterway and marker #123. Paddle southerly down the Wilderness Waterway into the end of Sunday Bay, as it funnels past marker #121. Slip into and through a few islands, passing marker #120. Shortly, come to marker #119. The channel to the south behind the two small isles is the beginning of the Huston River Route. Continue to move through the channel, passing an open bay to your left. Paddle directly to marker #117, and between two islands you will see marker #116. From marker #116, turn south to marker #115. All three markers cover only a short distance. Proceed southeasterly to marker #114 and the open water of Oyster Bay. This should not be confused with the Oyster Bay near Whitewater Bay. Stroke it south across this Oyster Bay for a flank of isles, passing markers #112 and #110. Bisect another flank of isles to open into Huston Bay and marker #108 at mile 3.

Head straight for the island fronted by an old house on stilts and skirt the east side of the island. This is the last built-on inholding in the park. Now paddle for the pass on the southeast end of Huston Bay at Wilderness Waterway marker #103. Past this pass is wide-open Last Huston Bay. This bay, like the previous two, is 2–4 feet deep, with brown-tinted clear water bordered by low mangrove. Stay with the south bank to the south corner of Last Huston Bay.

At the corner, progress beyond marker #101 into a channel. This channel splits at marker #100. To your right (west) is a channel leading to the Chatham River. You proceed left (southeasterly) and come to Wilderness

Waterway marker #99 at mile 7. Here, you intersect the Chatham River Route. It is 1.5 miles southwest down the Chatham River Route to the Watson's Place campsite, and it is 2 miles northeast up the Chatham River Route to Sweetwater chickee. The Darwin's Place Route starts here and heads southeasterly down the Wilderness Waterway 9.5 miles to Lostmans Five campsite.

Lopez River Route

Begin: Chokoloskee	End: Wilderness Waterway marker #125 at Crooked Creek
Distance: 7 miles	Time: 3.5 hours
Potential Tidal Influence: 3	Potential Wind Influence: 4
Navigational Challenge: 2	

Highlights: Gregorio Lopez homesite

Hazards: Motorboats in Chokoloskee Bay

Campsites: Lopez River

Connections: Hurddles Creek Route, Causeway Route

The Lopez River Route is a busy route for all boaters. It is the primary access route into the backcountry from Chokoloskee, tracing the Wilderness Waterway its entire course. The route starts at the landing on Chokoloskee and crosses open Chokoloskee Bay, which is fronted by the houses of Chokoloskee Island. It then enters the shoaly Lopez River, passing a homesite turned campsite on the south bank, and continues up the Lopez to Crooked Creek, and up the creek, which winds its way to an arm of Sunday Bay. Though this route is on the Wilderness Waterway, it is anything but wild. From the houses of Chokoloskee to the heavy motorboat use, it feels more like paddling around a marina. But it's the way to go if you are going to camp at Lopez River campsite, which is one of the park's better ground sites.

Leave the park service dock at Chokoloskee and paddle around the north point of the island, then stroke it southeast across Chokoloskee Bay.

The houses on the island will keep your eyes entertained, but watch for motorboats as you traverse the shallow body of water. Aim for the northeast shore of the bay, which is the mainland, and paddle parallel to it, passing channel markers indicating the deeper water.

Continue along the northeast shore and enter the mouth of the Lopez River. The mud bar extends far from shore here, but it shouldn't present a problem for paddlers. Notice the deep-water channel marker far out in the river. The Lopez funnels to around 140 feet wide. The shore is dense mangrove, except a couple of spots where there are grown-over shell mounds, before the river makes a couple of sharp bends. Come to the Lopez River campsite at 5 miles, also on a Calusa mound. This was settled and farmed by Gregorio Lopez, who came to the area from Spain in 1890. The landing here is a shoreline of shell. A cistern lies in view of the river. Water that ran off the roof of Lopez's house was stored in it for his use.

Pass the campsite and continue up the Lopez River as it tapers further before you reach Crooked Creek and Wilderness Waterway Marker #126 at mile 6. Turn your craft east up the mouth of Crooked Creek; it comes in at an acute angle to the Lopez. This stream winds and curves, building mud bars on its inside bends. Listen for motorboats coming around the sharp bends. Pass a white channel marker just before emerging onto an arm of Sunday Bay and Wilderness Waterway marker #125 at mile 7. From here it is 1.5 miles southeasterly to the Sunday Bay chickee on the Hurddles Creek Route. From the Sunday Bay chickee, continue southerly on the Wilderness Waterway via the Last Huston Bay Route. To the northwest, it is 5.5 miles back to Chokoloskee via the Hurddles Creek Route.

Pavilion Key Route

Begin: Picnic Key   End: Mormon Key

Distance: 15.5 miles   Time: 8 hours

Potential Tidal Influence: 5   Potential Wind Influence: 5

Navigational Challenge: 3

Highlights: Gulf paddling among the Ten Thousand Islands, good campsites

Hazards: Big Gulf wind and waves

Campsites: Picnic Key, Kingston Key chickee, Rabbit Key, Pavilion Key, Mormon Key

Connections: West Pass Route, Indian Key Pass Route, Rabbit Key Pass Route, Huston River Route, Chatham River Route, Turkey Key Route

---

Pavilion Key Route traverses the portion of the Ten Thousand Islands within the boundaries of the Everglades National Park. I like to island hop along the outermost keys that extend into the Gulf, but there are as many variations to the route as there are islands to check out along the way. Many campsites on the route make expanded stays and subsequent explorations of the vicinity possible. There is fantastic scenery everywhere you look. The route leaves Picnic Key just before Indian Key Pass, which links the Gulf to Chokoloskee. The nearby chickee at Kingston Key makes for another camping possibility. The paddle path is toward Jewel Key, then across open water to Rabbit Key, where you can also camp. The route then turns southerly to arrive at big Pavilion Key, yet another camping spot. From here, the route crosses Chatham Bend, where Mormon Key awaits, your final camping option. The paddling on this route can turn as scary as the route is beautiful. Unfavorable winds and tides can make the route formidable, especially out on Pavilion Key; more small craft have capsized between Pavilion Key and Mormon Key than anywhere else in the Everglades. Use good judgment in choosing your exact passage.

Leave Picnic Key and paddle south around the Stop Keys. Stay on the Gulf side of the Stop Keys shallows. Dead ahead is Indian Key, where there used to be a backcountry campsite. Aim for the lighted buoy adjacent to Indian Key, watching for boat traffic through the Indian Key Pass. To your east in the distance is the Kingston Key chickee. It is banked against the west side of Kingston Key at 2 miles. From the chickee, it is 6 miles to Gulf Coast Ranger Station via the Indian Key Pass Route. Past the chickee on the Pavilion Key Route, you can pull your boat over the sandy peninsula of Kingston Key and keep southeasterly. If you want to bypass the chickee, you can swing around the Gulf side of Kingston Key. Beyond Kingston Key, many other keys lie in the distance to the east. Pass what is left of Comer Key, which was nearly denuded of vegetation in a big storm. Jewel Key precedes Chokoloskee Pass. Chokoloskee Pass is marked by a large wooden post near Jewel Key, which is a good resting spot, though its beach is rocky by Everglades standards. Watch for shallows on the south side of Chokoloskee Pass.

From here, a direct line for Rabbit Key requires crossing wide-open water—if the waves are imposing, flank the islands closer to the mainland. From Jewel Key, Rabbit Key and the other islands appear to be uninterrupted shoreline. Make a compass bearing for Rabbit Key and stick with it. While in the open water, look past Turtle Key for the marked Rabbit Key Pass. It leads to Chokoloskee Bay. The Rabbit Key Pass Route leads 5.5 miles to Chokoloskee Island from Rabbit Key. On the Pavilion Key Route, come to Rabbit Key at mile 7. Approach the island on the north side, shooting for the strait between Rabbit and Lumber Keys. The Rabbit Key campsite is in a lagoon near the strait.

Taking a break at Jewel Key. Photo by W. W. Armstrong

Depart Rabbit Key and shoot southerly past Crate Key for Pavilion Key, which is the island farthest out on the horizon's Gulf side. Beyond Crate Key the mainland is hardly visible due to numerous islands to your east. Keep southerly toward Pavilion Key. As you approach this low-slung island, Little Pavilion Key will look like a dot against the much larger Pavilion Key.

As you near Pavilion, aim for the northern end of the island where the sandy spit meets the forest. This is where the camp lies. At low tide, Little Pavilion Key will reveal a sandbar to paddle around. In the early 1900s clam diggers used to live in small houses on stilts around Little Pavilion Key. They wore canvas "shoes" around their feet to protect them from getting cut yet still allow them to feel for clams, which they would harvest.

Come to Pavilion Key at mile 11. This key is a beach camper's dream come true. Other campers will be here, having had the same dream. Learn to share this Everglades National Park highlight.

Leave the northern tip of Pavilion Key, paddling toward the mainland, then southeasterly between some mangrove islands toward Mormon Key, which at this distance blends with the main shoreline. Cross open water, being mindful of the history of capsized craft in these waters. Duck Rock is off to your left. The treeless island used to be a rookery until it was stripped of vegetation by Hurricane Donna in 1960.

Between Pavilion Key and Mormon Key, the coastline turns from southeast running to south running. This coastal turn is known as Chatham Bend, for the Chatham River that flows into the Gulf at the bend. The high beach of Mormon Key will be facing you and will become visible as you come closer to the island. A smaller key south of Mormon Key will also have a visible beach.

Come to Mormon Key at mile 15.5. This island was once home to a man who lived here with his first and second wives, giving the island its name. It is now a fine backcountry campsite. From here it is 11 miles south to Lostmans Ranger Station along the Gulf on the Turkey Key Route. It is 4 miles east to Watson's Place on the Chatham River Route. It is 9 miles to Sunday Bay on the Huston River Route.

Rabbit Key Pass Route

Begin: Rabbit Key   End: Chokoloskee

Distance: 5.5 miles   Time: 3 hours

Potential Tidal Influence: 4   Potential Wind Influence: 4

Navigational Challenge: 2

Highlights: Short connection to Gulf

Hazards: Motorboats in Chokoloskee Bay

Campsites: Rabbit Key

Connections: Pavilion Key Route, Hurddles Creek Route, Lopez River Route, Causeway Route, Turner River Canoe Trail

---

Rabbit Key Pass Route is marked most of the way. It takes you from the beauty of the Ten Thousand islands back to the civilized world at Chokoloskee. It begins on the open Gulf, then enters the deep channel of Rabbit Key Pass to meander among some islands and open into Chokoloskee Bay. Here it passes along Chokoloskee Island, where you can get an eyeful of the changing face of this one-time shell mound.

From Rabbit Key campsite, paddle northward around the edge of Lumber Key toward Turtle Key. Just on the sandy east point of Turtle Key at mile 1 is the first marker for Rabbit Key Pass. These markers are not numbered, but all are wooden posts with a white triangular arrow pointing toward the deeper side of the channel. Paddlers need not be as concerned as other boaters with being on the deep side of the channel, just in the right direction with the channel.

Look northeast for more white markers. Trace the markers into the deep pass. Don't fall for the open-water trap, but head more northeasterly on the narrower route. Soon the waters open again, and there are two sets of markers at mile 2.5. One set continues easterly into an open bay, and another set heads left, northerly, through a much smaller channel. Follow the northerly, more sheltered route, which splits some islands. The markers confusingly turn back toward the Gulf for a moment but they are working around some shallows before veering Chokoloskee way again. The mangrove shoreline takes on a hilly appearance here, as the shorter

Canoeing around Rabbit Key at low tide. Photo by W. W. Armstrong

waterside trees give way to taller mangrove away from the water. The channel widens into Chokoloskee Bay—and the civilized world appears before you. There are some shallows ahead, which you will have to paddle around at low tide. Your best bet is to aim for Chokoloskee, then circle the island to the right.

Come to the south tip of the island at mile 4.5. Take in the scenery here as Chokoloskee changes from fishing village to tourist destination. The mouth of the Turner River appears on your right before you come to the park service landing at mile 5.5. From here it is 3 miles to the Gulf Coast Ranger Station via the Causeway Route. It is 8.5 miles to US 41 on the Turner River Canoe Trail. It is 5 miles to the Lopez River campsite via the Lopez River Route. It is 7 miles to Sunday Bay chickee via the Hurddles Creek Route.

Sandfly Island Route

Begin: Gulf Coast Ranger Station
Distance: 2 miles each way
Potential Tidal Influence: 3
Navigational Challenge: 1

End: Sandfly Island
Time: 1 hour each way
Potential Wind Influence: 4

Highlights: Nature trail on Sandfly Island

Hazards: Motor boats in Chokoloskee Bay

Campsites: None

Connections: Indian Key Pass Route, Pavilion Key Route, West Pass Route, Halfway Creek Canoe Trail, Causeway Route

---

The Sandfly Island Route is a short there-and-back day paddle that takes you away from the busy Gulf Coast Ranger Station into busy Chokoloskee Bay, then carries you back in time to Sandfly Island. The island was once inhabited by the Calusa, and then by white settlers until the national park era. At Sandfly Island, you can stretch your legs on the 1-mile Sandfly Nature Trail, which circles through a hammock forest atop the old Calusa shell mound. Before tackling the nature trail, inquire at the ranger station about bug conditions on Sandfly Island.

Start your paddle at the Gulf Coast Ranger Station canoe launch. Direct your craft almost due south from the launch into Chokoloskee Bay, passing between markers #5 and #6 and a manatee warning sign. You are now tracing the marked channel of Sandfly Pass. Keep south, passing a series of markers whose numerals decrease, and a sign welcoming you to Everglades National Park just before mile 1. Pass markers #1 and #2, then turn southwest to enter Sandfly Pass proper. The channel here is a good 110 feet wide and bordered by high mangrove.

The dock of Sandfly Island will come into view not long after you enter the pass. The push and pull of the tide is evident here in the pass. Look for a shell landing beneath the mangrove just before you reach the dock at mile 2. Pull up your craft onto the shell and tie up to a mangrove tree. The Sandfly Nature Trail starts near the dock.

Sandfly Nature Trail

Leave the dock and immediately pass the cistern, foundation, and spring of the Boggess family, who farmed the island, once cultivating more than 30 acres of tomatoes. They came here in 1912. As you walk the island, try imagining it as your permanent home, with no modern conveniences and sparse contact with the outside world. Imagine what the Boggess family would think of their "back of beyond" if they could see it today!

Along the Sandfly Island Nature Trail. Photo by author

The nature trail splits; take the left fork. The hammock forest here is rich with gumbo-limbo, poisonwood, and strangler fig. Mangrove drapes low-lying areas. Look for telltale tamarind trees, which indicate another dwelling. Swing around to the west side of the island, gaining glimpses of the water beyond Sandfly. Watch for a strangler fig engulfing a cabbage palm right on the path. The final feature of the trail is a boardwalk that extends over a creek and beneath a tall mangrove forest just before you complete the loop.

Turkey Key Route

Begin: Mormon Key	End: Lostmans River Ranger Station at Lostmans River
Distance: 11 miles	Time: 6 hours
Potential Tidal Influence: 5	Potential Wind Influence: 5
Navigational Challenge: 2	

Highlights: Beach campsites, historic islands

Hazards: Strong winds and big waves in the Gulf

Campsites: Mormon Key, New Turkey Key, Turkey Key, Hog Key

Connections: Pavilion Key Route, Chatham River Route, Highland Beach Route, Lostmans River Route

---

The Turkey Key Route encompasses several island campsites and even more keys as it heads down the Gulf to Lostmans Ranger Station at the mouth of the Lostmans River. Many of these once-inhabited islands have reverted to a more wild state. The points of these keys are often sandy, while the bulk of the isles are mangrove. There are shallows scattered among the islands that can be exposed at low tide, and the water can be extremely shallow by the mainland at all times. The mainland along this route is mangrove with an occasional bit of beach, with gnarled bleached trees adding variety. The wind may play a role in the exact paddle path you choose on this route. There are four campsites along the way, meaning you can stretch this leg of your journey out for days. Fishing can also be productive in these keys.

Start your route by leaving Mormon Key, where there is a fine backcountry campsite, and paddling around the west side of the island. Start south for a crowded group of keys. At low tide, you will have to stay on the Gulf side to keep from running aground, but bisect the keys if possible for the most scenery.

Once past these islands, aim for the channel between New Turkey Key and an unnamed mangrove key closer to the mainland. Tall pilings mark the channel. Watch for motorboats here. The best approach to the New Turkey Key campsite is from the southeast, beyond the pilings. The primary camping area is on the mainland side of this slender island, 2 miles from Mormon Key.

Paddle southeast from New Turkey Key to Turkey Key. The island is visible, 1 mile distant, and the signed camping area is directly in front of you, on the key's west side. I once spent two days here, trapped by gale-force winds. In pre-park days, this was a rendezvous point for fishermen who would turn in their catch to a boat from Chokoloskee and receive supplies from the same boat. It is now an excellent paddler's camp whose shallow approach discourages motor boaters.

Bird's nest at low tide in the Gulf.
Photo by W. W. Armstrong

Leave Turkey Key and paddle south past Buzzard Key into the Plover Keys. This is an attractive group of islands with scattered beach areas among the mangrove. The southeast side of Plover Key has the most extensive section of beach among these islands. Continue down the coast, aiming for Bird Key. The creatures that gave this key its name inhabit it still. The combination of nearby food and relative safety from predators makes this an attractive key for them.

The beach at Porpoise Point on Wood Key is visible from Bird Key. But first will come Boggess Point, facing west into the Gulf. If the winds are strong, you may want to take the inside route by Toms Bight. Either way you choose, pass Wood Key and look for coconut palms on the island's south side. They are a reminder of the days when this island was occupied by several families. There was once even a small school here. Traverse

Spanish bayonet on Hog Key. Photo by Ellen Connally

Wood Key Cove to Hog Key, arriving at mile 8. Here is an attractive beach campsite backed by Spanish bayonet and especially large sea grape. There are still hogs on Hog Key. Also note the large spreading tamarind tree. Leave Hog Key and swing southeast beside a long point of land leading into Lostmans River. At some pilings on the point, come to the Lostmans Ranger Station. The station tower will be visible before you can see the ranger station. This sandy high ground of the ranger station is fairly extensive. I have seen deer here. End your route at mile 11. From here it is 4 miles south to Highland Beach on the Highland Beach Route. It is 6 miles east to the Wilderness Waterway at marker #52 on the Lostmans River Route.

Turner River Canoe Trail

Begin: Tamiami Trail   End: Chokoloskee
Distance: 8.5 miles   Time: 5 hours

Potential Tidal Influence: 3   Potential Wind Influence: 2
Navigational Challenge: 4
Highlights: Diverse habitat
Hazards: Motorboats in Chokoloskee Bay
Campsites: None
Connections: Hurddles Creek Route, Rabbit Key Pass, Lopez River Route, Causeway Route

---

The Turner River Canoe Trail may be the most botanically diverse paddle in the Everglades. It starts on the Tamiami Trail in the Big Cypress National Preserve amid a freshwater environment dominated by towering cypress trees. It opens into sawgrass, broken by occasional tree islands, makes a tight squeeze through eerie tree tunnels, then transforms to classic mangrove-zone environment before intersecting the Hurddles Creek Route at Hurddles Creek. It continues down the Turner River as the river opens up and passes a high, historic Calusa mound before arriving at civilized Chokoloskee Island. In the 1950s a canal was dug near the upper Turner, diverting much of its water and altering the ecosystem. Now, the water is being rediverted to the Turner in an effort to restore the river.

This is a great day paddle or unconventional starting point for longer trips. The paddling on this trail can be tough. At the outset, shallow water and hydrilla, an underwater plant, combine to make the going slow. Next, the tunnels are very constricted, making steering and paddling difficult at best. Sea kayaks are untenable here; a double-bladed paddle simply can't work in the tight tunnels and sharp turns. To best enjoy this trail, take a canoe and consider getting an outfitter to provide shuttle for a one-way trip.

Put in at the landing adjacent to the bridge over the Turner River. To access this landing from Everglades City, drive north on State Road 29 to US 41. Drive east on US 41 for 6 miles to the Turner River. Put in and begin paddling south on a clear stream filled with hydrilla. The channel soon constricts to less than 15 feet. Your immediate surroundings are freshwater species: cypress, cattails, willows. The cattails, which have displaced some sawgrass, are a recent addition due to fertilizer runoff from the farming region north of the Everglades National Park.

Open area along the Turner River. Photo by W. W. Armstrong

This river was named for a guide, Richard B. Turner, who led U.S. forces up the waterway in search of Seminoles in 1857. The force, under John Parkhill, went upriver and destroyed some Indian villages. Later, Parkhill was killed in an ambush, and the bluecoats retreated to the Gulf.

Come to the first mangrove tunnel just a short distance into the paddle—here, the roots of red mangrove form a gauntlet for your craft. Overhead the leaves and branches of the trees crowd out the sun, leaving scant room for your canoe. Notice the profusion of epiphytes, air plants that grow on the mangrove branches. The water is shallow and crystalline. The going is slow. Briefly emerge into a pond. Stay right and reenter the mangrove tunnel to emerge finally into another environment—here, cattails, sawgrass, and willow provide an open and bright contrast to the cool shady tunnel.

Intersect an old canal and turn right; the canal is blocked off to the left. Continue in the open, occasionally passing sawgrass-ringed tree islands.

One of these islands of palm, on river left, provides a dry spot to take a break. The river here varies in width but stays deep enough to paddle with ease as you enter a very short second mangrove tunnel. There will be mangrove on river right and sawgrass on your left. Pay close attention here and look for another tunnel diverging right. This tunnel is marked by an orange stake.

Take this tunnel to the right, soon passing an Everglades National Park boundary sign at 3.5 miles. This third tunnel is a little more roomy than the first but is still a challenging paddle. After this tunnel opens, the vegetation becomes more typical of the park paddling zone: red and black mangrove and buttonwood, with a few palms thrown in. The Turner

Author on Turner River Canoe Trail. Photo by W. W. Armstrong

twists and turns and continues to vary in width. Keep your eyes peeled for orange tape tied to tree branches to help distinguish the main river from side streams. Another clue is the stronger tidal flow.

The banks become higher as you come to a large bay on river left; stay right and paddle a bit farther to intersect Hurddles Creek on your left. To your right the Turner River becomes much wider. The Hurddles Creek Route leads southerly 5.5 miles to the Sunday Bay chickee.

Paddle west on the Turner River, passing Left Hand Turner River on your right. Stay with the left-hand bank, looking for the nearly vertical bank of shell, here indicating a Calusa shell mound that reaches 19 feet at its highest elevation. Come to the mouth of the Turner River. The mouth is guarded by a few mangrove isles near Wilderness Waterway marker #129. Paddle westerly toward the park service boat ramp on the north end of Chokoloskee Island, near the Outdoor Resort, ending your route at 8.5 miles. From here, the Rabbit Key Pass Route leads 5.5 miles to Rabbit Key. The Lopez River Route leads 5 miles to Lopez River campsite. The Causeway Route leads 3 miles to the Gulf Coast Ranger Station.

West Pass Route

Begin: Gulf Coast Ranger Station   End: Picnic Key
Distance: 8.5 miles   Time: 5 hours
Potential Tidal Influence: 4   Potential Wind Influence: 4
Navigational Challenge: 4
Highlights: Numerous scenic islands, good beach camping
Hazards: Motor boats in Chokoloskee Bay
Campsites: Tiger Key, Picnic Key
Connections: Indian Key Pass Route, Pavilion Key Route, Causeway Route, Halfway Creek Canoe Trail

The West Pass Route takes you into the northernmost reaches of the park and into the midst of the Ten Thousand Islands. Three sorts of water are represented here: the busy Chokoloskee Bay, the riverine West Pass, and

Beyond the Barron River on the West Pass Route. Photo by W. W. Armstrong

the open water of the Gulf of Mexico. Boat traffic is heavy in Chokoloskee Bay, but it drops off as the route continues north along the mainland to enter West Pass. West Pass opens into the Gulf and Tiger Key, which overlooks the vast western horizon. Just around the corner is Picnic Key, another picturesque and popular camping destination.

Start your paddle at the Gulf Coast Ranger Station and paddle north in Chokoloskee Bay toward Lane Cove, passing marker #5, which indicates the channel into the Barron River. Keep northwest, crossing the marked channel that leads out Indian Key Pass, proceeding beyond some dredge-spoil islands and markers #29 and #30. Chokoloskee Bay is shallow on both sides of this channel.

Keep northwest in open water, passing a point on your right and paralleling Lane Cove. Scoot past some low-slung finger islands on your left. Note that other islands in the vicinity are comprised of a single mangrove tree. Veer west, leaving Lane Cove and paddling past the mouth of the Ferguson River at mile 3.5. The river is fronted by more islands, as you would expect in the Ten Thousand Islands. Stay close to the mouth of the Ferguson while making the passage for West Pass Bay. Notice how much more stout the mangrove is along the Ferguson River than on the nearby islands. It seems that mangrove thrives best when it is exposed to both saltwater and freshwater, alternating with the tides.

Clear the straits past the Ferguson River into West Pass Bay. Aim just south of due west for West Pass. A conspicuous island in the foreground makes a good aiming point. Stay just south of the conspicuous island and enter West Pass—it is about 80 feet wide, running south, then west. The waters are kept deep by daily tidal flows. Numerous tapered bays splinter off West Pass before it arrives in open waters at mile 6, where the Gulf of Mexico is visible. The northern tip of Tiger Key is also visible on the edge of the Gulf. Continue a southwesterly course beyond a few smaller islands, then swing around the northern tip of Tiger Key. The waters can be shallow here. Keep south and look for the beach and the signed Tiger Key campsite at mile 7.5. The white sands and Gulf view draw many campers here.

The West Pass Route continues south around the shallow south end of Tiger Key. The sandy camp of Picnic Key comes into view. Paddle east to the beach, lined with sea grape, and arrive at Picnic Key at mile 8.5. This encampment lures in Everglades enthusiasts, too. From Picnic Key, it is 7 miles back to Gulf Coast Ranger Station via the Indian Key Pass Route. It is 7 miles to Rabbit Key via the Pavilion Key Route.

Willy Willy Route

Begin: Lostmans Five campsite　　End: Willy Willy campsite
Distance: 9.5 miles　　Time: 5 hours
Potential Tidal Influence: 3　　Potential Wind Influence: 4
Navigational Challenge: 3
Highlights: Historic shell mounds
Hazards: Motor boats on Wilderness Waterway, wide-open bays
Campsites: Lostmans Five campsite, Willy Willy campsite
Connections: Darwin's Place Route, Lostmans River Route, Rodgers River Bay Route

The Willy Willy Route connects three historic ground sites to one another. It traces the Wilderness Waterway for most of the paddle through a series of big bays linked by channels to pass the east end of Lostmans River. There it leaves the Wilderness Waterway and crosses Big Lostmans Bay, to access a little-used creek leading to the Willy Willy campsite, an old Calusa shell mound adjacent to a freshwater creek at the edge of the marshy Glades. Along the way, it passes Onion Key, another bit of land with a storied past and present.

Start your route at the Lostmans Five campsite. Leave the dock and paddle west around a point to Wilderness Waterway marker #60. Notice how the land of Lostmans Five campsite continues to the point by the marker, as is evidenced by the hammock species on the shoreline. Paddle into a tapering inlet and a south-flowing stream, which is a good 50 feet wide and opens into Two Island Bay at marker #59.

There are no more islands in Two Island Bay. They were probably swept away by a hurricane. Head easterly for the peninsula protruding from the northern shore. Near the peninsula veer southeasterly toward another channel at marker #58. The waters are shallow at the entrance to this channel but should pose no problem to paddlers. Turn almost due south into this channel, which leads to 1-acre-square Onion Key.

Two stories predominate as to how Onion Key got its name. The first says the island was named for a forgotten farmer and his wife who settled here and cultivated onions on the island. The second story states that early Everglades pioneer Gregorio Lopez ate his last onion while camped on this island. Whatever the case, Onion Key's shell shoreline, as opposed to a mud and mangrove shoreline, gives it away as an Indian mound. Onion Key is the site of more than 1,000 years of occupation. Calusa, then Seminoles, were born and died here. In recent times, the 1920s, the headquarters of the Poinciana Company was based here; it went bust after the 1926 hurricane. The key has also been a park campsite. Now it is overgrown by a profusion of shrubby exotic Brazilian pepper.

Leave Onion Key, heading south, and come to marker #56. From here, enter Onion Key Bay, hugging the west shoreline to the point between the shoreline and the island. The reason the Wilderness Waterway goes the way it does is to stick to more sheltered, deeper waters for motorboats, for which it was originally designed. Pass marker #55 and continue southerly, shooting for marker #53, which is barely visible on the horizon. Shoot the channel south and come to Wilderness Waterway marker #52, at mile 3.5.

Here begins the Lostmans River Route. It heads west, where the Wilderness Waterway marker arrow is pointing, 6 miles to the Gulf and the Lostmans Ranger Station. The Willy Willy Route, however, swings southeasterly for a channel and marker #51. This short channel is very riverine in width, depth, and tidal pull. Follow its steep banks past marker #50, to marker #49. The arrow here points toward Third Bay, but you continue east another 100 yards, then turn south. Do not take the first southerly channel past marker #49; it leads back toward Lostmans River. The correct channel heads south, then turns almost due east into a nameless bay. Paddle almost due east across this bay, passing marker #47, then a tiny isle in the bay. Be sure to cross all the way to the far east end of the bay, to come to marker #45. Turn south, then east to marker #44 and Big Lostmans Bay, at mile 6.5. Note the large, gnarly buttonwoods here.

Leave the Wilderness Waterway and paddle just north of due east for a V-shaped inlet 1.5 miles across Big Lostmans Bay. Trust your compass on the crossing. At the back of the shallow inlet is a winding creek that heads generally east. This 15-foot-wide creek is plenty deep enough for self-propelled craft. Mudflats line the inside of the creek bends. Come to a split in the creek, and take the south channel. Pass an open sawgrass area before opening into Rocky Creek Bay.

Paddle east up Rocky Creek Bay, skirting a clump of palms on the south shore. Jump over to the north shore, noting the tall trees above the mangrove. Just ahead is the dock of the Willy Willy campsite at mile 9.5, by the mouth of a freshwater stream entering Rocky Creek Bay from the north. This is an old Indian shell-mound hammock that modern Everglades adventurers can spend a night on, and from which they can paddle the freshwater creeks of the interior glades. From here it is 5 miles to the Rodgers River chickee and 7 miles to Wilderness Waterway marker #26 at Broad River Bay via the Rodgers River Bay Route.

The Campsites

The Campsites

Everglades campers heading into the backcountry are required to stay in designated campsites. This concentrates the human impact into fewer and contained locations to minimize damage to natural resources. And out here, there aren't a whole lot of places to overnight, other than designated campsites, that are above water, especially on the "inside."

There are three types of campsites. Each type has its positive and negative characteristics. First, there are chickees, located where no dry land exists. These are elevated wooden platforms with open sides and sloped metal roofs. There is a vault toilet connected to the platform by a gangway. Double chickees have two platforms. There is limited room in these chickees.

The second type of campsite is a ground campsite. These are primarily old shell mounds built up over time by the Calusa and more recently used by white and Seminole settlers. They are often covered in tropical hammock vegetation and are as laden with bugs as with history. The third type of campsite is a beach campsite. These campsites are in the Gulf of Mexico on crushed-shell beaches. Access to them is strongly affected by winds and tides. On the beach, winds can blow your tent down. But the walking room of a beach camp can be a relief after being stuck in a boat all day.

For each campsite listed in this guide, you'll find a box that supplies easy-to-scan information for the Everglades camper. First, the type of campsite and the type of landing for your boat are listed. After that is a scenery rating, from 1 (poor) to 5 (excellent). Campsite use, on a scale from very low to high, is rated to help you know whether you are likely to have company or even be able to get on a site. Then maximum number of people and maximum number of parties allowed at the campsite are listed. When the maximum number of either people or parties is met, the campsite is full. For example, Lard Can campsite has a 10-person capacity and a 4-party limit. If one party of 10 people reserves a night at Lard Can campsite, then the campsite is full for that night. If 4 parties of 1 camper each reserve the same night at Lard Can, then the campsite is full for that night. The listing for maximum number of nights tells you the most nights in a row a camper can stay at that site. You can also learn which campsites allow fires and which have toilets.

Next to "on which route," you will find the exact route the campsite is on. If the campsite is at the terminus of two routes, then both routes are listed. Connecting routes nearby are also identified. Under "nearby campsites" are listed other camping possibilities in the same general area, in case the site you are trying to get is full and you want to be in the same vicinity.

Reserving Campsites

Campsites are to be reserved when you get your backcountry permit. Permits are issued in person up to 24 hours in advance, so have several campsites in mind for your trip, in case your first choices are full. A permit will be issued only to available campsites. Once you get an itinerary, you must stick to it. However, do not imperil yourself or your party by trying, no matter what, to stay on permit. Rangers will understand legitimate extenuating circumstances (big storms, injuries) that cause you to go off permit. On the other hand, if you just don't feel like paddling any farther, don't try to catch on at a campsite where you don't have reservations, especially a chickee. There simply isn't spare camping room available.

Florida Bay

Alligator Creek

Type of campsite: Ground	Landing: Ground
Scenery: 4	Use: Very low
Max. # of campers: 8	Max. # of parties: 3 Max. # of nights: 2
Fires: No	Toilet: No

On which route: West Lake Canoe Trail, Snake Bight Route

Nearby connecting routes: West Lake Canoe Trail, Snake Bight Route

Nearby campsites: Shark Point

If you like camping in solitude in a little-visited area of the Everglades backcountry, stay at Alligator Creek. Your camping buddies will be the wildlife, active day and night. This is a ground campsite located at the mouth of Alligator Creek where it enters Garfield Bight, a part of Florida Bay. The actual landing, which may be muddy at low tide, is on Alligator Creek, less than 100 feet from the bight. An alligator may be sunning itself at the landing. The camping area is on a flat marl prairie upon which grow dill weed, purslane, and other ground cover, though a portion of the campsite is worn to bare earth.

The mangrove along the shore of Alligator Creek and a few other trees provide a little shade. Foot trails extend into the prairie, where you can get partial views of Garfield Bight. Although the West Lake Canoe Trail is hand-propelled craft only, motorboaters can access the little-used campsite from Florida Bay, but few do, because Garfield Bight is so shallow.

Carl Ross Key

Type of campsite: Beach	Landing: Beach
Scenery: 5	Use: Medium
Max. # of campers: 9	Max. # of parties: 3 Max. # of nights: 2
Fires: Yes	Toilet: No

On which route: First American Bank Route, Man of War Route

Nearby connecting routes: First American Bank Route, Man of War Route
Nearby campsites: None

Carl Ross Key is a special place and one of the best backcountry campsites in the Everglades National Park. It is situated, along with Sandy Key, in the lonely west end of Florida Bay. This little comma-shaped island offers first-rate views in all directions. To your north is the low shoreline of Cape Sable, to your east the far-off keys of Florida Bay, and to your south Sandy Key—a protected nesting ground where many avian species can be seen. To your west are the open waters of the Gulf of Mexico.

Upon approaching Carl Ross Key from Flamingo, the first thing you'll see is a sandy shoreline punctuated with several large black mangrove. This is the primary camping area. A couple of palm trees give it the tropical touch. To your left is a shallow lagoon, then the sandy southern tip of the island, which overlooks the rookery of Sandy Key and a channel between the two islands. The interior of the island has a varied growth of grass, sea purslane, gumbo-limbo, and cactus. The west-facing side of the island is all beach. Overall, there is adequate beach to walk, about 300 yards along the perimeter of the island. The mosquitoes are few, making for a more positive camping experience.

Little Rabbit Key

Type of campsite: Ground	Landing: Dock	
Scenery: 4	Use: Low	
Max. # of campers: 12	Max. # of parties: 4	Max. # of nights: 2
Fires: No	Toilet: Yes	

On which route: Dildo Bank Route, Man of War Route
Nearby connecting routes: Dildo Bank Route, Man of War Route
Nearby campsites: None

Little Rabbit Key lies in the heart of Florida Bay. It is the second stop of the two-night, three-day Florida Bay loop. Its only other access is an all-day paddle from Flamingo. This small island is ringed by trees, with a grassy, brushy center covered with a creeping plant known as sea purslane. Red mangrove, with its prop roots, faces out on the ocean, with the more massive black mangrove growing a little more inland. Little Rabbit Key has no beach.

A small dock protrudes from an opening in the mangrove on the northwest side of the island. A clearing and the center of the island lie behind the dock. Camping areas are directly behind the dock and off to one side in the shade of some big black mangrove. The preferred tent sites are here, though you won't get much breeze.

A picnic table and vault toilet make Little Rabbit Key a bit more civilized. Little footpaths circle the perimeter of the key. Your only clear ocean views are from the dock and landing area. From here you can see Big Rabbit Key and the waters to the west. Come here for a fabulous sunset. Later, if you go out to the dock and shine your flashlight into the water, you'll see the shrimp, crabs, minnows, and other aquatic creatures that make up a strand of the web of life in Florida Bay.

North Nest Key

Type of campsite: Beach	Landing: Beach and dock	
Scenery: 5	Use: Medium	
Max. # of campers: 25	Max. # of parties: 7	Max. # of nights: 7
Fires: Yes	Toilet: Yes	
On which route: North Nest Key Loop		
Nearby connecting routes: None		
Nearby campsites: None		

The North Nest Key beach campsite lies all alone in northeast Florida Bay near Key Largo. But it deserves to be all alone, because it is in a class by itself. North Nest Key is a large island punctuated with small beaches amid its mangrove shoreline. The western side of the island has a swim beach, marked with "No Wake" buoys, whose shallow waters are ideal for wading. Just around the corner is the camping area. A 40 by 3–foot dock allows for easy landing of your craft, but the gentle beach here is paddler friendly, too. The colorful waters and green keys of Florida Bay offer a superlative view from the camping area.

Mangrove and buttonwood provide shade for small tent areas beneath their limbs. Footpaths lead farther into the island and to a couple of more open tent sites, next to a shallow pond. Other tent sites are right next to the bay. None of the camping areas are particularly large, but campers can disperse and get a little privacy if they so desire.

Shark Point

Type of campsite: Ground	Landing: Ground	
Scenery: 3	Use: Very low	
Max. # of campers: 8	Max. # of parties: 1	Max. # of nights: 3
Fires: No	Toilet: No	
On which route: Snake Bight Route		
Nearby connecting routes: West Lake Canoe Trail		
Nearby campsites: Alligator Creek		

This is a very seldom used ground campsite located on a spit of land that separates Garfield Bight from Rankin Bight in Florida Bay. The waters around the campsite are shallow, discouraging motorboats, and the Snake Bight Route is off the beaten path of many canoeists. This all translates to solitude. In fact, the campsite seems hardly used.

Shark Point juts into Florida Bay and is ringed by densely growing black mangrove with the exception of one "beach" barely wide enough to pull in a couple of sea kayaks or canoes. Walk a good 30 feet beyond the mangrove into a cleared area, where low-growing ground cover dominates the landscape and where you can pitch your tent on a marl mud flat in dry weather. Otherwise, you can tent on the ground cover. Surrounding you are many, many bleached skeletons of dead trees.

Mosquitoes can rule the scene here. This may be the buggiest backcountry campsite in the Everglades, but only one party is allowed per night at Shark Point, guaranteeing solitude for you and the mosquitoes.

Cape Sable, Whitewater Bay, and the South

Clubhouse Beach

Type of campsite: Beach	Landing: Beach
Scenery: 4	Use: Low
Max. # of campers: 24	Max. # of parties: 4 Max. # of nights: 3
Fires: Yes	Toilet: No

On which route: East Cape Route

Nearby connecting routes: Snake Bight Route, Buttonwood Canal Route, First National Bank Route, Dildo Key Route, Bear Lake Canoe Trail, Middle Cape Route

Nearby campsites: East Clubhouse Beach, East Cape

Clubhouse Beach campsite is just a few miles distant from East Clubhouse Beach campsite and closely resembles it. The beach here is more interspersed with mangrove on the shoreline, but the prairie is larger. The beach offers an equally good view of northern Florida Bay.

This beach was named by the Model Land Company, which was trying to develop the Cape Sable area during the Florida real estate boom in the early 1920s. The company built a large clubhouse on stilts, which extended out from the beach. Here company salespeople would entertain potential clients who were boated in from Miami and environs. I could find no remains of a clubhouse today. Hurricanes can be very rough on old wooden structures.

There are some good tent sites right where the beach meets the prairie, near the campsite marker, and you'll find plenty of trees in the vicinity to hunker behind should the weather become rough. There are also some tent sites on a clay flat behind the beach that would be adequate in dry weather, but should a rain come, this location will be a miry mess.

East Cape

Type of campsite: Beach   Landing: Beach
Scenery: 5   Use: Medium
Max. # of campers: 60   Max. # of parties: 15   Max. # of nights: 7
Fires: Yes   Toilet: No
On which route: East Cape Route, Middle Cape Route
Nearby connecting routes: East Cape Route, Middle Cape Route
Nearby campsites: Clubhouse Beach, Middle Cape

The large East Cape campsite occupies the most southerly tip of land in the mainland United States. The actual campsite starts at the most westerly creek that links Florida Bay with Lake Ingraham, which lies behind East Cape and Middle Cape. Just beside the creek is a flat tent site that looks south over Florida Bay. The rest of the campsite swings around the point of the cape. Old pilings of a dock, remnants of an old boat concession tour that landed here, mark the popular camping spot. There are tent sites for hundreds of yards along the beach.

The wide strip of beach is backed by a few coconut palms, along with cactus, grass, sea purslane, and Jamaica dogwood and other trees. Back in the 1830s the cape looked very different. It was the site of Fort Poinsett, when the U.S. Army and the Seminoles were at war. Army personnel thought that the Seminoles were getting arms from Spanish fishermen who operated in the area, and that Cape Sable was a meeting place for arms deals. The log fort was later abandoned.

East Clubhouse Beach

Type of campsite: Beach   Landing: Beach
Scenery: 4   Use: Low
Max. # of campers: 24   Max. # of parties: 4   Max. # of nights: 3
Fires: Yes   Toilet: No
On which route: East Cape Route

Nearby connecting routes: Snake Bight Route, Buttonwood Canal Route, First National Bank Route, Dildo Key Route, Bear Lake Canoe Trail, Middle Cape Route
Nearby campsites: Clubhouse Beach, East Cape

The East Clubhouse Beach campsite overlooks northwestern Florida Bay. It is a nice beach campsite, but not the best by the heady standards of Everglades National Park, where you'll find some of the best wilderness beach camping in all of the United States. This slender beach is punctuated with pockets of mangrove that grow right to the shoreline along its 300-yard length. Behind the beach is an open prairie of sea purslane, an edible plant, which extends far back to a dense woodland that sweeps around the prairie all the way to the shore west of the beach.

Here lie the remains of an old boat. Also in this area are a couple of tent sites that are shielded by the mangrove forest, should the weather be excessively windy or cold. Other good tent sites are on the shell beach right by the campsite sign and in a grassy section of prairie directly behind the sign. Beachcombers can go east for a decent walk, provided they don't mind having to go inland here and there and walk over the prairie.

Hells Bay

Type of campsite: Chickee	Landing: Dock	
Scenery: 3	Use: High	
Max. # of campers: 12	Max. # of parties: 2	Max. # of nights: 1
Fires: No	Toilet: Yes	

On which route: Hells Bay Canoe Trail, Lane River Route, East River Route
Nearby connecting routes: Hells Bay Canoe Trail, Lane River Route, East River Route
Nearby campsites: Pearl Bay chickee, Lane Bay chickee

Because the Hells Bay chickee stands at the confluence of three primary paddle routes east of Whitewater Bay, it is popular with campers. The most popular of the three approaches to the chickee is the marked Hells

Bay Canoe Trail, which comes from Main Park Road. This campsite is also often a stop for paddlers coming up the East River from lower White-water Bay.

The surrounding water is shallow and clear, with a coffee-colored tint. Do not swim here, and be careful getting water from around the chickee, because there is a food-habituated alligator that makes Hells Bay part of his territory. He's known as Old Snaggle and will try to bum scraps from you. Never feed this or any other alligator or wild animal. They lose their wildness when people feed them.

This double chickee lies at the south end of Hells Bay in a small cove of low mangrove. It is well away from the shoreline, which makes for adequate breezes and fewer insects. The structure faces east, which means a great sunrise followed by an early blazing sun. But your best views are to the north and the bulk of Hells Bay, so named because it is hell to get into and hell to get out of.

Joe River

Type of campsite: Chickee	Landing: Dock	
Scenery: 2	Use: High	
Max. # of campers: 12	Max. # of parties: 2	Max. # of nights: 1
Fires: No	Toilet: Yes	
On which route: Cormorant Pass Route, Joe River Route		
Nearby connecting routes: Big Sable Route, Cormorant Pass Route, Joe River Route		
Nearby campsites: South Joe River chickee, Oyster Bay chickee		

Joe River is a very sturdy newer chickee that doesn't sway as you walk around it, as some of the older ones do. It is set in a tiny cove off the east side of a bend in Joe River, just south of Oyster Bay. There is a somewhat limited view either up or down the Joe River. Behind the southwest-facing chickee is a tall forest of mangrove on three sides, broken by two small creeks flowing into and out of the tiny cove. This creates daily tidal flow directly under the chickee.

Two 13 by 13–foot platforms with 6-foot-wide gangplanks come together at a common vault toilet. The whole camping area is set 20 feet away from the mangrove, which may help some as far as insects, but don't expect too much of a breeze here. This campsite has the high use you would expect on a popular paddling route.

Lane Bay

Type of campsite: Chickee	Landing: Dock	
Scenery: 4	Use: Medium	
Max. # of campers: 6	Max. # of parties: 1	Max. # of nights: 1
Fires: No	Toilet: Yes	
On which route: Lane River Route		
Nearby connecting routes: Hells Bay Canoe Trail, Roberts River Route		
Nearby campsites: Hells Bay chickee, Roberts River chickee		

The Lane Bay single-camping-party chickee is backed against a hardwood hammock at the north end of Lane Bay. A south-facing platform, even with a roof it gets its share of sun, but the view of Lane Bay is worth it. This perch offers campers a commanding view of wooded shores with a larger variety of vegetation than the average mangrove waterfront. The hardwood hammock directly behind the chickee gives you close-up views of the setting—ferns, wax myrtle, and coco plums—though this forest may contribute to insect problems at times. In the bay directly in front of the chickee is the beginning of the Lane River.

A user-friendly design makes this chickee even more attractive. The standard camping platform is connected to the vault toilet by a 4-foot-wide sloping gangplank, which also gets the camper closer to the water for unloading and loading gear from their craft than at many other chickees. Such a low gangplank can function only in waters with the minimal tide variation of Lane Bay. Off the gangplank, too, is a small ladder for swimmers who want to enjoy the shallow waters.

Lard Can

Type of campsite: Ground	Landing: Ground
Scenery: 3	Use: Low
Max. # of campers: 10	Max. # of parties: 4 Max. # of nights: 2
Fires: No	Toilet: Yes

On which route: Hells Bay Canoe Trail
Nearby connecting routes: Lane River Route, East River Route
Nearby campsites: Pearl Bay, Hells Bay

Lard Can is an old spot of heavily wooded solid ground that humans have inhabited since the Calusa discovered it hundreds of years ago. In pre-park days, gladesmen often set up base camps here for hunting and fishing. At these camps they stored supplies in big lard cans made of tin, which were the driest storage available—hence the name.

A ring of mangrove borders the water, except for a small landing split by a tree, where two canoes can pull up onto mud and roots. There is a small clearing surrounded by ferns, palm trees, and coco plums.

This low-use campsite with three decent tent sites makes for a good first night's stop, especially if you are getting a late start or the chickees are full. It is good for solitude as well; I've never seen anyone else camped on it. Even if you angle for bass and freshwater species in the ponds on the way in, you won't have to worry about making a frenzied paddle to camp before dark because it is only three miles from Main Park Road.

Set in dense woods, Lard Can will be very buggy following rains. It can be muddy as well. Before you camp here, check the gauge (PVC pipe marked in inches) on the left of the Hells Bay Canoe Trail dock. If the gauge reads 2 feet or the dock is submerged, Lard Can will be pretty sloppy, too.

Middle Cape

Type of campsite: Beach	Landing: Beach
Scenery: 5	Use: Medium

Max. # of campers: 60   Max. # of parties: 15   Max. # of nights: 7
Fires: Yes   Toilet: No
On which route: Middle Cape Route
Nearby connecting routes: East Cape Route, Big Sable Route
Nearby campsites: East Cape, Northwest Cape

A long stretch of beach, including Middle Cape itself, makes up the Middle Cape campsite. On the south end of the cape is an open, palm-dotted field paralleling the beach. A few old pilings, exposed at low tide, mark the start of the popular camping section of the beach. Shade here is nonexistent. Closer to the cape are some gumbo-limbo and Jamaica dogwood, along with some agave, whose barren flower stalks tower in the air.

The cape itself offers relatively high ground at its sharp tip and tremendous views both north and south and, of course, into the Gulf of Mexico. North of the cape are some excellent tent sites. Then the beach narrows beside a small grassy field, which gives way to mangroves that grow to the Gulf's edge.

Middle Cape was once known as Palm Point. According to legend, several tall palms grew at the cape and passing mariners used them as a guide to their location. In the early 1800s the palms were cut down, but the spot was still known as Palm Point until the Coast and Geodetic Survey renamed it.

North River

Type of campsite: Chickee   Landing: Dock
Scenery: 2   Use: Medium
Max. # of campers: 6   Max. # of parties: 1   Max. # of nights: 1
Fires: No   Toilet: Yes
On which route: The Cutoff Route
Nearby connecting routes: North River Route, The Labyrinth Route, Roberts River Route, Cormorant Pass Route
Nearby campsites: Watson River chickee, Roberts River chickee

---

The North River chickee is actually not on the North River, but on the river north of the North River. This river has no name. The covered camping platform named for the nearby North River lies on the east side of a small mangrove island less than 100 feet in diameter that sits in the middle of this unnamed river, which is only a couple of hundred feet in width itself here.

This is an older chickee of standard size connected to a vault toilet by a 3-foot-wide gangplank. There is also a built-in ladder leading to shallow clear waters that deepen quickly, making for good swimming possibilities. The view is somewhat limited by mangrove branches that extend around three sides of the structure, which overlooks the main river channel and a creek separated by low mangrove. This small island will not present much in the way of bug problems.

Be prepared for an early-morning sun here. Arise early to enjoy the sunrise and get moving before the rays really heat up the chickee. At night, the lights of Miami will shimmer across the water, but with minimal powerboat traffic and a lot of bird life your sense of solitude in nature will remain overpowering. By day, you can investigate the upper reaches of the North River above The Cutoff.

Northwest Cape

Type of campsite: Beach	Landing: Beach
Scenery: 5	Use: Medium
Max. # of campers: 36	Max. # of parties: 9 Max. # of nights: 7
Fires: Yes	Toilet: No

On which route: Middle Cape Route, Big Sable Route

Nearby connecting routes: Middle Cape Route, Big Sable Route, Ponce De Leon Bay Route

Nearby campsites: Middle Cape, Graveyard Creek

The Northwest is my favorite of the cape campsites. It gets the least use of these campsites because it is the hardest to access. You get a real sense of going back in time to a long-ago Florida here. This is as beautiful as any spot in the country.

At Northwest Cape campsite. Photo by author

The beach follows the gentle contour lines of Northwest Cape. The sand is wide enough to camp anywhere in the immediate vicinity of the cape. Behind the beach is a pretty grass plain that goes back a good half mile and is punctuated with palm trees and a few hardwood hammocks. In spots, Jamaica dogwood grows right along the beach line. Patches of agave grow among the grass.

Northwest Cape curves gently north. Up the way, palms grow right along the beach. An interesting hammock of gumbo-limbo and dildo cactus grow right behind some palm trunks that now stand upright in the sea. The beach extends a little way farther north until it hits a healthy stand of mangrove at the ocean's edge. There is fine camping all along here.

Oyster Bay

Type of campsite: Chickee   Landing: Dock

Scenery: 2   Use: High

Max. # of campers: 12   Max. # of parties: 2   Max. # of nights: 1

Fires: No   Toilet: Yes

On which route: Big Sable Route, Cormorant Pass Route, Shark Cutoff Route

Nearby connecting routes: Big Sable Route, Cormorant Pass Route, Whitewater Bay Route, Joe River Route, Shark Cutoff Route
Nearby campsites: Shark River chickee, Joe River chickee

Oyster Bay is one of the larger double chickees, and it sees use from both paddlers and motorboaters. It is on the route for those who circle Cape Sable and for those who loop Whitewater Bay. Being so close to the Wilderness Waterway keeps it hopping, too.

The camping platform lies just west of Cormorant Pass in northern Oyster Bay. Two 14 by 12–foot platforms are connected by 7-foot-wide gangplanks that meet at a common vault toilet. A central ladder reaches into the water. All this makes for extra room for walking around. Also, you can set up your tent earlier in the day and still have room to do things on a larger than average chickee.

Situated among a group of mostly small islands, the chickee faces east and will get some early-morning sun. But the west side backs up to a mangrove island a mere 15 feet distant. This chickee does not offer outstanding views, but it is sheltered from the elements by these islands. Wind can be a good thing when the bugs are out, and on my three stays here I have had problems with no-see-ums each time. Maybe it was just my bad luck.

Pearl Bay

Type of campsite: Chickee	Landing: Dock	
Scenery: 3	Use: High	
Max. # of campers: 12	Max. # of parties: 2	Max. # of nights: 1
Fires: No	Toilet: Yes	
On which route: Hells Bay Canoe Trail		
Nearby connecting routes: East River Route, Lane River Route		
Nearby campsites: Lard Can, Hells Bay chickee		

Pearl Bay campsite is the Cadillac of chickees—the largest and best built. It serves an additional important function by being the park's only handicapped-accessible backcountry campsite.

This accessibility starts with a covered canoe slip. Astride this slip are two canoe-length steps with metal handrails, which lead to an extra-wide 15 by 15–foot chickee. Wooden guardrails border the platform, yet these guardrails have conspicuous openings to access the water around the chickee. A 6-foot-wide gangway leads to a large handicapped-accessible toilet. Another gangway leads to an adjoining equally large chickee that also has wooden guardrails and a correspondingly large roof. All this translates to extra room to move around in for campers who feel cramped in their boats.

The Pearl Bay chickee lies at the north end of Pearl Bay and looks south over the bulk of the inlet. There are a good 30 feet between the chickee and the shoreline behind it, which reduces potential insect problems. During the day, canoers paddling the Hells Bay Canoe Trail may pass by, but by evening it will be just you and the permanent residents of the Everglades.

Roberts River

Type of campsite: Chickee	Landing: Dock	
Scenery: 4	Use: Medium	
Max. # of campers: 12	Max. # of parties: 2	Max. # of nights: 1
Fires: No	Toilet: Yes	

On which route: Roberts River Route, The Cutoff Route

Nearby connecting routes: Roberts River Route, The Cutoff Route, Lane River Route

Nearby campsites: Lane Bay chickee, North River chickee

Roberts River chickee is a two-camper group affair tucked in a little cove at the head of an elongated stretch of the Roberts River. It is a newer chickee, with wider (6-foot) walkways than the older chickees. The walkways connect the covered camping platforms with a common vault toilet.

Just a stone's throw away is an old wooded hammock with ample dry ground land that was an old camping ground for all kinds of folks who traversed this section of the Everglades. The hammock, now home to huge ferns, tall trees, and a few palms, may have inspired the decision to locate this west-facing chickee where it is.

Having the bulk of the bay in front of the chickee means warm sunsets, and the woods so close behind delay the morning sun from becoming hot too early. The chickee's overall protection from the elements makes for a nice camp in inclement weather, but it could be a little on the buggy side, which hasn't been the case on any of my stays here.

Roberts River chickee makes a good base camp for exploring the headwaters of the Roberts River, which splits off into several streamlets above The Cutoff, less than a mile distant. It is also good for peace and quiet, as it is off the beaten path of the motorboating crowd.

South Joe River

Type of campsite: Chickee	Landing: Dock	
Scenery: 3	Use: High	
Max. # of campers: 12	Max. # of parties: 2	Max. # of nights: 1
Fires: No	Toilet: Yes	
On which route: Joe River Route		
Nearby connecting routes: Cormorant Pass Route, Whitewater Bay Route, Buttonwood Canal Route, East River Route		
Nearby campsites: Joe River chickee		

The South Joe River camping platform is a popular first night's destination for paddlers who depart from Flamingo. It is located in a side bay of the Joe River, off the main waterway, which adds the advantage of quiet. This bay has two creeks that drain it, so you are able to enter the bay from two directions, depending on which part of the Joe River you are coming from.

This east-facing chickee has a commanding view of the entire bay. The two camping platforms are 12 feet square, with 5 by 15–foot gangplanks merging to a common vault toilet. The whole chickee is a good 40 feet from the one mangrove shore. This spells fewer insects and better breezes. Expect company here on weekends, mainly paddlers. In pre-park days, gladesmen used to hunt and camp on patches of land west of the river.

Watson River

Type of campsite: Chickee	Landing: Dock
Scenery: 3	Use: High
Max. # of campers: 6	Max. # of parties: 1 Max. # of nights: 1
Fires: No	Toilet: Yes

On which route: The Cutoff Route, Cormorant Pass Route, The Labyrinth Route

Nearby connecting routes: The Cutoff Route, Cormorant Pass Route, The Labyrinth Route, Whitewater Bay Route, Shark Cutoff Route

Nearby campsites: North River chickee, Shark River chickee, Oyster Bay chickee

Watson River chickee is set into a mangrove stand on the north side of a Whitewater Bay key, somewhat protected by a couple of other small keys nearby. From here you can access the big bay, small streamlets, and the little-paddled Watson River. It is a single-party covered chickee, an older model with weathered boards and a short, narrow walkway leading to a vault toilet. The camping platform faces north and, since it is surrounded on three sides by mangrove, north is its only view, scanning the beginning of the Watson River. Chilly north winds, a periodic occurrence in the Everglades during the paddling season, may bear down on the camper here.

This shady spot is welcome on a hot day, though the nearby mangrove could lead to bug problems and also visits from raccoons, usually not a problem at chickees. During the day you may hear powerboats, but at night, there won't be another person for miles—just the mangrove, the water, and the stars.

The Central Rivers Area

Broad River

Type of campsite: Ground   Landing: Dock

Scenery: 3   Use: Low

Max. # of campers: 10   Max. # of parties: 3   Max. # of nights: 2

Fires: No   Toilet: Yes

On which route: Broad River Route

Nearby connecting routes: Highland Beach Route, The Nightmare Route, Rodgers River Route, Wood River Route

Nearby campsites: Highland Beach

Broad River campsite is set on a piece of dry ground 2 miles up the south bank of the Broad River from the Gulf of Mexico. It is also a 10-minute paddle from the north end of The Nightmare. Many paddlers camp here, waiting for the right tides to paddle The Nightmare. This mostly open ground site gets some shade from Jamaica dogwood, palm, and Brazilian pepper. Assorted vines such as morning glory complement the more substantial vegetation, which has been cleared back recently, allowing for more camping space. A few small mangrove front the Broad River.

The campsite is accessed by an inventive dock that helps paddlers load and unload their craft in this area of major tidal variation. The main dock forms a U. The first part heads into the water, then turns left, then left again to a vault toilet. Parallel to the part jutting into the water is a sloped platform that descends into the river. This platform allows you to access your craft even if it lies far below the dock. The other section of the dock allows for tying up your boat. There is also a very small ground landing if there are multiple boats here.

Several tent sites are scattered on the land, including secluded sites far from the water. You can have any variation of sun and shade you desire. Two picnic tables make cooking and eating easier. You may be making breakfast as quickly as possible to escape the mosquitoes.

Camp Lonesome

Type of campsite: Ground	Landing: Dock
Scenery: 4	Use: Low
Max. # of campers: 10	Max. # of parties: 3 Max. # of nights: 3
Fires: No	Toilet: Yes

On which route: Broad River Route, Wood River Route

Nearby connecting routes: Broad River Route, Wood River Route, Rodgers River Bay Route

Nearby campsites: Rodgers River chickee

Camp Lonesome is an old shell mound that has been lived on and camped on for an untold number of years. The original Everglades settlers, the Calusa, augmented these bits of land by piling up discarded shells, which combined with soil that accumulated over time to produce mounds on which they stayed. Seminoles occupied this locale as late as the 1940s as a homesite and trading post.

Today, there is a T-shaped dock that leads into a mound of land on which grow palms, fig, and a very tall gumbo-limbo. Ferns, brush, and vines enclose this campsite on all sides, so the fresh water of the Broad River is visible only from the dock.

A couple of picnic tables make this mound more camper friendly. Expect to share the very small campsite with weekend motorboaters who come here to fish. Despite the usual company and very tight quarters, this site exudes an aura of the wild Everglades, especially during the week.

Canepatch

Type of campsite: Ground	Landing: Dock
Scenery: 4	Use: Medium
Max. # of campers: 12	Max. # of parties: 4 Max. # of nights: 3
Fires: No	Toilet: Yes

On which route: North Harney River Route, Harney River Route

Nearby connecting routes: North Harney River Route, Harney River Route, Shark Cutoff Route
Nearby campsites: None

The Canepatch ground site is a historic mound used for centuries by the Calusa, then by Seminole and white settlers. It was known for a long time as Avocado Mound, for the avocado trees planted by Seminoles. Its final agricultural incarnation was as a cane, lemon, and banana farm. Today, you can see remnants of all three plants growing on the mound.

To reach the campsite, come to the T-shaped dock on your arrival. Then follow a long gangway from the water onto the mound and come to a clearing amid numerous banana trees, which dominate the campsite. A few palms and gumbo-limbo add to the heavy peripheral vegetation. Though the center of the clearing is unshaded, there are shaded tent spots about. The mound itself is sizable, but the area is very overgrown, leaving a small camping area. Intrepid explorers who don't mind being bug bit and scratched up can investigate the site. Remember, if you stumble on an artifact, leave it for others to discover and enjoy as you did.

Expect motorboat campers on weekend nights in the peak season. Try to come during the week and stay a couple of nights to check out other feeder streams and Little Banana Patch, 2 miles up Rookery Branch. Make friends with your fellow campers here—the close quarters demand it. Also, watch out for raccoons. They are notorious for their banditry here.

Graveyard Creek

Type of campsite: Ground	Landing: Beach and ground
Scenery: 5	Use: Medium
Max. # of campers: 12	Max. # of parties: 4 Max. # of nights: 3
Fires: No	Toilet: Yes

On which route: Highland Beach Route, Graveyard Creek Route, Ponce De Leon Bay Route

Nearby connecting routes: Highland Beach Route, Graveyard Creek Route, Ponce De Leon Bay Route, Harney River Route
Nearby campsites: Harney River chickee, Shark River chickee

The Graveyard Creek campsite, lying on the northern edge of a small inlet where Graveyard Creek meets the Gulf of Mexico, is officially designated a ground campsite but has characteristics of both a ground and a beach campsite. The camping area is on a spit of high ground that runs along the Gulf of Mexico, then doglegs back east along Graveyard Creek. There are ample shaded tent sites here. Behind the spit is a marshy mangrove wood. There are broken mangrove and sand fronting the Gulf and a small beach area along Graveyard Creek.

Two coconut palms mark the northern end of the campsite. Then comes the first of a few sea hibiscus trees. These naturalized trees have large heart-shaped leaves and flowers that evolve from yellow to red. Scattered mangrove parallels the beach on Graveyard Creek. This beach gets steeper as you head up the creek. The best access for this campsite is up Graveyard Creek. The creek is deepest here and will allow exit and entry to the campsite no matter what the water level, as falling tides can leave some access points high and dry. At the end of the beach by the deep water is a vault toilet. The other campsite amenities are picnic tables.

Harney River

Type of campsite: Chickee	Landing: Dock	
Scenery: 3	Use: High	
Max. # of campers: 6	Max. # of parties: 1	Max. # of nights: 1
Fires: No	Toilet: Yes	

On which route: Harney River Route, The Nightmare Route
Nearby connecting routes: Harney River Route, The Nightmare Route, North Harney River Route, Highland Beach Route
Nearby campsites: None

Harney River chickee is a single camping platform located 4 miles east of the Gulf beside an island in the middle of the Harney River. It is strategically placed at the south end of an overgrown and tidally influenced area of the Wilderness Waterway. From this chickee you can paddle on a rising or high tide through heavily vegetated Broad Creek and sometimes shallow Nightmare on The Nightmare Route. Because of its strategic location, the campsite is a bottleneck for those traveling the length of the Wilderness Waterway and can be difficult to reserve.

This 12-foot square platform with a covered roof is backed up against red mangrove on the north side the island in the center of the Harney. This makes for shade nearly all day long. The renovated chickee (it used to sway with your every move) has a 4-foot-wide gangplank leading to a vault toilet and a ladder into the water. Variations of 4 feet between the tidal high and low are not uncommon at this chickee, making loading and unloading your craft, especially sea kayaks, difficult at times.

Highland Beach

Type of campsite: Beach	Landing: Beach	
Scenery: 5	Use: Medium	
Max. # of campers: 24	Max. # of parties: 4	Max. # of nights: 3
Fires: Yes	Toilet: No	
On which route: Highland Beach Route, Broad River Route		
Nearby connecting routes: Broad River Route, Wood River Route, Highland Beach Route, The Nightmare Route, Lostmans River Route		
Nearby campsites: Broad River		

Highland Beach is one of my favorite campsites. It's a classic natural beach that takes effort for paddlers to access. And for the Everglades it is high ground. The long shell ridge was formed by the wave action of the Gulf of Mexico. In pre-park days, this high land was farmed by the Rewis family, but it has reverted to what seems an undisturbed coastline.

The beach starts at the northern edge of the bay formed by the Rodgers and Broad Rivers. The beach continues north and becomes higher the

An "Everglades portage" at Highland Beach. Photo by W. W. Armstrong

farther north you go. A grass prairie backs the sand and is dotted with cabbage palm, Spanish bayonet, and an occasional Jamaica dogwood and cactus. Mangrove guards the back side of the prairie. Palms grow thickest at the beach's edge where the sand is highest. Finally, the sandy shore gives way to mangrove a couple of miles north of the bay.

Beware of the shallow approach to the beach on a low tide. Conversely, you may be left high and dry at this campsite until the tide has risen sufficiently to allow your departure. Due to this shallow water and to its distance from either Everglades departure point, this campsite is not heavily used. Expect to see a few motorboats zipping around the vicinity, though.

Rodgers River

Type of campsite: Chickee	Landing: Dock
Scenery: 3	Use: Medium
Max. # of campers: 12	Max. # of parties: 2 Max. # of nights: 1
Fires: No	Toilet: Yes

On which route: Willy Willy Route, Cabbage Island Shortcut, Rodgers River Route, Toms Creek Route

Nearby connecting routes: Willy Willy Route, Cabbage Island Shortcut, Rodgers River Route, Toms Creek Route
Nearby campsites: Willy Willy

Rodgers River is a double chickee located a mile west of the Wilderness Waterway in the south portion of Rodgers River Bay. Since it is situated in the dead center of the Everglades paddling area, canoeists and sea kayakers must put forth considerable effort to get to it.

The view from here may be worth it. All of Rodgers River Bay lies before you to the south, the direction in which the chickee faces. Behind you is a shallow inlet. The mangrove shoreline is more than 40 feet distant, making bug problems minimal. Conversely, you had better weight down your gear because if the wind blows there is little to block it. I once spent a cold rainy evening huddling behind my tent while cooking and eating dinner.

The platforms are 11 by 13 feet and have gangways leading to a common vault toilet. The shelter overhead will provide some shade, but a south-facing chickee bears the brunt of the sun. If you share the site at all, you will more than likely be sharing it with fellow paddlers.

Shark River

Type of campsite: Chickee	Landing: Dock	
Scenery: 3	Use: High	
Max. # of campers: 6	Max. # of parties: 1	Max. # of nights: 1
Fires: No	Toilet: Yes	

On which route: Shark Cutoff Route, The Labyrinth Route, Graveyard Creek Route

Nearby connecting routes: Shark Cutoff Route, The Labyrinth Route, Graveyard Creek Route, Big Sable Route, Cormorant Pass Route

Nearby campsites: Graveyard Creek, Oyster Bay chickee, Watson River chickee

---

Shark River is a vestige of the original chickee system put together by the park service in the 1970s. It is a single 10 by 12–foot camping platform that is backed up against red mangrove on a side creek of the Little Shark River. A slender 2-foot-wide gangway leads to a vault toilet and a small ladder extending into the water. This platform has the least overall square footage of all the chickees.

The chickee's north-facing posture makes this a shady place. The close proximity of the mangrove can result in fewer breezes and more bugs, but only in comparison to other chickees. Overall, it is a quiet, pleasant spot, but its being a single chickee on the Wilderness Waterway can lead to high demand.

The side creek of the Shark River chickee is also the beginning of The Labyrinth. The Graveyard Creek route leads west from here to Graveyard Creek campsite. The Wilderness Waterway continues northeast on the Shark Rivers and southwest through the Shark Cutoff to Whitewater Bay.

Willy Willy

Type of campsite: Ground	Landing: Dock	
Scenery: 4	Use: Low	
Max. # of campers: 10	Max. # of parties: 3	Max. # of nights: 3
Fires: No	Toilet: Yes	

On which route: Willy Willy Route, Rodgers River Bay Route

Nearby connecting routes: Willy Willy Route, Rodgers River Bay Route, Lostmans River Route, Rodgers River Route, Cabbage Island Shortcut, Toms Creek Route

Nearby campsites: Rodgers River chickee

Willy Willy is an old shell mound turned campsite deep in the eastern part of the Everglades paddling area, near the Big Cypress National Preserve. Freshwater creeks are all around this shady hammock of gumbo-limbo, palm, ferns, and dense undergrowth. An L-shaped dock connects the shell mound to the water. Pull your boat alongside the dock and enter the camp. Two picnic tables and a vault toilet add to campers' convenience.

This high mound drains well; it is sloped, by Everglades standards. But Willy Willy does have level tent sites. The campsite is limited in size and crowded in by vegetation, so stay friends with your camping neighbors. On weekends there are likely to be motorboaters who have brought the kitchen sink with them. Try to stay here during the week for a couple of nights to explore the adjacent freshwater creeks, using a topographic map.

Ten Thousand Islands

Darwin's Place

Type of campsite: Ground	Landing: Ground
Scenery: 4	Use: Medium
Max. # of campers: 8	Max. # of parties: 2 Max. # of nights: 3
Fires: No	Toilet: Yes

On which route: Darwin's Place Route

Nearby connecting routes: Chatham River Route, Last Huston Bay Route, Gopher Key Route

Nearby campsites: Sweetwater chickee, Plate Creek chickee

Darwin's Place is a ground camp with a lot of good and a little bit of bad. It is located atop an old Calusa mound by a small creek connecting Chevelier and Cannon Bays. This mound was the home of the last man to homestead in Everglades National Park. Arthur Leslie Darwin was a hermit whose house foundation adorns the site. He moved here in 1945 and grew bananas to sell, living out his days on Possum Key, the common name given the shell mound here. You can still see the outline of his concrete house.

Possum Key was much more open in Darwin's day and has grown in. But the park service has cleared the mound some, eliminating the exotic Brazilian pepper and leaving fig, gumbo-limbo, Simpson stopper, a lone coconut palm, and a few cabbage palms.

Expect fellow campers to be occupying one of the many tent sites here on weekends. If you stay here, consider a layover day or a short day to explore Gopher Key, via the Gopher Key Route.

Hog Key

Type of campsite: Beach   Landing: Beach
Scenery: 5   Use: Medium
Max. # of campers: 8   Max. # of parties: 2 Max. # of nights: 2
Fires: Yes   Toilet: No
On which route: Turkey Key Route
Nearby connecting routes: Lostmans River Route, Highland Beach Route
Nearby campsites: Turkey Key, New Turkey Key

Hog Key is really not an island, but a peninsula jutting out into the Gulf of Mexico. From shallows in the water, the beach slopes up more than 6 feet to a narrow plain of prickly pear cactus, sea oats, and grass. Behind

Horseshoe crabs on the beach at Hog Key. Photo by author

this is an extensive forest of sea grape, cabbage palm, and some of the largest Spanish bayonet I have ever seen. Look for the giant tamarind tree spreading its branches over the campsite. Your view is of Wood Key and the Plover Keys.

It may be hard to find a perfectly level tent site here, but you will certainly be above the high-tide line. Speaking of tides, try to time your arrival with a rising tide, as the shallow approach can make this a hard camp to get to at the same time it makes it the domain of sea kayakers and canoers.

This area was settled by Richard Hamilton in the early 1900s. He ran hogs here, but the swines' diet of oysters and crabs left them inedible. To make them edible, the hogs were changed to a diet of table scraps, which made their flesh more tolerable. Wild hogs are still here today—I've seen one while camped here.

Kingston Key

Type of campsite: Chickee   Landing: Dock

Scenery: 4   Use: Medium

Max. # of campers: 6   Max. # of parties: 2   Max. # of nights: 1

Fires: No   Toilet: Yes

On which route: Indian Key Pass Route, Pavilion Key Route

Nearby connecting routes: Indian Key Pass Route, Pavilion Key Route, West Pass Route

Nearby campsites: Picnic Key, Tiger Key

Kingston Key chickee has a design very different from that of most other chickees. It is also novel in other ways. For starters, it is the only chickee in the Gulf of Mexico. It began its existence as a dock for campers staying at Kingston Key. As can happen over time, Kingston Key shifted, leaving the park service with a dock beside an island in a bay. A camping platform was added to the dock, and Kingston Key chickee was born. It now lies nearly 100 feet from the west side of the island in a lagoon. Across the

Kingston Key chickee from Kingston Key. Photo by W. W. Armstrong

water are Indian Key and Indian Key Pass. A beach on Kingston Key nearby is unsuitable for camping because it is often submerged at higher tides.

The north-facing camping platform is 50 by 10 feet and is covered by two 20 by 10–foot roofs. The center portion of the spacious platform is open. Three ladders extend into the water. The old dock supports a vault toilet.

Lopez River

Type of campsite: Ground	Landing: Ground	
Scenery: 3	Use: High	
Max. # of campers: 12	Max. # of parties: 3	Max. # of nights: 2
Fires: No	Toilet: Yes	
On which route: Lopez River Route		
Nearby connecting routes: Last Huston Bay Route, Hurddles Creek Route, Rabbit Key Pass Route		
Nearby campsites: Sunday Bay chickee		

Lopez River campsite is an old shell mound first occupied by the Calusa and later by Gregorio Lopez, who came to the area in the 1890s. The boat landing is actually part of the shell mound that extends into the river. There are a few small landing spots, but the primary landing is right in front of an old cistern, one of the remains of the Lopez place. The year "1892" appears on part of the cistern right by the river. Mangrove fronts the rest of the campsite. Modern amenities include several picnic tables and a vault toilet, located near the cistern.

The ground here is high and dry. Shady tent sites are located beneath a large buttonwood and a few gumbo-limbo trees upriver of the cistern. Another more isolated tent site is below the cistern near an old tamarind tree. Dense thickets that include the shrub blackbead enclose the main camping area away from the river, but the shell mound extends in both directions along the Lopez.

Lostmans Five

Type of campsite: Ground	Landing: Dock	
Scenery: 3	Use: Low	
Max. # of campers: 15	Max. # of parties: 3	Max. # of nights: 3
Fires: No	Toilet: Yes	
On which route: Darwin's Place Route, Willy Willy Route		
Nearby connecting routes: Darwin's Place Route, Willy Willy Route, Lostmans River Route		
Nearby campsites: Plate Creek chickee		

The Lostmans Five ground site is very low and is noted for being muddy at times. And it can be, but the setting is attractive. Most of the ground sites in the interior are blocked from a water view by heavy vegetation. But Lostmans Five is right on the water, and about half the campsite looks over Lostmans Five Bay at the mouth of Lostmans Creek. A T-shaped dock extends into the water for easy landing. There is a vault toilet on the dock. Picnic tables make the campsite more user friendly.

Buttonwood, ferns, and small bushes such as saffron plum surround the mostly open part of the campsite that doesn't abut the bay. A few palm trees break up the open area. Even though the site is open, shaded tent sites are available on the camp's perimeter.

Concrete blocks and old pilings indicate a previous presence, perhaps from the Poinciana land operation, headquartered on nearby Onion Key. In the 1920s, potential land buyers were driven to Pinecrest, off the Tamiami Trail, and then walked to a canoe landing at Lostmans Five, where they boated about a mile to Onion Key. This spot is very likely the canoe landing. The 1926 hurricane ended the Poinciana development. Lostmans Five was later a site for a cabin on stilts.

The potential muddiness of the site scares off a lot of campers, so you will likely have the camp to yourself, especially during the week. If it hasn't rained lately, I recommend this camp. Take some time to paddle toward the freshwater Glades up Lostmans Five Creek.

Mormon Key

Type of campsite: Beach	Landing: Beach	
Scenery: 4	Use: High	
Max. # of campers: 12	Max. # of parties: 2	Max. # of nights: 3
Fires: Yes	Toilet: No	

On which route: Pavilion Key Route, Huston River Route, Chatham River Route, Turkey Key Route

Nearby connecting routes: Pavilion Key Route, Huston River Route, Chatham River Route, Turkey Key Route

Nearby campsites: Pavilion Key, New Turkey Key, Watson's Place

Mormon Key lies at the mouth of the Chatham River in an area occupied for a long time and known as Chatham Bend. The Calusa stayed here; you can see their broken conch and clam shells. Later the site was occupied by white settlers, one of whom lived here with his first and second wives simultaneously, which gave it the name Mormon Key. At low tide, concrete remnants of a dock can be seen at the west point of the island.

The northwest-facing beach here is high but small. A grass, cactus, and brush field parallels the beach. Behind this clearing are buttonwood, sea grape, and mangrove. Other hammock species are in the interior of the island. This signed key has several flat tent sites, but they are mostly out in the open, affording little privacy if you have neighbors. This openness allows views across Chatham Bend to the mouth of the Chatham River, Gun Rock Point, Pavilion Key, and other points north.

Even though the beach is small, you can stretch your legs by circling Mormon Key at low tide. Watch out for sharp clumps of oysters. It's interesting to think of this island comprising the limits of your home—two houses stood here until 1960, when they were flattened by Hurricane Donna.

New Turkey Key

Type of campsite: Beach	Landing: Beach	
Scenery: 4	Use: High	
Max. # of campers: 10	Max. # of parties: 2	Max. # of nights: 2
Fires: Yes	Toilet: Yes	
On which route: Turkey Key Route		
Nearby connecting routes: Pavilion Key Route, Huston River Route, Chatham River Route		
Nearby campsites: Mormon Key, Turkey Key		

New Turkey Key campsite lies in the center of a very slender, small island at the extreme south end of the Ten Thousand Islands. The north tip of New Turkey faces the mainland and is sandy, but it is subject to flooding when high tides and winds mix. I found this out the hard way—do not camp here. The center portion of the island is buffered with black mangrove and a little sea grape. Access can be from both the Gulf and the mainland side of the island. I recommend the mainland side, as a deep channel runs beside the island here. The primary tent sites here are in a grassy area by the vault toilet. There is another isolated tent site on a grassy flat punctuated with Spanish bayonet on the south end of the key.

This small key has a two-party limit. On weekdays you will usually have it to yourself. Expect motorboat campers on weekends—they like the deep channel that allows them to pull their boats close to shore without leaving them stranded in the shallows.

Pavilion Key

Type of campsite: Beach	Landing: Beach	
Scenery: 5	Use: High	
Max. # of campers: 20	Max. # of parties: 4	Max. # of nights: 3
Fires: Yes	Toilet: Yes	
On which route: Pavilion Key Route		
Nearby connecting routes: Chatham River Route, Huston River Route, Rabbit key Pass Route		
Nearby campsites: Rabbit Key, Mormon Key		

Pavilion Key is the largest island campsite in the Everglades Ten Thousand Islands. The primary camping area is on the northern tip of the island, where a long sandy spit extends out from the forested part of the island. Vegetation on the peninsula includes sea oats, grass, and a couple

Dusky campfire at Pavilion Key. Photo by W. W. Armstrong

of buttonwoods. There is not much shade here. On the plus side are the ocean views and breezes from both sides of the spit. But if the wind is gusty, your tent could be blown away.

Farther from the spit is a beach area that is forested on its south side by sea grape, sea hibiscus, mangrove, and a tangle of vines. This growth acts as a buffer that slows some winds, especially from the south. There are some tent sites along this stretch of beach, where you can also beachcomb a fair distance.

If you are looking for solitude, don't come here. This is a large-capacity campsite, as is evidenced by its having two vault toilets. It is a popular site for paddlers and some motorboaters, because it is far out in the Gulf and has such a large beach. This popularity is not lost on Pavilion's raccoons, who lurk under cover of darkness to steal food and water. Store your goods appropriately.

Picnic Key

Type of campsite: Beach	Landing: Beach	
Scenery: 5	Use: High	
Max. # of campers: 16	Max. # of parties: 3	Max. # of nights: 3
Fires: Yes	Toilet: Yes	

On which route: Indian Key Pass Route, West Pass Route, Pavilion Key Route

Nearby connecting routes: Indian Key Pass Route, West Pass Route, Pavilion Key Route

Nearby campsites: Tiger Key, Kingston Key chickee

Picnic Key campsite is located in the heart of the Ten Thousand Islands, 7 miles from the Gulf Coast Ranger Station, just north of Indian Key Pass. Most of the U-shaped island is mangrove, but a southwest-facing beach makes it a camping pleasure. A park service sign marks the beach; the only other park presence is a vault toilet. This beach runs more than 100 yards in length and is backed by sea oats, palms, and a multitude of sea grape trees. Some mangrove is mixed among these trees, as is sea hibis-

Campfires are allowed at beach campsites like Picnic Key. Photo by W. W. Armstrong

cus and Jamaica dogwood. In pre-park days, residents of Chokoloskee used to come to Picnic Key in the fall to harvest sea grapes, spreading their blankets under the trees and shaking the fruits from them, turning the event into a picnic. Later, they turned the sea grapes into a tasty jam.

Your view from this busy camp is of the Gulf of Mexico and nearby Tiger Key to the west and the Stop Keys to the south. Welcome morning shade is provided by the woods east of the beach. A word of caution: Be careful while wading or swimming near the beach—there are a few rocks here.

Plate Creek

Type of campsite: Chickee	Landing: Dock	
Scenery: 4	Use: Medium	
Max. # of campers: 6	Max. # of parties: 1	Max. # of nights: 1
Fires: No	Toilet: Yes	
On which route: Darwin's Place Route		
Nearby connecting routes: Willy Willy Route, Lostmans River Route		
Nearby campsites: Lostmans Five		

Plate Creek is the most unusual chickee in the park. It is a single unit with more room than most double chickees. It was built on the pilings of an old land development office. The large pilings of the shaded portion of the platform are from an old water tower that fed the various floating buildings here. Park chickee builders used these and other leftover pilings imaginatively. First, they built a 50 by 4–foot dock with a vault toilet at one end. A short gangway leads to the main platform. This platform, 20 by 14 feet, is only partly covered, but it is more than adequate for a paddler's tent. Spread your gear out on the rest of the platform and walk the dock to stretch your legs.

Plate Creek chickee is located on the east side of an island in the center of Plate Creek Bay, which is graced with lots of palms. Since the chickee is backed up against this island, the island stops a cold northwest wind but allows possible insect and critter problems. Store your food with care.

Rabbit Key

Type of campsite: Beach   Landing: Beach
Scenery: 4   Use: High
Max. # of campers: 8   Max. # of parties: 2   Max. # of nights: 2
Fires: Yes   Toilet: Yes
On which route: Rabbit Key Pass Route, Pavilion Key Route
Nearby connecting routes: Rabbit Key Pass Route, Pavilion Key Route
Nearby campsites: Pavilion Key

Rabbit Key, an island campsite, is located at the southern end of the Ten Thousand Islands adjacent to the Gulf of Mexico, but the primary camping area faces north and east, toward the mainland. In view are Lumber and Crate Keys, and an unnamed key across a lagoon from the camp. Expect to share Rabbit Key with other campers on weekends and most weekdays. It is popular for its scenic blend of sand and trees.

The primary camping area is limited in space. It is on a small beach backed with grass and mangrove beside a tiny rill that drains a pond in the center of the island. There is another tent site south of the island's vault toilet, under some trees by the grass, sea purslane, and prickly pear cactus. The west side of the island has a couple of shaded tent sites that can be used when the weather is cool and windy—otherwise these spots will be too buggy.

Sunday Bay

Type of campsite: Chickee	Landing: Dock	
Scenery: 3	Use: High	
Max. # of campers: 12	Max. # of parties: 2	Max. # of nights: 1
Fires: No	Toilet: Yes	
On which route: Hurddles Creek Route, Huston Bay Route		
Nearby connecting routes: Lopez River Route, Huston River Route, Last Huston Bay Route		
Nearby campsites: Lopez River		

Sunday Bay chickee is an excellent first night's destination from Chokoloskee. It is not too far to paddle and is one of the larger double chickees, with a special treat for one of the two groups that can stay here. This south-facing platform is located one-half mile from the Wilderness Waterway on the north edge of a small bay that splinters off larger Sunday Bay. The close proximity of Chokoloskee and the Wilderness Waterway make it a popular camping destination, so expect to have company, especially on weekends.

The two 11 by 13–foot shaded platforms are connected to a central vault toilet by 4-foot-wide gangways. One of the platforms has the added bonus of a bench seat built along its north edge, where campers can sit and overlook the bay. The first campers to arrive at the chickee always take this platform. The whole structure lies a good 30 feet distant from the mangrove, making for fewer bugs.

Sweetwater

Type of campsite: Chickee   Landing: Dock

Scenery: 4   Use: High

Max. # of campers: 12   Max. # of parties: 2   Max. # of nights: 1

Fires: No   Toilet: Yes

On which route: Chatham River Route

Nearby connecting routes: Last Huston Bay Route, Darwin's Place Route

Nearby campsites: Watson's Place, Darwin's Place

Sweetwater chickee is off the beaten path. It is two miles up Sweetwater Creek, off the Wilderness Waterway, near the Chatham River. *You cannot access Sweetwater chickee via Last Huston Bay, only from Sweetwater Creek.* The mouth of Sweetwater Creek is narrow and hard to find, but once you get here, this camping platform will reward your determination. Few motorboaters use this area, since the creek ends toward the freshwater Glades and is not on a commonly traveled waterway, making it a quiet setting.

Sea kayakers load up at Sweetwater chickee. Photo by W. W. Armstrong

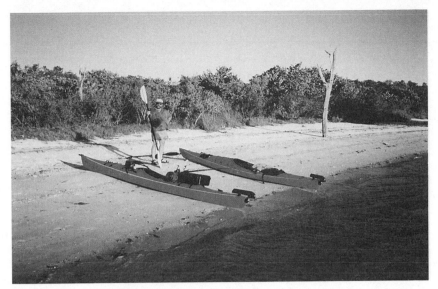

Bill Armstrong after landing at Tiger Key. Photo by author

The camping platforms are 12 by 13 feet and are connected to a common vault toilet by 5-foot-wide gangways. Situated in a lagoon of the creek, the chickee faces south. A palm-topped island is nearby, but not too close, just like the rest of the shore. The 50 feet of water between the camping platform and the mangrove minimizes insect problems. Tidal variations are small this far from the Gulf, making loading your craft easier.

Tiger Key

Type of campsite: Beach   Landing: Beach
Scenery: 5   Use: High
Max. # of campers: 12   Max. # of parties: 3   Max. # of nights: 3
Fires: Yes   Toilet: No
On which route: West Pass Route
Nearby connecting routes: Indian Key Pass Route, Pavilion Key Route
Nearby campsites: Picnic Key, Kingston Key chickee

Tiger Key is the most northerly of all the campsites in the Everglades National Park. It is a west-facing beach camp on the outer edge of the Ten Thousand Islands. No matter which way you access this key, you must paddle out to the Gulf side of the island to a shallow cove where the campsite is located, near the island's center. Try to avoid low tide when approaching this camp, or you may have to portage your boat and gear a fair distance to the key.

A sign marks the long beach where campers stay. Two skeleton trees rise from the white sand. To find a tent site above the high-tide line, you may have to sleep at an angle on the sloping sand or set up in the grass, which is dotted with prickly pear cactus. Behind this grass is dense brush, occasional sea grape, buttonwood, and a lot of mangrove. Occasional mangrove interrupts the beach. Your view is of the expansive Gulf, Camp Lulu Key, and the Ten Thousand Islands Wildlife Refuge.

Turkey Key

Type of campsite: Beach	Landing: Beach	
Scenery: 4	Use: Medium	
Max. # of campers: 12	Max. # of parties: 3	Max. # of nights: 3
Fires: Yes	Toilet: No	
On which route: Turkey Key Route		
Nearby connecting routes: Chatham River Route, Pavilion Key Route, Huston River Route		
Nearby campsites: New Turkey Key, Mormon Key		

Turkey Key is a beach campsite on a mangrove island a little south of the Chatham River. Running north-south, the island is just a short distance off the mainland. The primary camping areas are on a west-facing beach marked with a park service sign. Other, smaller camping sites are located farther south and on the south tip of the island.

Vegetation is mostly mangrove, with scattered growths of sea hibiscus and sea grape. Grass and sea oats stabilize the beach areas, which are broken by mangrove extending to the water. Be apprised of the shallow approach to the key; if the tide is out, you will be carrying your gear to the beach. This is what is known as an Everglades "portage." The shallow approach makes it mostly a paddlers' campsite. While on the beach, note the amazing quantity of clam and conch shells. The preponderance of shells suggests a commercial operation in times past. Turkey Key was once the site of fishing shacks and was a rendezvous point for fishermen and their suppliers.

Watson's Place

Type of campsite: Ground   Landing: Dock

Scenery: 3   Use: High

Max. # of campers: 20   Max. # of parties: 5   Max. # of nights: 2

Fires: No   Toilet: Yes

On which route: Chatham River Route

Nearby connecting routes: Last Huston Bay Route, Darwin's Place Route, Huston River Route

Nearby campsites: Sweetwater chickee, Mormon Key

Watson's Place campsite lies on the north bank of the Chatham River, about 3 miles inland from the Gulf. It was once a thriving cane and vegetable farm of 35 acres, on an old Indian shell mound. The farm, known as Chatham Bend, was operated by the notorious Ed Watson, who murdered several people on the site. Now, the cleared area is less than an acre, but you can see the remains of a syrup kettle, a cistern, and farm implements. Determined explorers who venture through the thickets to see more evidence of Watson's operation should be aware that the bodies of several Watson victims were never found. . . .

Others lived here after Watson, but the park service let the place grow over. A T-shaped dock has a walkway that connects the land to a long landing where boats can tie up. There is also a vault toilet on the dock. A shell landing lies on the far side of a buttonwood and a Jamaica dogwood tree fronting the river. These trees provide one of the few shady spots at this campsite, with the exception of a tamarind tree by the tall part of the mound, where Watson's house was. Dense brush borders the other sides of the campsite, which has picnic tables.

With the campsite's capacity of 5 parties or 20 campers, expect company here, especially on weekends. And if you are here by yourself, don't be surprised if the spirits of Watson's victims keep you company, whispering in the wind.

Appendix

Route Chart

This chart combines the numerical information given at the beginning of each route description. "Wind" is potential wind influence. "Tide" is potential tide influence. "Nav" is navigational challenge on a scale of 1 to 5, 1 being low and 5 being high.

Route	Start	End	Miles	Wind	Tide	Nav
Florida Bay						
Dildo Key Bank Route	Little Rabbit Key	Flamingo	12.5	5	5	3
East Cape Route	Flamingo	East Cape	10	5	5	2
First National Bank Route	Flamingo	Carl Ross Key	10	5	5	3
Man of War Route	Carl Ross Key	Little Rabbit Key	13.5	5	5	3
North Nest Key Loop	Key Largo	Key Largo	16	4	5	3
Snake Bight Route	Alligator Creek	Flamingo	12	4	5	3
Cape Sable, Whitewater Bay, and the South						
Bear Lake Canoe Trail	Buttonwood Canal	East Cape	10.5	3	2	1
Big Sable Route	Northwest Cape	Oyster Bay chickee	13	5	5	2
Buttonwood Canal Route	Flamingo	CG marker #10	5	2	2	1
Cormorant Pass Route	Joe River chickee	Watson River chickee	12	3	4	3
The Cutoff Route	Roberts River chickee	Watson River chickee	6	3	4	3
East River Route	CG marker #10	Hells Bay chickee	5.5	2	4	3
Hells Bay Canoe Trail	Main Park Road	Hells Bay chickee	6	1	2	1
Joe River Route	CG marker #10	Joe River chickee	12	3	3	2
The Labyrinth Route	Watson River chickee	Shark River chickee	6	2	1	5
Lane River Route	Confluence Roberts R./Lane R.	Hells Bay chickee	5	2	3	3
Middle Cape Route	East Cape	Northwest Cape	9.5	5	5	2
Mud Lake Loop	Main Park Road	Main Park Road	7	2	3	2
Nine Mile Pond Loop	Main Park Road	Main Park Road	5.2	1	3	1
Noble Hammock Loop	Main Park Road	Main Park Road	2	1	2	1
North River Route	CG marker # 32	Cutoff at North River	4.5	2	3	2

Route Chart—continued

Route	Start	End	Miles	Wind	Tide	Nav
Roberts River Route	CG marker #18	Roberts R. Chickee	5.5	2	4	2
West Lake Canoe Trail	Main Park Road	Garfield Bight	8.5	2	2	3
Whitewater Bay Route	CG marker #10	CG marker #40	12	2	5	1
The Central Rivers Area						
Broad River Route	Gulf	Camp Lonesome	11.5	4	3	2
Cabbage Island Shortcut	Rodgers River chickee	Broad River	3.5	2	2	3
Graveyard Creek Route	Shark River chickee	Graveyard Creek	7	4	3	3
Harney River Route	Canepatch	Gulf	13.5	4	3	2
Highland Beach Route	Lostmans Ranger Station	Graveyard Creek	13	4	5	2
Lostmans River Route	WW marker #52	Lostmans Ranger Station	6	4	3	2
The Nightmare Route	Broad River campsite	Harney River chickee	8.5	2	2	4
North Harney River Route	WW marker #11	Canepatch	10.5	4	3	4
Ponce De Leon Bay Route	Shark River Island	Graveyard Creek	4	4	5	2
Rodgers River Route	Gulf	Rodgers River chickee	10.5	3	3	3
Rodgers River Bay Route	Willy Willy	WW #26 at Broad R. Bay	7	2	3	3
Shark Cutoff Route	WW marker #9 @ Tarpon Bay	Oyster Bay chickee	7.5	4	2	2
Toms Creek Route	Rodgers River chickee	Lostmans River	7	3	3	3
Wood River Route	Camp Lonesome	Broad River	10	2	2	2
Ten Thousand Islands						
Causeway Route	Chokoloskee	Gulf Coast Ranger Station	3	4	3	2
Chatham River Route	Mormon Key	Sweetwater Bay chickee	7.5	4	3	3

Route	From	To					
Darwin's Place Route	WW marker # 99 @ Chatham R.	Lostmans Five	9.5	2	2	4	2
Gopher Key Route	Darwin's Place	Gopher Key	3	2	2	2	3
Halfway Creek Canoe Trail	Tamiami Trail	Gulf Coast Ranger Station	7.5	3	3	2	3
Hurddles Creek Route	Chokoloskee	Sunday Bay chickee	7	3	3	2	3
Huston River Route	WW marker #119 @ Sunday B.	Mormon Key	9	4	4	4	2
Indian Key Pass Route	Gulf Coast Ranger Station	Picnic Key	7	5	3	3	2
Last Huston Bay Route	Sunday Bay chickee	WW marker # 99 at Chatham R.	7	2	2	4	2
Lopez River Route	Chokoloskee	WW marker #125 at Crooked C.	7	3	3	4	2
Pavilion Key Route	Picnic Key	Mormon Key	15.5	5	5	5	3
Rabbit Key Pass Route	Rabbit Key	Chokoloskee	5.5	4	4	4	2
Sandfly Island Route	Gulf Coast Ranger Station	Sandfly Island	2	3	3	4	1
Turkey Key Route	Mormon Key	Lostmans Ranger Station	11	5	5	5	2
Turner River Canoe Trail	Tamiami Trail	Chokoloskee	8.5	3	3	2	4
West Pass Route	Gulf Coast Ranger Station	Picnic Key	8.5	4	4	4	4
Willy Willy Route	Lostmans Five	Willy Willy	9.5	3	3	4	4

Campsite Chart

This chart combines information for the backcountry campsites in the paddling region of the Everglades National Park. The length-of-stay limits indicated apply to peak-use season, November through April. Campsite capacities apply year-round. Campsite capacities are subject to change; check at a ranger station before departing. Campsites must be vacated by noon.

Campsite	Type of Site	# of people	# of parties	# of nights	Toilet	Table	Dock	Use
Florida Bay								
Alligator Creek	Ground	8	3	2				L
Carl Ross Key	Beach	12	4	2				M
Little Rabbit Key	Ground	12	4	2	*	*	*	L
North Nest Key	Beach	25	7	7	*	*		M
Shark Point	Ground	8	1	3				L
Cape Sable, Whitewater Bay, and the South								
Clubhouse Beach	Beach	24	4	3				L
East Cape	Beach	60	15	7				M
East Clubhouse Beach	Beach	24	4	3				L
Hells Bay	Chickee	12	2	1	*	*		H
Joe River	Chickee	12	2	1	*	*		H
Lane Bay	Chickee	6	1	1	*	*		M
Lard Can	Ground	10	4	2	*			L
Middle Cape	Beach	60	15	7				M
North River	Chickee	6	1	1	*	*		M
Northwest Cape	Beach	36	9	7				M
Oyster Bay	Chickee	12	2	2	*	*		H
Pearl Bay	Chickee	12	2	1	*	*		H
Roberts River	Chickee	12	2	1	*	*		M

Campsite Chart—continued

Campsite	Type of Site	# of people	# of parties	# of nights	Toilet	Table	Dock	Use
South Joe River	Chickee	12	2	1	*	*		H
Watson River	Chickee	6	1	1	*	*		H
The Central Rivers Area								
Broad River	Ground	10	3	2	*	*	*	L
Camp Lonesome	Ground	10	3	3	*	*	*	L
Canepatch	Ground	12	4	3	*	*	*	M
Graveyard Creek	Ground	12	4	3	*	*		M
Harney River	Chickee	6	1	1	*	*		H
Highland Beach	Beach	24	4	3				M
Rodgers River	Chickee	12	2	1	*	*		M
Shark River	Chickee	6	1	1	*	*		H
Willy Willy	Ground	10	3	3	*	*	*	L
Ten Thousand Islands								
Darwin's Place	Ground	8	2	3	*	*		M
Hog Key	Beach	8	2	2				L

Site	Type							Rating
Kingston Key	Chickee	12	2	1	*	*		M
Lopez River	Ground	12	3	2	*	*		H
Lostmans Five	Ground	15	3	3	*	*	*	L
Mormon Key	Beach	12	2	3				M
New Turkey Key	Beach	10	2	2	*			H
Pavilion Key	Beach	20	4	3				H
Picnic Key	Beach	16	3	3				H
Plate Creek	Chickee	6	1	1	*	*		M
Rabbit Key	Beach	8	2	2				H
Sunday Bay	Chickee	12	2	1	*	*		H
Sweetwater	Chickee	12	2	1	*	*		H
Tiger Key	Beach	12	3	3				H
Turkey Key	Beach	12	3	3				M
Watson's Place	Ground	20	5	2	*	*	*	H

Paddler's Checklist

____   Coast Guard–approved life vest

____   Paddles, with spare for each person in boat

____   Bailer

____   Bow and stern lines

____   Waterproof bags for gear

____   Flares

____   Light for operating at night

____   Waterproof nautical chart

____   Compass, with spare

____   Tide chart

____   Binoculars

____   Backcountry permit

____   Fishing license and regulations

____   Weather forecast

____   Freestanding tent with no-see-um netting

____   Sleeping bag comfort rated to 40

____   Sleeping pad

____   Water—one gallon per person per day

____   Food, with extra day's supply

____   Raccoon-proof storage container for food and water

____   Portable stove or grill

____   Fuel for stove

____   Waterproof matches and lighter

____   Cooking gear and utensils

____   Biodegradable soap

____   Rain gear

____   Cold- and warm-weather clothing

____   Long-sleeved shirt and long pants for sun protection

____   Wide-brimmed hat

____   First-aid kit

____   Knife, with spare stowed away

____   Wristwatch for calculating tides

____ Sunglasses

____ Sunscreen and chapstick

____ Insect repellent

____ Transistor or weather radio for weather forecasts

____ Personal items—toothbrush, etc.

____ Trowel

____ Biodegradable toilet paper

Boat Rentals and Outfitters

Everglades City:

North American Canoe Tours, Inc.

Post Office Box 5038

Everglades City, FL 34139

(941) 695-3299

www.evergladesadventures.com

These folks rent canoes, kayaks, and gear, lead tours, and provide shuttles. They also offer showers and overnight lodging at Ivey House, which is located adjacent to North American Canoe Tours in Everglades City.

Florida City:

Everglades International Hostel

20 SW 2nd Avenue

Florida City, FL 33034

(305) 372-3874

http://members.xoom.com/gladeshostel

This outfit provides inexpensive lodging and canoe rentals. It's only 15 minutes from the east entrance to Everglades National Park.

Miami:

Jet's Florida Outdoors

9696 Bird Road

Miami, FL 33165

(305) 221-1371

www.jetsfloridaoutdoors.com

This is the most comprehensive outdoor store in the Miami area. It sells every item a paddler can want or need. The staff will also give practical advice for adventuring in the Everglades.

Flamingo:
Flamingo Lodge Marina & Outpost Resort
1 Flamingo Lodge Highway
Flamingo, FL 33034
(941) 695-3101
www.flamingolodge.com
High on convenience and price, this bunch offers canoes and kayaks for rent from the main jumping-off spot for the Southern Everglades. Showers are available as well.

Key Largo:
Florida Bay Outfitters
104050 Overseas Highway
Key Largo, FL 33037
(305) 451-3018
www.pennekamp.com/fbout/
Florida Bay Outfitters is your Keys connection for canoe and kayak rentals. They also sell all paddling gear and boats and offer guided tours of from half a day to a week.

Suggested Reading

Here are other books about the Everglades and surrounding environs that may interest you.

Beach and Coastal Camping in Florida, by Johnny Molloy (University Press of Florida, 1999). This book chronicles the 24 best places to camp and explore the coast of Florida. It simplifies the coastal camping experience on both the Atlantic and Gulf coasts, from the Keys to the Panhandle.

The Everglades: An Environmental History, by David McCally (University Press of Florida, 1999). This is the story of the negative human impact on the Everglades and the attempts to restore the ecosystem to a semblance of its former self.

Fishing the Everglades, by John A. Kumiski (Argonaut Publishing Company, 1993). Angling paddlers will appreciate all the helpful information in this book, which includes detailed information about the species that inhabit the Everglades.

Gladesmen, by Glen Simmons and Laura Ogden (University Press of Florida, 1998). This is a fascinating firsthand account of gator hunter and Everglades explorer Glen Simmons, who rambled much of the park before 1947.

Man in the Everglades, by Charlton W. Tebeau (University of Miami Press, 1964). This book concentrates on the human residents of the Everglades, from the Calusa to the white settlers and Seminoles who lived there before it became a national park.

River of Grass, by Marjory Stoneman Douglas (Mockingbird Books, 1947). This is the Everglades classic that opened the eyes of thousands to the natural wonders and history of the Everglades. The descriptive passages bring the park to life.

Swamp Screamer: At Large with the Florida Panther, by Charles Fergus (University Press of Florida, 1998). This book is an eye-opening account of attempts to save and perpetuate the Florida panther. The tangle of government agencies and private interests of South Florida will give you an idea of how people and public policies affect our wild lands and animals.

Totch, A Life in the Everglades, by Loren G. "Totch" Brown (University Press of Florida, 1993). This book is the firsthand story of an Everglades resident who lived there as a boy and of where life led him after the park was established. His adventures continue into the 1980s.

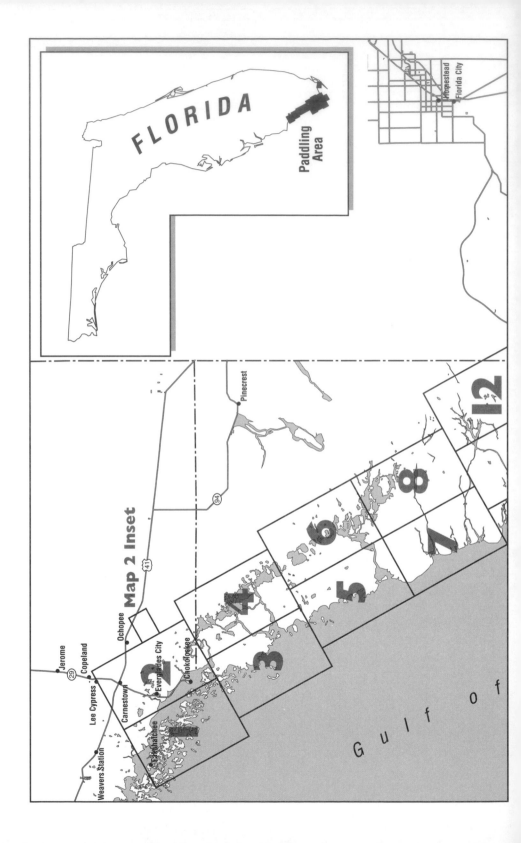

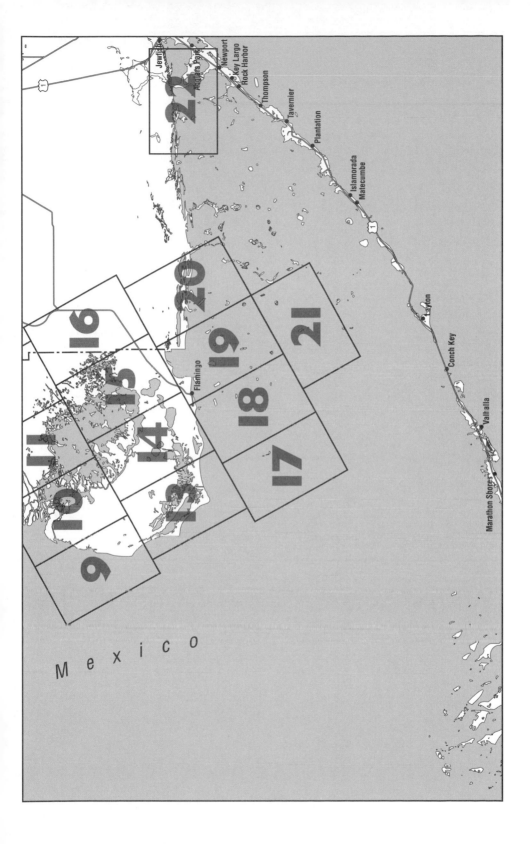

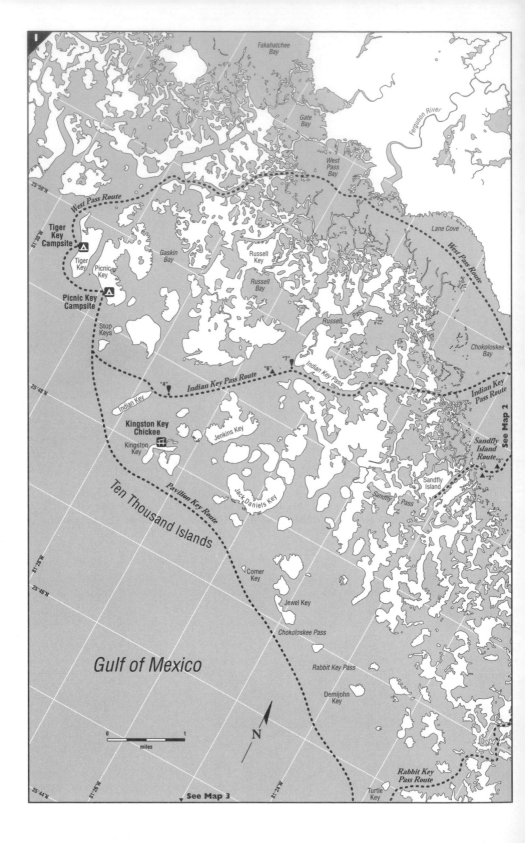

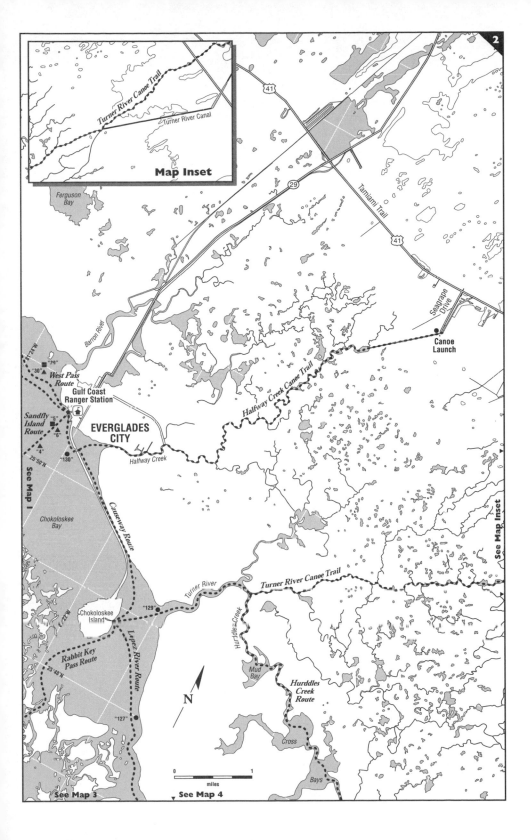

Map Inset

Turner River Canoe Trail

Turner River Canal

Ferguson
Bay

Tamiami Trail

41

29

Barron River

Seagrape
Drive

Canoe
Launch

Halfway Creek Canoe Trail

"29"
"30" ▲ West Pass
Route
Gulf Coast
Ranger Station

Sandfly
Island
Route "5" ▲
"6" ▲
"4" ▲

EVERGLADES
CITY

"130"

Halfway Creek

See Map 1

Chokoloskee
Bay

Causeway Route

Turner River

Turner River Canoe Trail

Chokoloskee
Island

"129"

Hurdle Creek

Rabbit Key
Pass Route

Lopez River Route

25°48'N

"127"

N

Mud
Bay

Hurddles
Creek
Route

Cross

0   1
miles

Bays

See Map 3

See Map 4

See Map Inset

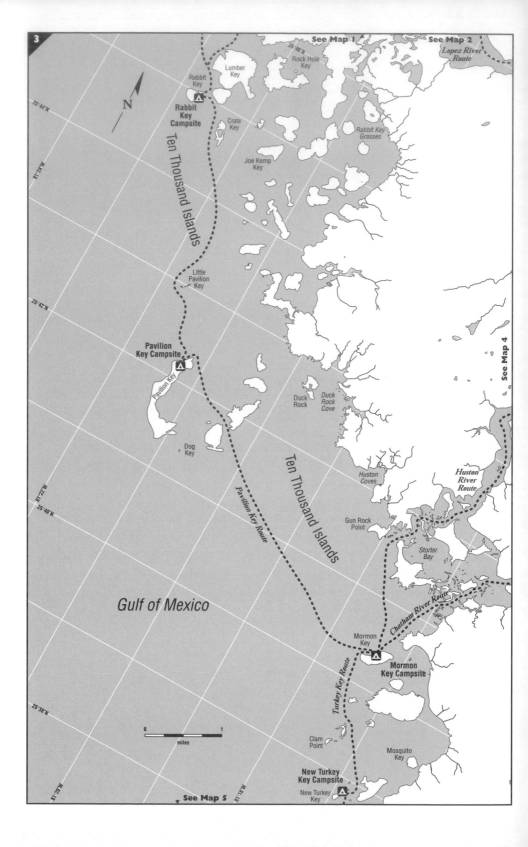

See Map 1
See Map 2

Lopez River Route

25°46'N

Rock Hole Key

Rabbit Key

Lumber Key

Rabbit Key Campsite

Crate Key

Rabbit Key Grasses

25°44'N

81°24'W

N

Joe Kemp Key

Ten Thousand Islands

Little Pavilion Key

25°42'N

Pavilion Key Campsite

Pavilion Key

Duck Rock

Duck Rock Cove

See Map 4

Dog Key

Huston Coves

Huston River Route

81°22'W

25°40'N

Gun Rock Point

Ten Thousand Islands

Pavilion Key Route

Storter Bay

Gulf of Mexico

Chatham River Route

Mormon Key

25°38'N

Mormon Key Campsite

Turkey Key Route

0   1

miles

Clam Point

Mosquito Key

25°36'N

81°20'W

New Turkey Key Campsite

New Turkey Key

81°21'W

See Map 5

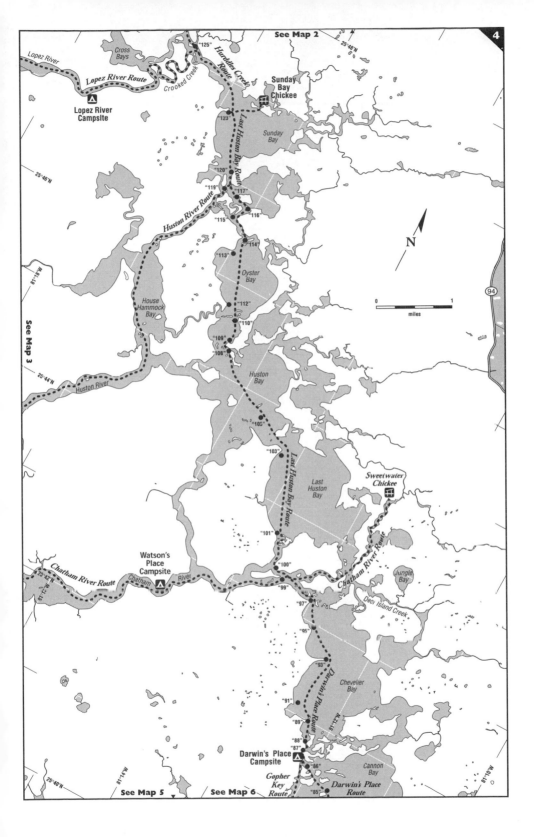

See Map 2

25°48'N

Lopez River

Cross
Bays

Lopez River Route

Crooked Creek

Hurddles Creek Route

"125"

Sunday
Bay
Chickee

Lopez River
Campsite

"123"

Sunday
Bay

25°46'N

"120"

Last Huston Bay Route

"119"

Huston River Route

"117"

"116"

"115"

N

"114"

"113"

Oyster
Bay

House
Hammock
Bay

"112"

"110"

0   1
miles

"109"

"108"

81°18'W

See Map 3

25°44'N

Huston
Bay

Huston River

"105"

"103"

Last Huston Bay Route

Last
Huston
Bay

Sweetwater
Chickee

"101"

Watson's
Place
Campsite

Chatham River Route

"100"

Chatham River Route

Jungle
Bay

25°42'N

81°16'W

Chatham River Route

Chatham   River

"99"

"97"

Deer Island Creek

"95"

Darwin's Place Route

"93"

Chevelier
Bay

"91"

81°16'W

"89"

"88"

"87"

Darwin's Place
Campsite

"86"

Cannon
Bay

81°14'W

25°40'N

81°14'W

Gopher
Key
Route

"85"

Darwin's Place
Route

See Map 5   See Map 6

94

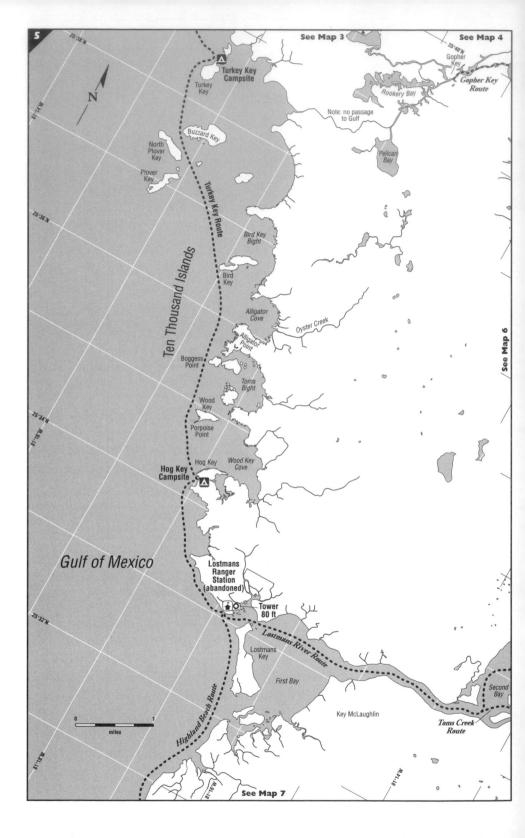

25°38'N

25°40'N
Gopher
Key

*Gopher Key
Route*

△
**Turkey Key
Campsite**

81°14'W

N

Turkey
Key

Rookery Bay

Buzzard Key

Note: no passage
to Gulf

Pelican
Bay

North
Plover
Key

Plover
Key

25°36'N

*Bird Key
Bight*

Ten Thousand Islands

Turkey Key Route

Bird
Key

*Alligator
Cove*

Oyster Creek

*Alligator
Point*

Boggess
Point

81°16'W

*Toms
Bight*

25°34'N

Wood
Key

Porpoise
Point

Hog Key

*Wood Key
Cove*

**Hog Key
Campsite**
△

Gulf of Mexico

**Lostmans
Ranger
Station
(abandoned)**

🏠 ○ **Tower
80 ft**

25°32'N

Lostmans River Route

Lostmans
Key

81°16'W

First Bay

Highland Beach Route

Second
Bay

0   1

miles

Key McLaughlin

*Toms Creek
Route*

81°15'W

81°14'W

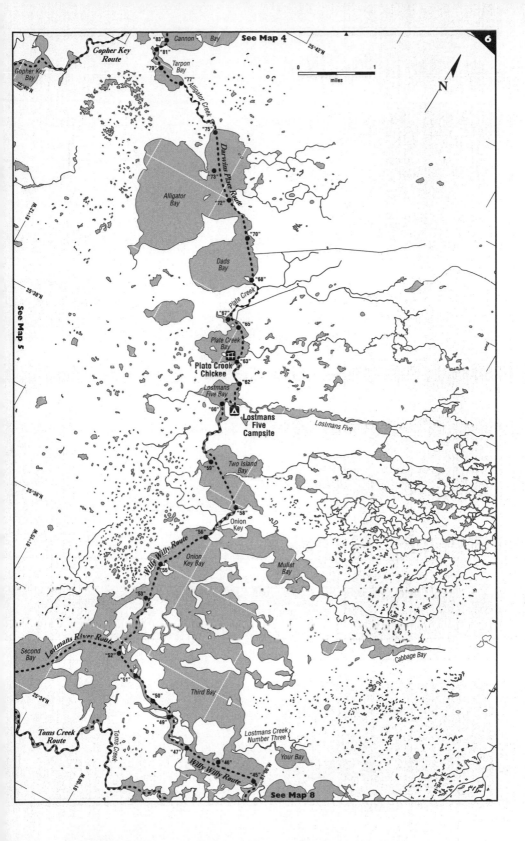

See Map 4

See Map 5

See Map 8

N

0   1
miles

Gopher Key Route

Gopher Key Bay

25°40'N

Cannon Bay

"83"

"81"

"79"

Tarpon Bay

"77"

Alligator Creek

"75"

Darwins Place Route

"73"

"72"

Alligator Bay

"70"

Dads Bay

25°38'N

Plate Creek

"68"

"67"

"65"

Plate Creek Bay

"63"

Plate Creek Chickee

"62"

Lostmans Five Bay

"60"

Lostmans Five Campsite

Lostmans Five

"59"

Two Island Bay

"58"

Onion Key

"56"

Willy Willy Route

Onion Key Bay

55

"53"

Mullet Bay

Cabbage Bay

Lostmans River Route

Second Bay

"52"

"51"

"50"

Third Bay

25°34'N

"49"

Toms Creek Route

"47"

"46"

"45"

Willy Willy Route

Toms Creek

Lostmans Creek Number Three

Your Bay

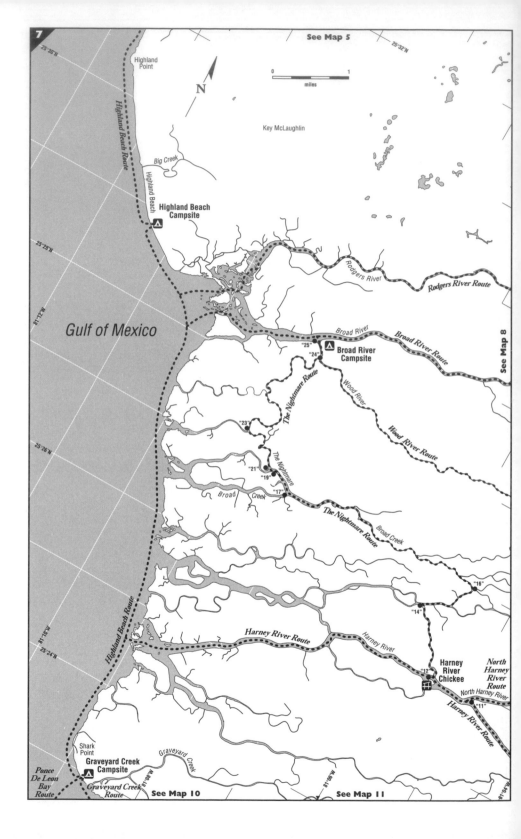

See Map 5

25°30'N

25°32'N

Highland Point

N

0   1
miles

Key McLaughlin

Highland Beach Route

Big Creek

25°28'N

Highland Beach

**Highland Beach
Campsite**

81°32'W

Rodgers River

Rodgers River Route

See Map 8

Gulf of Mexico

Broad River

Broad River Route

"25"

"24"   **Broad River
Campsite**

The Nightmare Route

Wood River

25°26'N

"23"

Wood River Route

"21"

"19"

The Nightmare

"17"

Broad   Creek

The Nightmare Route

Broad Creek

"16"

"14"

Harney River Route

Harney River

25°24'N

81°10'W

81°08'W

**Harney
River
Chickee**

*North
Harney
River
Route*

"12"

North Harney River

Harney River Route

"11"

Shark
Point

**Graveyard Creek
Campsite**

Graveyard   Creek

*Ponce
De Leon
Bay
Route*

Graveyard Creek
Route

81°08'W

81°06'W

See Map 10

See Map 11

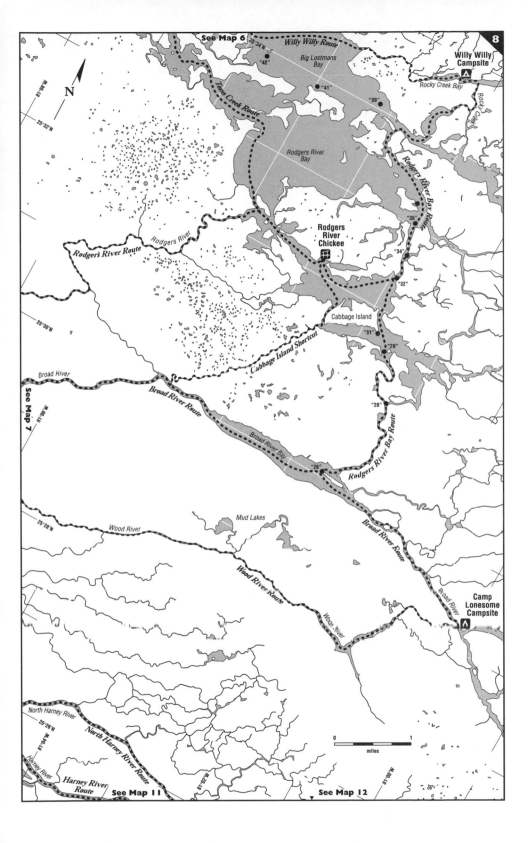

See Map 6

Willy Willy Route

"25°34'N

"42"

Big Lostmans Bay

Willy Willy Campsite

Rocky Creek Bay

Rocky Creek

Tavel Creek Route

"41"

"39"

Rodgers River Bay

Rodgers River Bay Route

"35"

Rodgers River Route

Rodgers River

Rodgers River Chickee

"34"

"32"

25°30'N

Cabbage Island

"31"

Cabbage Island Shortcut

"29"

Broad River

81°38'W

See Map 7

Broad River Route

Broad River Bay

"28"

Broad River Route

Rodgers River Bay Route

"26"

Mud Lakes

25°28'N

Wood River

Wood River Route

Broad River Route

Wood River

Broad River

Camp Lonesome Campsite

North Harney River

25°26'N

North Harney River Route

81°28'W

Harney River

Harney River Route

See Map 11

81°30'W

See Map 12

81°00'W

0   1
miles

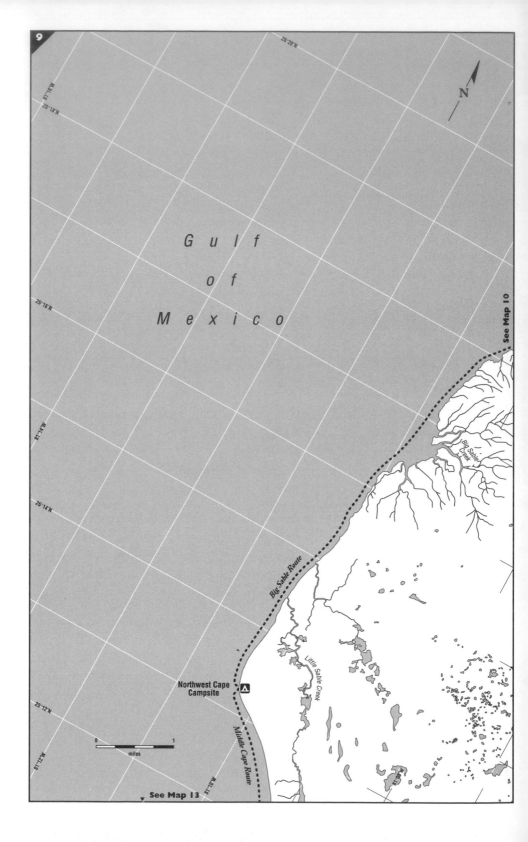

N

28°20'N

25°18'N

G u l f

o f

M e x i c o

25°16'N

25°14'N

See Map 10

Big Sable Creek

Big Sable Route

Little Sable Creek

Middle Cape Route

Northwest Cape Campsite

25°12'N

0   1
miles

See Map 13

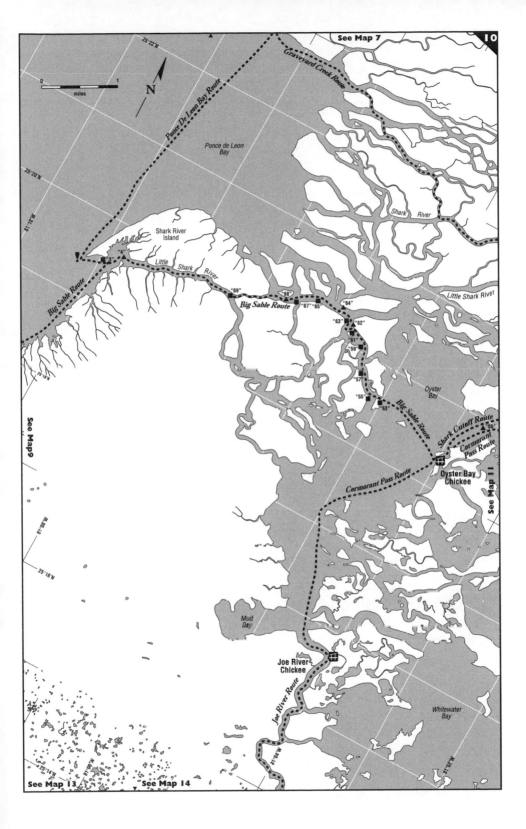

25°22'N

Graveyard Creek Route

Ponce De Leon Bay Route

N

miles

Ponce de Leon
Bay

25°20'N

81°10'W

Shark River

Shark River
Island

25°18'N

Little   Shark   River

Little Shark River

Big Sable Route

"69"

"68"

Big Sable Route

"67" "65"

"64"

"63"

"62"

"61"

"59"

Oyster
Bay

"57"

"55"

81°08'W

"53"

Big Sable Route

Shark Cutoff Route

"50"

Cormorant
Pass Route

See Map9

Oyster Bay
Chickee

Cormorant Pass Route

See Map 11

25°16'N

Mud
Bay

Joe River
Chickee

Joe River Route

Whitewater
Bay

81°06'W

25°14'N

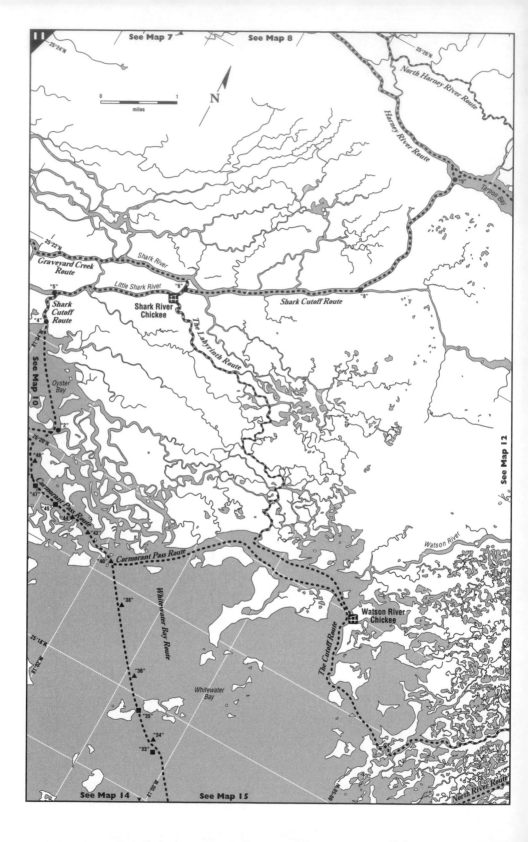

11

25°24'N

25°26'N

North Harney River Route

Harney River Route

Tarpon Bay

"9"

25°22'N

Shark River

Graveyard Creek Route

Little Shark River

"5"   "6"

Shark Cutoff Route   "8"

Shark Cutoff Route

Shark River Chickee

"4"

The Labyrinth Route

See Map 10

Oyster Bay

"2"

See 12

25°20'N

"46"

"47"

Cormorant Pass Route

"45"

"44"

"42"

Watson River

"40"

Cormorant Pass Route

Whitewater Bay Route

Watson River Chickee

"38"

The Cutoff Route

25°18'N

81°20'W

"36"

Whitewater Bay

"35"

"34"

"33"

81°30'W

North River Route

N

0   1
miles

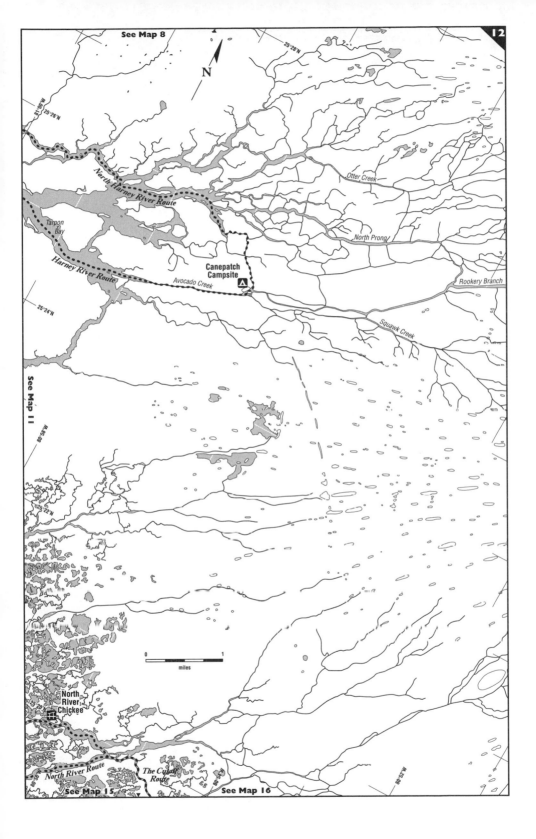

N

12

25°28'N

Otter Creek

North Harney River Route

Tarpon Bay

North Prong

Rookery Branch

Harney River Route

Canepatch
Campsite

Avocado Creek

25°24'N

Squawk Creek

See Map 11

25°22'N

miles
0   1

North
River
Chickee

25°20'

North River Route

The Canal
Route

See Map 15

See Map 16

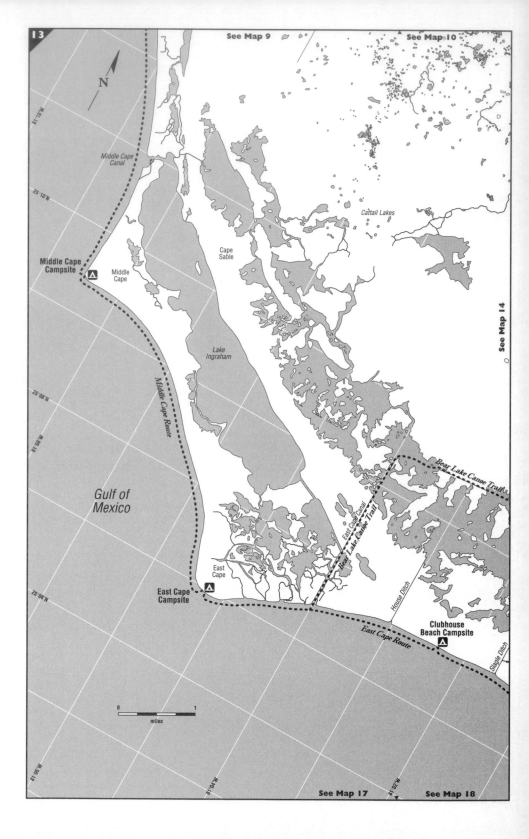

N

See Map 9
See Map 10

Middle Cape
Canal

25°10'N

Cattail Lakes

Cape
Sable

See Map 14

Middle Cape
Campsite

Middle
Cape

Lake
Ingraham

25°08'N

Middle Cape Route

81°11'W

81°10'W

Gulf of
Mexico

Bear Lake Canoe Trail

East Cape Canal

Bear Lake Canoe Trail

25°06'N

East
Cape

East Cape
Campsite

House Ditch

Clubhouse
Beach Campsite

East Cape Route

Slagle Ditch

0   1
miles

81°05'W

81°04'W

81°03'W

81°02'W

See Map 17
See Map 18

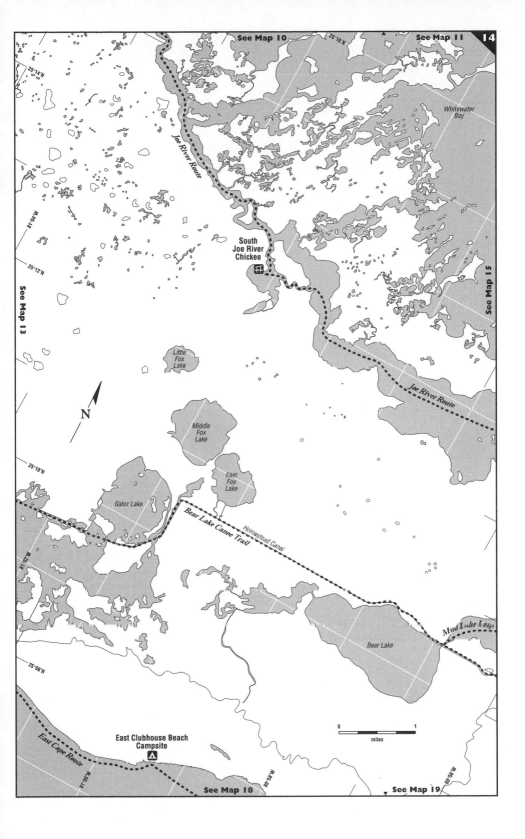

Whitewater
Bay

See Map 15

See Map 13

Joe River Route

South
Joe River
Chickee

Little
Fox
Lake

Joe River Route

N

Middle
Fox
Lake

East
Fox
Lake

Gator Lake

Bear Lake Canoe Trail

Homestead Canal

Bear Lake

Mud Lake Loop

East Cape Route

East Clubhouse Beach
Campsite

0   1
miles

See Map 18

See Map 19

25°14'N

25°12'N

25°10'N

25°08'N

81°04'W

81°02'W

80°58'W

80°56'W

25°16'N

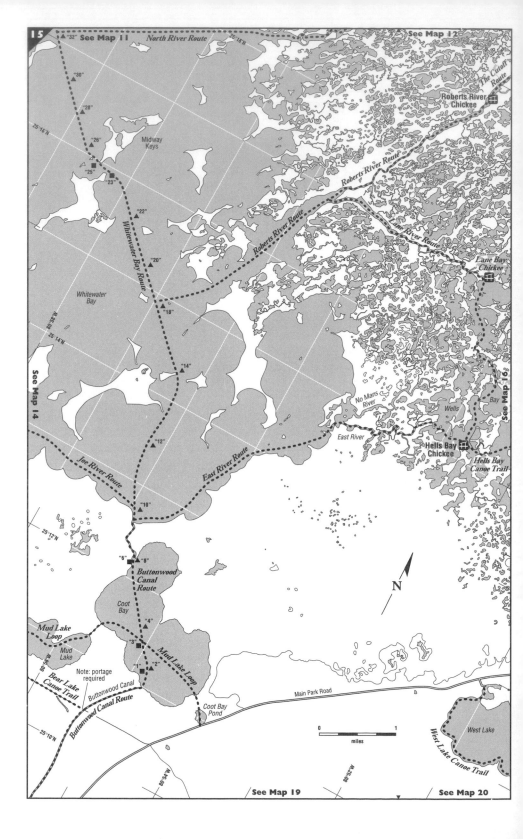

See Map 11
See Map 12
See Map 14
See Map 16
See Map 19
See Map 20

North River Route

"32"

"30"

"28"

"26"

25°16'N

"25"

"23"

Midway Keys

"22"

Whitewater Bay Route

"20"

Whitewater Bay

25°14'N

"18"

Roberts River Route

Roberts River Chickee

Roberts River Route

Lane River Route

The Cutoff Route

Lane Bay Chickee

"14"

"12"

East River Route

No Mans River

Wells

Bay

Joe River Route

Hells Bay Chickee

Hells Bay Canoe Trail

East River

"10"

25°12'N

"6" "8"

Buttonwood Canal Route

Coot Bay

Mud Lake Loop

"4"

Mud Lake

"3"

Mud Lake Loop

Bear Lake Canoe Trail

Note: portage required

"1" "2"

Buttonwood Canal

Coot Bay Pond

Main Park Road

West Lake

West Lake Canoe Trail

25°10'N

Buttonwood Canal Route

N

0   1
miles

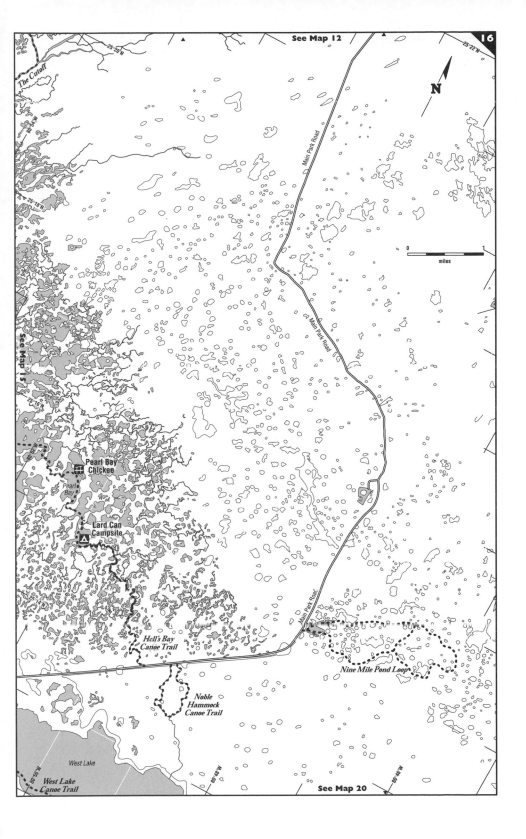

25°20'N

25°22'N

N

The Cutoff

80°54'W

25°18'N

Main Park Road

0   1
miles

See Map 15

25°16'N

80°52'W

Main Park Road

Pearl Bay
Chickee

Pearl
Bay

Lard Can
Campsite

25°22'N

Main Park Road

Hell's Bay
Canoe Trail

Nine Mile Pond Loop

Noble
Hammock
Canoe Trail

West Lake

80°48'W

80°46'W

West Lake
Canoe Trail

80°50'W

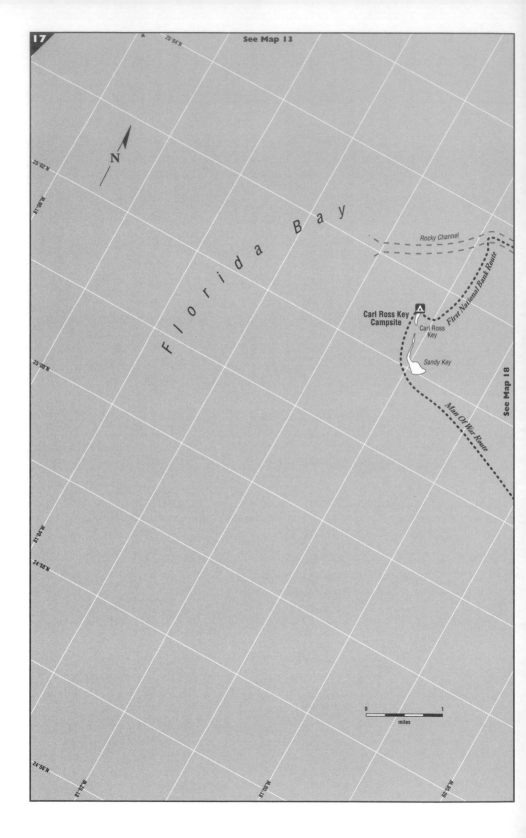

25°04'N

25°02'N

81°08'W

F l o r i d a   B a y

Rocky Channel

First National Bank Route

Carl Ross Key
Campsite

Carl Ross
Key

25°00'N

Sandy Key

See Map 18

Man O' War Route

81°04'W

24°58'N

81°06'W

0   1

miles

81°02'W

81°00'W

80°58'W

24°56'N

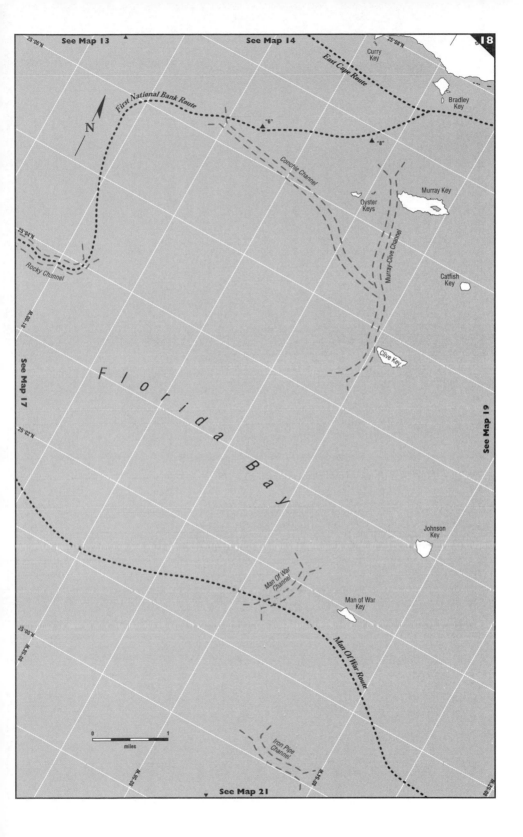

See Map 13
See Map 14

25°06'N

East Cape Route

Curry Key

Bradley Key

25°08'N

First National Bank Route

N

"6"

"8"

Conchie Channel

Murray Key

Oyster Keys

Murray-Clive Channel

Catfish Key

25°04'N

81°00'W

Rocky Channel

Clive Key

F l o r i d a   B a y

25°02'N

See Map 17

See Map 19

Johnson Key

Man Of War Channel

Man of War Key

25°00'N

80°54'W

Man Of War Route

0   1
miles

Iron Pipe Channel

80°56'W

80°55'W

80°52'W

See Map 21

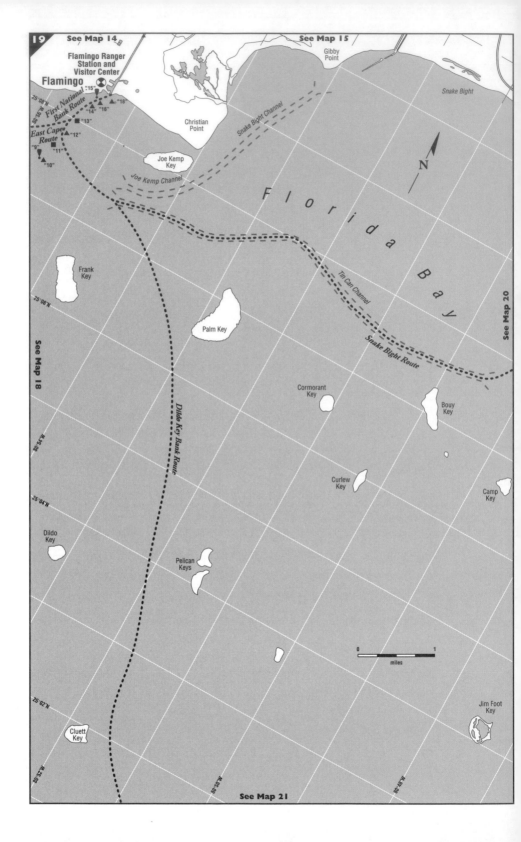

See Map 14
See Map 15

Flamingo Ranger
Station and
Visitor Center

Flamingo

Gibby
Point

Snake Bight

First National
Bank Route

"15"

"14" "16" "18"

"13"

East Cape
Route

"9" "12"

"11"

"10"

Christian
Point

Snake Bight Channel

Joe Kemp
Key

Joe Kemp Channel

F l o r i d a   B a y

N

Frank
Key

Palm Key

Tin Can Channel

Dildo Key Bank Route

Cormorant
Key

Bouy
Key

Snake Bight Route

See Map 18

See Map 20

Curlew
Key

Camp
Key

Dildo
Key

Pelican
Keys

0   1
miles

Cluett
Key

Jim Foot
Key

See Map 21

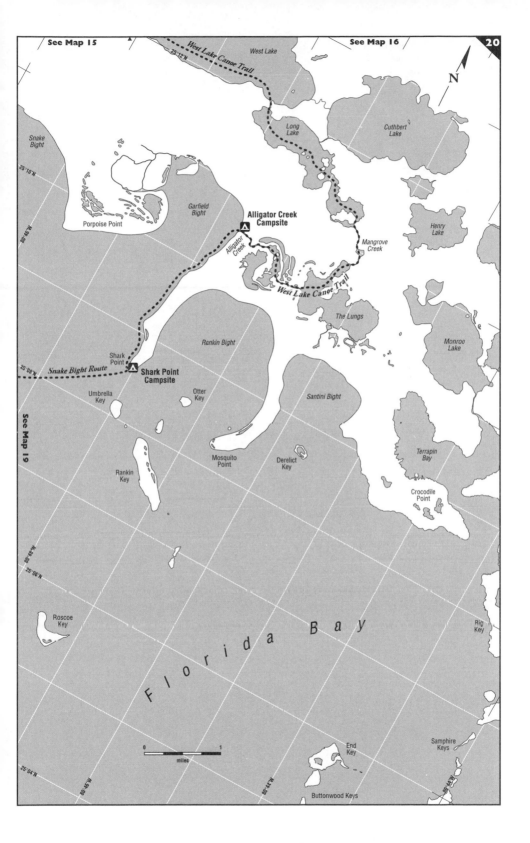

N

West Lake Canoe Trail

25°12'N

West Lake

Long
Lake

Cuthbert
Lake

Snake
Bight

25°10'N

80°50'W

Garfield
Bight

Porpoise Point

Henry
Lake

**Alligator Creek
Campsite**

Alligator
Creek

Mangrove
Creek

West Lake Canoe Trail

The Lungs

Monroe
Lake

Rankin Bight

Shark
Point

25°08'N

Snake Bight Route

**Shark Point
Campsite**

Umbrella
Key

Otter
Key

Santini Bight

Terrapin
Bay

Mosquito
Point

Derelict
Key

Rankin
Key

Crocodile
Point

80°48'W

25°06'N

Roscoe
Key

F l o r i d a   B a y

Rig
Key

0   1
miles

25°04'N

80°46'W

80°44'W

End
Key

Samphire
Keys

80°42'W

Buttonwood Keys

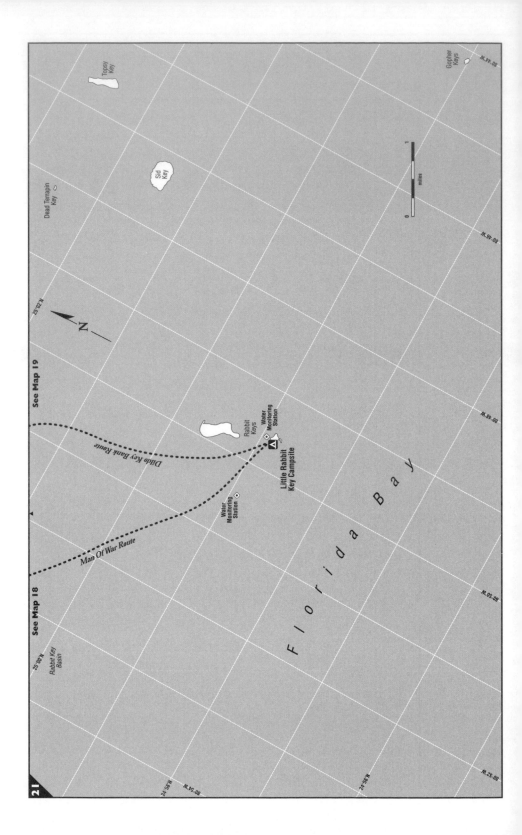

Topsy Key

Gopher Keys

80.44.W

Sid Key

Dead Terrapin Key

25.02.N

See Map 19

N

miles

80.46.W

Rabbit Keys

Dildo Key Bank Route

Water Monitoring Station

80.48.W

Water Monitoring Station

Little Rabbit Key Campsite

Man Of War Route

See Map 18

Florida Bay

25.00.N

Rabbit Key Basin

80.50.W

24.58.N

80.54.W

24.56.N

80.52.W

21

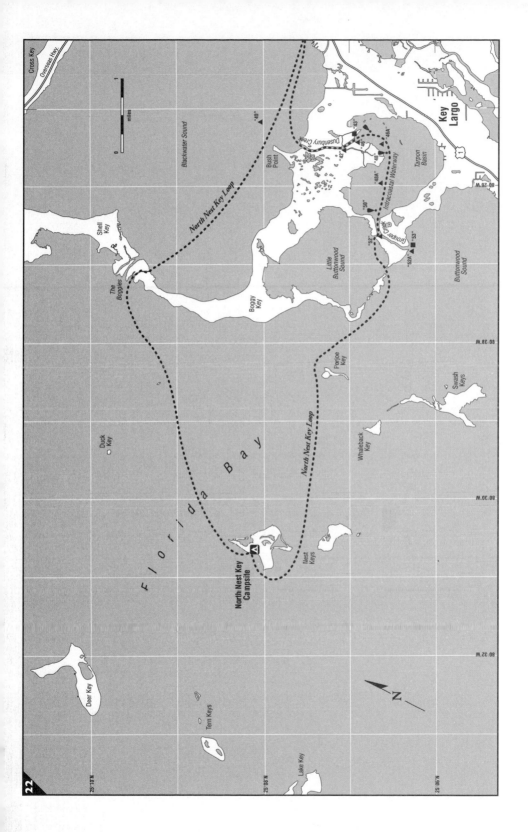